Bravo Troop

Bravo Troop
A Forward Observer's Vietnam Memoir

WILLIAM WATSON

McFarland & Company, Inc., Publishers
Jefferson, North Carolina

ISBN (print) 978-1-4766-8846-6
ISBN (ebook) 978-1-4766-4603-9

LIBRARY OF CONGRESS AND BRITISH LIBRARY
CATALOGUING DATA ARE AVAILABLE

Library of Congress Control Number 2022022390

© 2022 William Watson. All rights reserved

No part of this book may be reproduced or transmitted in any form or by any means, electronic or mechanical, including photocopying or recording, or by any information storage and retrieval system, without permission in writing from the publisher.

Front cover: A Sheridan in the field with Bravo Troop in February.
Note the damage to the locally added chain link screen.
These screens were eventually abandoned.
(National Archives photograph number CC55197)

Printed in the United States of America

McFarland & Company, Inc., Publishers
Box 611, Jefferson, North Carolina 28640
www.mcfarlandpub.com

To the men of Bravo Troop,
3rd Squadron, 4th Cavalry, with whom I served

Table of Contents

Preface   1

1–Getting There   5
2–Welcome Aboard   23
3–Ap Bien Hoa   32
4–Little Rubber   51
5–First Boi Loi   66
6–Second Boi Loi   86
7–Long Trench   99
8–Cau Khoi Rubber   115
9–The Citadel   128
10–Country Store   140
11–Helmet Fight   159
12–War Correspondents   169
13–Sergeant Major Turner   176
14–Hoi Chan Fight   188
15–Baby Dumpling   201
16–CRIP   217
17–Defending Tay Ninh   226
18–Checking Out   242

Glossary   263
The Author's Service Record   267
Index   269

Preface

I have worked on this book in fits and starts for almost fifty years. Initially, I gave little thought to why I wanted to write a book. Perhaps it was little more than a conceited desire to tell my story. Then I realized I also wanted to tell the story of the men who had served with me.

When I joined Bravo Troop, I assumed that the others would do their jobs and I only needed to do mine. I have learned since that was not true for every unit. Fortunately, it was true for Bravo Troop. Men I would never have met otherwise did their jobs with courage, usually facing more danger than I did. My respect for them demands telling our story, the troop's story. I can think of no higher praise than for one of them to say, "I remember Foxy. He was one of us."

When I got to details, I worked to explain artillery procedures and to show how much of our time was spent on repetitive routine with an indefinite threat to life and limb. I have included as much routine as I could with any hope that the book would be read. The real ratio of routine to excitement involved much more routine than I have reported.

Before I left Vietnam I marked a 1:100,000 map with the places and dates of our fights to take home. I also made a copy of an Army tape recording of the Squadron's radio net for most of the fight on June 19. When I got home, my parents gave me the letters and cassette tapes I had sent them. Those were the records I had to supplement my memory when I started making notes of various events and conversations.

To help combining my notes into a book, I got copies of the Squadron Duty Officer's Log for January through July from the National Archives. Those logs are written summaries of reports and messages on the Squadron's radio net. They confirmed the dates I remembered, reported the troop's movements and provided other details.

All three of the Commanding Officers I served with reviewed my first draft for the time I was their Forward Observer and provided corrections and additions. I incorporated some of those. I left out most of the things they knew or saw that I didn't. If one of them remembered something that didn't match what I remembered clearly, I stayed with what I remembered.

Our fight at Ap Bien Hoa on January 26 is a special case. Several people who were there have read my account and said I misreported details of the battle, including the Troop's disposition. They all knew more than I did at the time, but I have still reported what I knew then.

It is clear now that I was often unaware of much that was going on around me then.

Many names in the book are made up because I don't remember someone's name. Even at the time, there were many men I knew only by a nickname at best. Many of the names I do remember have been changed because I didn't know how to contact them. McGowan, Headley, Jackson, Wells and Carlson are real names.

A substantial part of what I think I said or heard is shown in quotes rather than paraphrasing or summarizing it. My editor calls that "remembered dialog." If anyone says I couldn't possibly remember word for word so much dialog from so many people over fifty years later, they would be right. I don't claim that all of it is word for word exact. There isn't an official record of any of it. It is just what I remember. Much of it was written down by me two or three years after it happened, not fifty.

When I review what I remember vividly and why, I am surprised that many of my most vivid memories were and are of longer statements and conversations. An example is the welcoming briefing at Long Binh. The flat, staccato style of the Lieutenant, who probably had given the same briefing to every bus that arrived there for some time, was memorable. Memory of the details was reinforced by the fact that it was the first comprehensive instructions I had received since I got to Vietnam and that almost everything in the briefing was something that I did or confirmed by the end of the next day. The briefing on arrival at Cu Chi was similar in style and prompt confirmation.

The interviews with the DIVARTY commander were memorable because of my relation to the two other new arrivals. They were both of lower rank but had unit experience that I did not. They were both invited to join their battalions immediately while my battalion left me where I was.

There are similar explanations for the essential accuracy of all of my longer remembered dialog.

If I don't claim all of my remembered dialog is exact, what do I claim? Nothing in it refers to an event that didn't happen or misrepresents one that did. All of it is consistent with the records I have about the troop. None of it was questioned by any of the troop's three commanding officers.

All of it is as trustworthy as if I had told the same story without using quotes.

The map of Bravo Troop's Primary Area of Operations shows almost all of the roads, towns, geographic features and checkpoints referred to in the book. Words that may not be immediately familiar are defined in the Glossary.

1

Getting There

January 10, 1969

My tip to Vietnam began with a civilian flight from Tulsa to San Francisco, then a bus trip to Travis Air Force Base. The Travis terminal resembled a train station with everybody in uniform. A bored Air Force NCO gave me a flight number and told where to check my bags.

I changed in a restroom from dress greens to short sleeve khakis. There were several others making the same change and about an equal number changing the other way. The men going home had more ribbons.

A chartered World Airways DC8 got us to Honolulu. We took off with a new crew and crossed the International Date Line into tomorrow between Honolulu and Wake Island.

January 11

After Wake Island, Okinawa was our last stop before Vietnam, where we deplaned at Bien Hoa airport, passing a welcoming committee of troops taking our plane home. In one corner of the terminal two Special Forces officers in tiger stripe camouflage sat on the floor with a group of Cambodian irregulars and their families. They were the only ones in the terminal carrying weapons.

A large sign in the terminal pointed where to go. The bus was an olive drab school bus. The passenger windows were covered by a heavy wire mesh. The driver was a PFC with an M16 with one magazine. We drove through a gate in the Bien Hoa perimeter. Soon we were close to alone, traveling between flat fields of brown grass.

The last training film I saw at Ft. Sill was about convoys in Vietnam. Every convoy in Vietnam was supposed to be ready to fight. That meant every man was armed and briefed on how to react in an ambush. Our bus had one rifle.

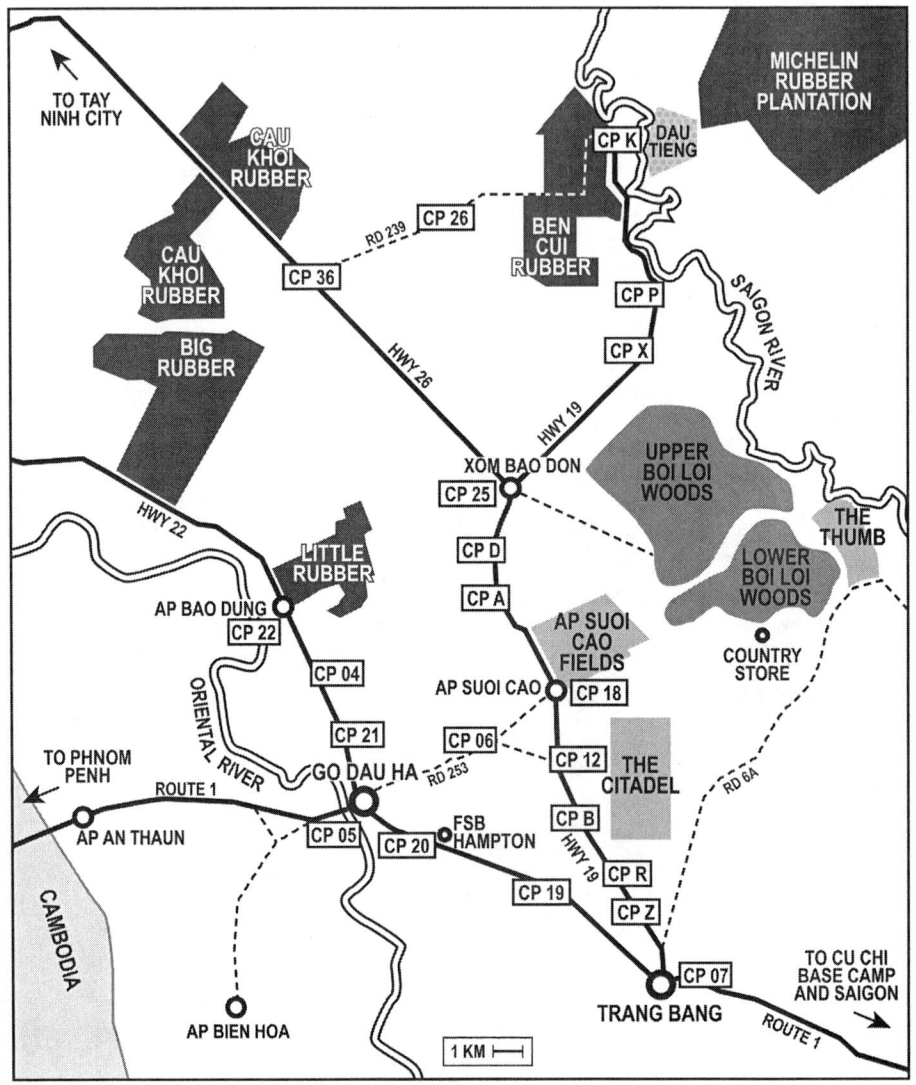

Bravo Troop's primary operating area (Brightwood Creative).

We went through two small towns then turned onto a wider road. A little further on a barbed wire fence appeared on our left. There were sandbag bunkers about two hundred feet apart just inside the wire. We turned into a gate. The driver pulled ahead about fifty feet and turned to us: "This is the 287th Replacement Company for officers. The 90th Replacement Battalion for enlisted personnel is the next stop up the road. Officers should dismount here."

1—Getting There

As the bus left, a Second Lieutenant with a clipboard appeared out of a small building on the side of the road and asked us to check in with him. He checked our names off his list and assigned barracks numbers. He pointed out the Company Headquarters, but said that we should have no reason to need it. He said that at ten next morning there would be a bus to the supply point.

"You have one day's grace for stateside uniforms, but after that the uniform of the day is jungle fatigues, so get your issue on time. Buy your insignia and name tapes at the same time. Do not have your fatigues tailored. There are several Vietnamese concessions in the building next to the issue point that sell insignia and will sew them on. They all know where everything goes better than I do, but don't let them tailor your fatigues."

He turned and pointed toward the end of the row of buildings. "The mess hall is the last building in the left row of buildings. Dinner is served from seventeen hundred to eighteen thirty. Breakfast is from oh six hundred to oh eight hundred. Lunch from eleven thirty to thirteen hundred. There are no charges at the mess. The Army assumes you are eating three Army meals a day while you are in Nam and just keeps your subsistence allowance. Same with quarters allowance. The barracks are free, but the Army keeps your quarters allowance."

"There is an orientation film at nineteen hundred tonight that each of you is required to see. Even if this isn't your first tour, you are still required to see the film. It may have changed since last time."

"Assignments are posted twice a day on the bulletin board outside the Company Headquarters. Check the board after breakfast and after lunch. When your name is posted, come into the Clerk's office and get a copy of your travel instructions. You should get an assignment the day after tomorrow, but don't think that you've been forgotten until two days after that. If you haven't been assigned by then, check with the Duty Officer."

He pointed to a door in the building closest to where we were standing. "Before you go to your barracks, go through currency exchange. You are no longer allowed to have greenbacks. You will be given Military Payment Certificates for all the cash you are carrying, including change. Failing to exchange all of your greenbacks is a serious offense. You may pay a Vietnamese at any concession inside the post with MPCs. You should not give MPCs to a Vietnamese except at a concession. You are not allowed to leave the Long Binh compound until you have been assigned, so you shouldn't need any local currency."

He pointed to a building a bit away from the rest, further down the road from the gate. "That's the nurse and WAC barracks. It is off limits to all male personnel. We have WAC enlisted personnel as well as officers staying there. The enlisted WACs are authorized to use the officers' mess, but not the officers' club. The enlisted WACs and enlisted personnel in this company are excused from saluting company grade officers and warrant officers in the company area. All company grade officers and warrant officers are excused from saluting each other in the company area. Too many of us to go around saluting."

Turning to face the other side of the road, he nodded to the only nearby building on the other side. "That is the officers' club. It opens at oh eight hundred and closes at twenty two hundred. Cold beer and soda, no hard liquor. It is the only air-conditioned building in the Company area, except the CO's quarters. Don't feel bad about the air-conditioning. Both the NCO club and the EM club in the replacement battalion area are air-conditioned. Are there any questions?"

"How do we find the barracks you assigned us to?"

"The numbers are painted on the doors. Any other questions? All right, that's it. Don't forget the movie."

The currency exchange went fast. The orientation film wasn't too bad. The Vietnamese have an ancient and sophisticated culture and we are guests in their country to assist them in defeating antidemocratic subversives and outside invaders. If we are not polite guests we will lose the people's respect and trust and will waste the benefits of the military victories that we are winning in cooperation with the Army of the Republic of Vietnam. Besides the ARVNs, the South Vietnamese have Regional Forces, RFs, like our National Guard, and Popular Forces, PFs, who serve in their own villages, like a militia. We should never pat children on the head. What we consider a friendly gesture is an insult to the Vietnamese because of the Buddhist belief that a person's soul is in his head. The film wasn't too bad, and it wasn't too long.

After the movie, I went to the officers' club. The club was cool and the beer was cold and cheap. The MPCs were about half the size of real money. All of the bills were the same design with different colors for the different denominations. The picture on the front of each bill was a submarine sailing on the surface. I hadn't seen any submarines yet. I sat there with a pocket full of five cent, ten cent, twenty-five cent and one dollar MPCs sipping beer until I thought I could go to sleep.

January 12

After breakfast I took the bus to the supply point. It was a long building with a long line at one end and individuals dribbling out at the other end carrying full bags. By the time I got off the bus the first officers off the bus had cut the line. The troops in line took little note so I did the same. After drawing all of my new gear, I went to a concession shop in the next building and had name tags and insignia sewn on my five new jungle fatigue blouses. The Vietnamese woman at the sewing machine said very little and finished quickly.

When I got back, I changed into my new jungle fatigues. They were looser and cooler. When I walked out I found two Lieutenants hard at work putting their web gear together. I went back, got mine out and joined them. When we finished, we speculated about assignment. The conversation paled quickly. We stopped at the bulletin board on the way to the club. I was not posted.

January 13

I woke up about 0700. Three Lieutenants I didn't know were sitting on a bunk at the other end of the building listening to the Super Bowl.

"Who's winning?"

"Jets. Its just about over and the Jets are way ahead. The fuckin' Jets."

I was posted to the 25th Infantry Division. The bus to the airstrip for the plane to the 25th was scheduled for 0830. The C-123 came at 0930. Half an hour later our planeload was boarding a bus at the Cu Chi airstrip. It was a short ride to a cluster of huts like the ones at Long Binh.

"Welcome to the 25th Infantry Division, the Tropic Lightning Division. I am Lieutenant Krause, officer in charge of the 25th Replacement Detachment. You will be staying here until you have completed the division orientation course. It is a five day course with a new class beginning every other day. A class began today, but you are too late for that, so you will begin the course the day after tomorrow."

"Officers' quarters are the first building on the left over there. E6 and above use the next building. E5 and below, the five barracks after that. Take any open bunk. Officers will be advised of their assignments as they are made. There is a formation for all enlisted men at oh seven hundred every morning and assignments will be announced at that formation. The mess hall is behind this building. All meals are served at normal hours. When you go to the orientation course, your lunch will be C-rations picked up at the back of this building before formation. If you insist on getting in trouble, please wait until you have left us. That's it."

"Wait one. All Field Artillery officers are to report to the Division Artillery Headquarters tomorrow at oh nine hundred. Divarty is over there. Headquarters is the building next to the tower." He pointed to a thirty foot wooden observation tower about a hundred meters away. "OK, that's it."

January 14

There were three of us at DIVARTY. The other two were Second Lieutenants. We were met by the Assistant S1. He explained we would have an interview with the DIVARTY commanding officer, tour the DIVARTY complex and then meet with the CO again to get our unit assignments.

We were ushered into the CO's office. "Good morning gentlemen." We replied, almost in unison, "Good morning sir."

The CO, a full Colonel, stood up behind his desk. He was the highest ranking Black officer I had ever met. "Please stand easy. Lieutenant Watson, you're senior. Do you have any troop experience?" "No sir. Only officers' basic and jump school."

He asked the others the same question, also by name. The first said, "Yes sir. Three months as the Assistant Executive Officer of a one oh five battery." The second, "Yes sir. Four months as Assistant Fire Direction Officer of an eight inch battery."

"You can be assured that there are jobs for all of you here. Because you had a free day before you start the orientation course, we wanted to have you come over and see what we do here. Be sure to find our officers' club and come by the club any time. After you finish your tour, come back here and we should have your assignments."

All four of us smiled, three of us said "thank you sir," and left.

The DIVARTY complex wasn't really all that much. The Captain who was our guide took us through two office buildings about the same as the barracks I'd seen since arrival. The first building was S1 and S4, personnel and supplies. The second, S2 and S3, intelligence and operations.

"Now the TOC" the Captain said as he pointed to a huge sandbag bunker with walls about eight feet high and a sandbag roof. "Excuse me, sir," said one of the Second Lieutenants, "what's a tock?" "TOC is tactical operations center. That's where the S2 and S3 sections really do their work."

Inside the bunker were two rooms. One was full of radios with an operator for every two radios. "We try to listen in on everything that is happening in the Division. We use the information to plan resupply and the like. The Artillery battalions advise us every time one of their Forward Observers or Liaison Officers reports a contact and we try to monitor the FO's frequency. Sometimes we report the progress of a battle to Division faster than the maneuver unit does."

In the next room he pointed to a huge map of the Division, "This map shows the location of every firing battery in the Division. Right now all of them are in semi-permanent fire support bases, usually shared with an infantry battalion. We also show all of the ARVN artillery in the area. We rarely ask them for fire support, but it is nice to know where they are if support is needed. There is only a slight overlap in our areas of activity anyway. The shaded areas are free fire areas. Anywhere else we have to get the permission of the Vietnamese civilian authorities before we fire, but in the shaded areas we already have permission to fire and only have to worry about friendly units. The battalion FDC, you know, the fire direction center, responsible for each area keeps detailed track of all US units in the area and of any RF or PF operations or ambushes."

"How do you know where the US units are?"

"Mostly from the forward observers. They call in the location of the company that they are attached to as it moves around." He glanced at his watch. "I think we can go back to the CO now."

We were shown in as soon as we got back. "Gentlemen, welcome back. Did you see what we're doing?"

"Yes sir." "Good. I have your assignments."

He spoke to the other two first. The first was assigned to the 7th Battalion, 11th Artillery. "They're a towed one oh five unit. They're sending a jeep over to the Replacement Detachment to pick you up. They want you to stay with them during the orientation"

The second one was assigned to the 3rd Battalion, 13th Artillery. "They only have one battery of eight inch, but they should be able to use your experience. They're picking you up too. Both of them will take you to and from the course."

"Lieutenant Watson, you'll be with the Automatic Eighth, 1st Battalion, 8th Artillery, one oh fives. Their S1 says their officers' huts are full up so you'll be staying at the Replacement Detachment through your orientation. Call them when the training is over and they will come and get you. They'll have a bunk by then. Do any of you have any questions?"

"No sir." "Good. Good luck."

I went to dinner early then to the DIVARTY officers' club. It was a small hooch on the edge of the DIVARTY area close to the Replacement Detachment area. There was an NCO behind a small bar, four stools at the bar and a few tables and chairs. Cold beers and sodas were in a refrigerator behind the bar. For me the big attraction was a TV behind the bar. There was only the AFVN channel, but it was American TV programming. I sipped a couple of beers until I was almost tired, then went back to my hooch.

January 15

Shave, shower and breakfast, then I picked up a C-ration for lunch. The enlisted men were called into a formation. Officers were not required to march to the class, but I didn't know where it was. When the formation marched off, I followed. Each man was carrying a C-ration box, like a small cardboard lunch box without a handle, so they didn't look very military.

Our morning instruction was about enemy organization. The class sat on a small bleacher facing the instructor. The instructor talked about VC local forces and main force battalions and NVA regulars. He showed posters of typical VC military unit organization charts and typical strength figures. The VC platoons and companies had nominal strengths about half of U.S. platoons and companies. The sergeant said that actual strength of most of the VC military units was less than half their nominal strength, because of the Tet offensive. He said that the local forces still set mines and booby traps, guided main force units and made general trouble, but were no longer significant military assets. The VC main force battalions had spearheaded the Tet attacks and taken very high casualties. They had been rebuilt with NVA regulars as replacements. That meant that they didn't know much more about the countryside than we did. It also meant that they were probably better equipped and trained than they had been before Tet.

The description of regular NVA units started with a map that showed almost all of the south half of South Vietnam. It showed several NVA division headquarters just over the border in Cambodia and Laos and two or three regiments for each division near the border on either side. The ones closest to us were two NVA regiments and a division headquarters west of us inside Cambodia and another regiment north of Tay Ninh City, just on our side of the Cambodian border. The Sergeant said that the NVA rarely concentrated anything larger than a battalion inside Vietnam. They operated mostly by sending company sized units into our area for a while and spent most of their time in Cambodia.

"An NVA trooper in Vietnam spends most of his time hiding, hiding from you, hiding from our gunships and hiding from our bombers. When we locate an NVA unit inside Vietnam they usually suffer horrible casualties. When they attack something before we find them, they usually get smashed. Then they sneak back to Cambodia, put the unit back together and try it again. If you run into an NVA soldier, he will not be ten feet tall, he will probably be scared, tired and hungry. However, don't get too cocky, he will also be tough, well trained and highly motivated."

He continued with a display of enemy equipment and uniforms. When we left the bleachers for lunch, my C-ration was more food than I wanted. I sampled the stuff in the cans and ate the big chocolate covered dinner mint.

The afternoon's instruction was about enemy weapons. The most

1—Getting There

common of them was the AK47 assault rifle. They showed us a light machine gun that looked a lot like an AK47 with a longer barrel. The RPG2 rocket propelled grenade launcher was little more than a straight light metal tube with a handle near one end. The RPG7 launcher had a wooden cover for much of the tube and a flash suppressor at the back end. We got a chance to handle the enemy weapons. I think that was to make them less frightening.

On the way back to the Replacement Detachment I stopped at the DIVARTY Officers' Club for two cold Cokes. I was so dirty I went to the back door and took the cans to the barracks with me. After cleaning up and dinner I went back to the DIVARTY Officers' Club for a couple of beers and AFVN.

January 16

"Good morning. This morning we're going over enemy booby traps and mines."

The instructor had a flip chart on an easel that showed common VC booby traps. He talked about the posters as he moved through them slowly. The last poster showed our jungle boots. "Your Army issue jungle boots came with nylon mesh insoles inside. Do not take them out. If you have taken them out or lost them, go to the supply room and get replacements. They will not stop everything, but they will stop some spikes from penetrating the sole of your boot and will reduce the injury if something does penetrate your boot."

Then came another set of posters and more details on mines. He went over pressure fuses and trip wires. "Trip wires are hard to see, but they are visible. Keeping your eyes open will keep you alive. If you are looking carefully where you are going, you should also notice surface disturbance if a mine has been buried recently."

He had two samples to show us. "Not all of the enemy's mines are primitive." He held up a round grey mine the size of a really big pie plate three inches thick. "This is a Czech anti-tank mine. The gooks get a small number of manufactured mines from their Commie friends."

He put the anti-tank mine down and picked up the other one. It was dark green, about half again as big as a beer can. "Some day when you're out in the boonies and getting sloppy about keeping you eyes open, I hope you remember this little honey." He held it out toward the class in the palm of his right hand, about level with his eyes. "This is a Chicom nut cutter."

He took a smaller green cylinder out of the middle of it. "This is the business end. This mine is always set on the surface or partially buried, with one or more trip wires. If you trip one you will hear a very small explosion first, less noise than a firecracker. That little explosion pops this center part up in the air. Don't worry about what to do then, it's already too late. The second fuse is almost instantaneous. As soon as the business part is belt high, it will go off. If you are lucky, it will only blow off your nuts."

He paused for about three seconds then turned and put the mine on the table behind him. "Are there any questions?"

"Sarge, is it true that if you hear the click when you step on a mine and don't lift your foot off, the mine won't go off?"

"I've heard the story, but I've never met anyone who saw it happen. There are a few manufactured mines that are cocked with the initial pressure and triggered by the release. If you step on something and it clicks, but doesn't go off, you should freeze and ask for help. What you really should do is keep your eyes open and don't step on it to start with. Don't bet your life on getting a second chance. Okay, break for lunch."

At 1300 a new Sergeant stepped in front of the bleachers and a few stragglers ran to sit down. The afternoon's training was malaria prevention and first aid. I didn't care all that much about the short history of malaria, but I did pay attention to the prevention instructions. Two pills. The big white one, once a day at breakfast, starting tomorrow. The little yellow one, once a week; one tomorrow and then on your unit's schedule. Take both, no malaria; screw up and you could get very sick.

The best part of the first aid refresher was about use of the standard field dressing that came in a brown heavy paper package. The paper was plastic coated on the inside and the package was sealed to keep the dressing dry and sterile until the paper was torn. The field dressing itself was a white gauze pad a little smaller than a paperback book with a long white gauze strap on each corner. The straps were long enough to tie around someone's chest. For a wound in the head or arm or leg, the straps were wrapped around more than once then tied. The instructor called a kid down from the bleachers to be his demonstration dummy and showed the basic ways to tie the dressing over a wound and how to use it as a sling for an injured arm.

"Who remembers what a sucking chest wound is?" He pointed at a trooper in the first row: "A hole in your lung." "Good. That's right, a punctured lung. How do you identify a sucking chest wound?" He pointed at another trooper: "You hear sucking." Another kid yelled out, "Pink stuff around the hole."

"You're both right. If the punctured lung is still trying to work, you can hear air being sucked in the hole. The blood and air may make a pink froth around the hole. If you see pink foam on a chest wound instead of red blood, it's a sucking chest wound. How do we use the field dressing on a sucking chest wound?"

The sergeant pointed at a new trooper, "Use the paper!" The sergeant pointed to the next kid in the row, "Take off his pistol belt." The next kid drew a blank, but someone behind him yelled out, "Bandage on the outside." "Slow down. Slow down. I can see you, remember." As he talked, the instructor did what he said. "For a sucking chest wound, we do use the wrapper. Open the dressing and save the wrapper. Spread out the paper, sterile side closest to the wound. Hold this."

His demonstration dummy held the paper up against his chest where the sergeant had put it. The sergeant held the dressing in one hand and pointed at the wrapper on the kid's chest with the other. "Do not fuck around cutting clothes or undressing the wounded man. His best chance of living is having the hole stopped so that his chest stops leaking. Get him to the doctors alive and let them worry about cleaning up the hole. All right, next put on the field dressing over the wrapper."

The sergeant put the dressing in place and reached around the kid to tie the straps across his back, "This is the most important thing, for a sucking chest wound the wrapper is the real bandage and the field dressing is just to hold the wrapper over the hole. What's next?"

"Put a belt over it," one of the kids yelled out. "That's right, put a belt over it." The sergeant took off his dummy's pistol belt and let it out a little, then spoke as he put it back on around the kid's chest, over the field dressing. "Let the man's belt out a little, but not too much. Keep it tight around his chest. The field dressing sticks up a little and the pistol belt pushes it down to keep the wrapper on tight. How's that feel?" "Tight, Sarge."

"Good. Last point. How should this man lie down?" He looked at the bleachers, waiting. "On the wound." "That's right. When a man with a sucking chest wound lies down, he must lie on the wounded side, not on his back, not on his stomach and not on the good side. He's only got one good lung left and if he's going to live to get to the doctors, you've got to keep that good lung high and dry. We want all the blood and crap inside his body to drain into the lung that already isn't working. He's not going to like it because it will hurt to lie on the wounded side. It hurts a lot. He will curse you and cry from the pain, but if you want him to live, you've got to keep him lying on the wounded side. Any questions?"

The class was silent. "All right son, take off the belt and put the dressing and wrapper in that trash drum." He looked back at the bleachers. "A sucking chest wound is the wound that how you treat your buddy is going to make the biggest difference. Wrapper, sterile side in, then the field dressing to hold it in place, then a tight pistol belt to keep the hole closed. The wounded man lies on his wounded side, no matter how much he bitches. This has been a sharp class. I think you all know enough to keep your buddy alive. That's it for today."

January 17

Next morning's class began with U.S. hand grenades. The instructor had posters showing all the parts and insides of three different U.S. grenades. When he was done with the posters, he passed samples of all three through the bleachers. "These are all deactivated. If you want to check, screw out the fuse assembly and look inside. There is no explosive inside the body of these grenades and the gain at the bottom of the fuse has been removed. Do not pull the pin. Once the striker has been released these are hard to reassemble."

The grenades were passed from hand to hand and some people did unscrew the fuse assembly from the body of the grenade, look inside then screw it back together. "You can see how easy it is to unscrew and put back in. That's one of the reasons you should never use a grenade that you find in the field. Sometimes the gooks find a grenade, unscrew the fuse, remove the delay element from the fuse, put it back together and leave it by the side of a trail for you to pick up. If you pick up that grenade and throw it later, it will go off as it leaves your hand, not a few seconds later."

One of the grenades was the standard pineapple grenade. A hand-size steel oblong body with deep criss-crossed grooves on the outside that announced that it would break up into half inch square steel fragments when it went off. The second one had a spherical steel body just about the size of a baseball with no grooves. Its surface was a little rough, an unfinished casting. The third had the same general shape and size as the pineapple grenade, but its surface was very smooth. It looked like its body was made from two pieces of stamped sheet metal.

"Most of the grenades you get in the field will be the smooth lemon shaped one. There are still a few pineapples in stock, but they aren't being made any more. There a few of the baseball grenades too, but not many. Somebody thought that since you all know how to throw a baseball our grenades should be like baseballs. They're okay, but the lemon shape is still easier to handle and throw. You all know how the pineapple breaks up to make fragments. The baseball grenade breaks into a lot more smaller pieces because the steel it is made from shatters. The lemon grenade is even better. The outside is just a thin metal skin. The fragments come from a long piece of spring steel that is wound tightly inside the covering, just waiting to get out. That spring shatters even better than the baseball grenade, it makes thousands of tiny fragments. The fragments from the lemon grenade are so small that it takes a surgeon hours to find them all if a casualty survives."

We took a break then started over for smoke grenades, parachute flares, star clusters and Claymore mines. Not much to a smoke grenade, just a can about the size of a beer can painted flat grey. The same kind of a fuse assembly as a regular grenade was screwed in one end and one band of color around the body matched the color of the smoke. The sergeant showed all the parts and colors on another set of posters. Then he picked up a grenade, pointed to the purple ring around the body and said, "purple." He pulled the pin and tossed the grenade onto a dirt patch about ten meters further away from the bleachers. You could hear the striker hit when the spoon flew off. The grenade hit the ground and rolled a little before the purple smoke started coming out the fuse end. Then there was so much smoke that you couldn't see the grenade. The sergeant pointed out that smoke grenades looked a lot like tear gas grenades. He showed us a tear gas grenade. It had a black band around the body with "CS" in yellow all around the black band about every two inches.

"Look at this again boys. You pop smoke for an incoming helicopter with one of these CS grenades and you will make lots of people very unhappy."

Next were hand held parachute flares and star clusters. Both looked the same on the outside, an aluminum cylinder 14 inches long about two inches in diameter, with a cap about three inches long at one end. Again there was a poster for each to show the parts and what was inside. Inside the end without the cap was primer and the cap had a pointed spike on the inside of its closed end. The way the flare or star cluster came, the cap covered the open end of the cylinder. The sergeant showed with a real one that when you wanted to fire it, you took the cap off, put the cap over the other end, held the cylinder in one fist with the open end pointed the way you wanted it to go then, without actually doing it, said you hit the cap with your other hand to launch it. Hitting the repositioned cap drove its spike into the primer and fired the star cluster or flare. He demonstrated the drill again without firing then called for a volunteer. One of the kids in the front row stood up and the sergeant called him out. "Do it as I talk you through. Okay, take the cap off. Put it on the other end. Don't worry, it's not a hair trigger. Just don't point it at anyone. Okay, hold it in your fist, open end pointed straight up, out away from your body, about face high. Looks good. Okay, now slap your other hand up against the bottom."

The kid slapped it as soon as the sergeant said to and something whooshed out of his hands. Four green balls of light popped about a hundred meters up. They went up a little more, started back down and burned out in a few seconds. "Okay, good job, put the trash in that barrel and sit down. That's what a starcluster looks like, just like a roman candle. They come in different colors and are used for signaling, mostly at night. You may get an order that a green star cluster means something and you'd better remember what it is, because it will be something so important that it needs to be communicated to a lot of people all at once."

"We're not going to put up a flare, because they are more of a fire hazard. It works just the same, except when it pops open it's a magnesium flare suspended under a little parachute. It's not pretty, but it throws a lot of light for a little while. The parachute usually keeps the flare in the air as long as it burns, but sometimes the flare is still burning when it lands, and that's the fire hazard. You could use a flare as a signal or to show where you were, but usually they're used to provide light when VC are about. Any questions? Okay, take five and come back for Claymores."

When we came back he had a new poster up and a Claymore mine on the table. A Claymore mine had a green plastic outside, ten inches by six inches and an inch and a half thick. It curved a little on its long axis. "Most of you know what this is; a Claymore mine. This is used for ambushes and to defend our perimeters. The business end is the outside of the curve." He ran his hand over the outside of the curve. "What does it say here? Who knows?"

Someone in the front row yelled, "Front toward enemy!" "Hell, you can read it from there. He's right though, front toward enemy. If it's dark, remember the outside of the curve points toward the enemy. If you ever put one out backwards, you may kill yourself. Which side goes toward the enemy?" Most of the class joined in answering, "the outside of the curve."

"Right, outside of the curve toward the enemy. There are about two hundred steel ball bearings just under this plastic cover and that's what gets blown out when you set this off. You can set it up with these little folding feet on the back or whatever is handy at the time, but set it up like a drive-in movie screen, with the outside of the curve pointed at the enemy. The Claymore can be rigged with a trip wire, but most of the time it will be set with one of these hand detonators." He held up a box-like thing a little smaller than a pack of cigarettes with a lever sticking up from one end of a long side.

"Squeeze this lever and it makes enough electricity to set the mine off, if you remembered to insert the fuse on the other end of the wire that comes attached to this. When you put Claymores out, you put the fuses in and make sure the safety pin is in the hand detonator until you want to set it off. In the morning, it you're picking up Claymores, be sure the safety pins are in and take the fuse out of the mine before you pick it up. When you are carrying a Claymore, do not put the hand detonators and fuses in the same bag or pouch with the mine. The explosive in a Claymore is C4.

1—Getting There

C4 is hard to set off, but that's what the fuse is designed to do. Don't carry them together. Okay, that's it. Break for lunch. Back here at 1300."

The afternoon's training was field stripping the M16. It began with the instructor going over it step by step for the class in the bleachers. Then he went through it again. Then he did it a third time calling on people in the bleachers to tell him the next step. All of the instruction was peppered with other information, loading procedures, proper cleaning techniques, and pointing out specific improvements in the rifle's design.

Next the class moved out of the bleachers to several rough tables with an M16 for each student to practice on. First a walk through, doing just one step at a time as the instructor called out the steps, taking the rifle apart and putting it back together. Then a second time "by the numbers." All the while several assistant instructors walked around the tables looking for anyone who was having any trouble. Then we were told to do it on our own at our own speed. The instructor joined his assistants. A few stragglers needed help to disassemble. Then we put it back together. Again a few stragglers needed help. Then the same again, disassemble and reassemble, with fewer stragglers. Then most of the class was given a break while the instructors worked personally with anyone who was still having problems. Finally the class was called back together for a summary, and the day's classes were over. There had been few problems because most of the class had gone through basic training with an M16. My rifle training had been with an M1 five years ago. All I knew about an M16, I had just learned.

January 18

The morning was weak courses on the M60 and .50 caliber machine guns. But, I learned enough to be able to load and fire both.

Lunch break ended when two buses pulled up next to the training area. We took a short ride to a stop on the road inside the Cu Chi perimeter. We stopped midway between two bunkers where there was a path through gaps in five separate barriers of barbed wire fence and entanglements. Next to each gap was a movable barbed wire barrier that had been opened to create the path. At the end of the path there were six tables with two folding chairs and a spotting scope in front of one. We were divided into six groups and told to wait behind a table. When the Captain in my group called first was done, the instructor called me forward.

"Sergeant, I've never fired an M16." "No problem sir, there are five rounds in this magazine. Put it in and let's see what we can do. Seat the magazine firmly. Now, pull the cocking handle at the rear of the receiver back as far as it will go and release it. Now, get in a firing position. This is the safety, release it, aim and fire at the target as soon as I'm looking through the scope."

He put his eye to the scope and I fired. "Right and low. Try two clicks up and four clicks left." He saw I didn't know what he was talking about. He pointed to two tiny knobs on the rear sight. "This is up and down, clockwise is up. This is left and right, clockwise is left. You can feel the clicks when you move them."

Three more shots called for minor adjustments and I think I followed his instructions. "That looks about right. Try it again." I fired my fifth round. "Looks good. By the way sir, this is the lever that selects semiautomatic or automatic fire. In the other position, it fires full automatic. The magazine holds twenty rounds, but if you only load eighteen it's less likely to jam. Everyone picks up their own empty cartridges, sir. Put them in the pail behind the middle of the firing line."

As I walked to the pail, I wondered if I had actually adjusted the sight properly or had just come to the end of my five rounds. When I was issued my own M16, I never adjusted the sights or took the selector off full automatic.

Buses took us back to the training area and we were released for the day.

January 19

The last day of the course was about enemy ambushes. The morning was classroom presentations about how the VC set up an ambush, how ambushes worked and how the ambushed formation should react. After lunch, a series of ambush drills were scheduled. Officers were excused from the drills. Instead of drifting away, I followed the class to watch.

After the fourth unrealistic ambush drill, the class was sent back to the bleachers and the lead instructor closed the course. "Everybody gets the same course because everybody needs to know what's going on around us. For those of you going to line units, the things we have talked about here are the things that will keep you alive. Stay focused, keep your head in the game, stay alive, keep your buddy alive." He stared at the bleachers for a moment. "Dismissed."

After dinner I went to the DIVARTY Officers' Club. Like the nights before, I nursed two or three beers then left to go to bed. I walked out of the club more bored than tired and noticed parachute flares drifting down on the perimeter half a mile away with the muffled sound of machine gun fire coming from the same direction, live ammunition fired with purpose.

January 20

There was an extra day of training in calling in helicopter gunships and artillery fire required for officers and NCOs going to infantry units. All other officers and NCOs had been encouraged to take it. Most of my Artillery training had been about calling in artillery fire but I took the class.

When I got back to the Replacement Detachment, I phoned the S1 of my Artillery battalion and he sent a jeep over. When I got there the S1 was waiting in his office. He was a fat First Lieutenant who seemed incapable of looking you in the eye. He directed me to their transient hooch. It didn't look like anyone had used it while I was in the training course.

At dinner the S1 said the CO wanted to see me after dinner in the battalion's officers' club. I went there promptly after dinner and had a Coke while I waited. The CO, a Lieutenant Colonel, came in a bit later with a Major and I was called over to join them at the bar. I was on the CO's left and the Major on his right. He asked some standard questions. When he heard I was from Tulsa, he asked if I knew some families in Dallas that he knew. When I said that I didn't, he appeared to lose interest.

January 21

While I was eating breakfast the S1 found me and told me to go see the S2, the S3 and the XO. The S2 and S3 briefings amounted to nothing. The S3 told me to report to the Operations Sergeant and read the rules for firing artillery near the Cambodian border. He was adamant that I was required to sign that I had read the rules. I found the Operations Sergeant and he got out the form for me to sign. When I asked where the rules were, he seemed irritated. He suggested again that I sign the form and read the rules later at my convenience. When I made it clear that I wasn't going to sign until I had read the rules, he started looking for them. It took him some time to find them.

Within one thousand meters of the Cambodian border all adjusting fire had to be done with a single gun. Standard fire adjustment was done with the center two guns of a six gun battery. Within a thousand meters of the Cambodian border, no adjustment could be more than fifty meters. Standard procedures let the forward observer decide how far to move the rounds in an adjustment. Obviously, near Cambodia, we were supposed to be more delicate. After I read the rules, I signed the form and left.

The Executive Officer was the Major I had met at the Officers' Club with the Commanding Officer. He was brusk. He asked if I had been briefed by the S2 and S3. "Yes sir."

He gave a short speech that all lieutenants coming to the battalion started in the field as forward observers and that I would be assigned as a forward observer, but they didn't know where yet. After six months or so I would be probably be moved to a firing battery or battalion headquarters. He said that I should expect as little as five minutes' notice and have my gear ready to go. I said "yes sir" again and was dismissed.

At dinner I met two of the battalion's First Lieutenants who were spending their last days in base camp before going home. Each had been out as a forward observer for an infantry company for their full year. They were planning to visit several of the officers' clubs scattered around Cu Chi and invited me to join them. I accepted and soon we were leaving in a jeep they had gotten somewhere.

Every battalion and higher headquarters in the Cu Chi base camp had its own officers' club. Most were essentially the same as the DIVARTY club, a hooch with a bar, refrigerator, TV, some chairs and tables and an NCO bartender. The first two clubs we visited were almost empty and we left each after a single beer. The third at Second Brigade headquarters had a crowd in it and some music playing. We stayed there longer.

One of the ex-FOs said that he had been offered a chance to come in to a job at battalion after about six months. He turned it down, volunteering to stay with his infantry company. "There's just too much chickenshit stuff at battalion headquarters." The other nodded in agreement, "Damn straight."

I told them that I would be going out as an FO because of the battalion policy that all lieutenants start as FOs. They both smiled. "Our S1, that little shit, hasn't been out anywhere. But don't worry, being an FO isn't all that bad. Your company will make contact with the VC about every thirty days. You'll get to fire a mission about every ninety days or so. Your Liaison Officer will shoot most of the fire missions from a chopper. Don't worry, there's just not that much to it. You'll just tell him where your CO wants it and if they're too close." He took a pull on his beer and paused a second. "Except if you get the Three Quarter Cav. They haven't had an FO leave yet wasn't wounded or dead."

The other nodded again, "Damn straight."

2

Welcome Aboard

January 22

After breakfast I was called to see the S3. "Lieutenant Watson, you are going to be the forward observer for Bravo Troop, 3rd Squadron, 4th Cavalry. They're in Cu Chi on stand down. Get your gear together and bring it back here. Your Recon Sergeant is on the way over now to pick you up outside. Any questions?" "No sir."

A Recon Sergeant was part of the standard forward observer team who was trained to be the FO's backup and assistant. The rest of the team was the Forward Observer, me, and a Radio Telephone Operator, a Spec4 or PFC who took care of the team's radio. A jeep pulled up next to the battalion's headquarters building and two men got out. The driver was a twenty something white guy and the other was a younger Black guy. The driver led as they approached stopped and saluted. I returned the salute. I already knew it was an unusually formal greeting.

"Lieutenant Watson, I'm Fontana, your Recon Sergeant. This is Charlie, your RTO. We borrowed a Cav jeep." I looked at the Black kid and he nodded. He was wearing a Private's single chevron on his collar. Fontana wore a Spec4 insignia. "Is this all of your gear sir?" As Fontana asked, he and Charlie picked up my gear. "Yes, thank you. Let's go."

My gear and Charlie went in the back. I took the passenger seat and Fontana drove off. Cu Chi was spread out, with space between clusters of buildings and storage yards. The streets in unit areas were just oiled dirt, but the main roads were asphalt. I didn't know where we were going, but eventually we turned off into a unit area across the road from one end of the Cu Chi airstrip. We passed a motor pool crammed with twenty or so armored personnel carriers in varying stages of disassembly.

We parked next to an armored personnel carrier backed up to the edge of the lot next to two hooches. The APC had its back ramp down. The top rear corner on each side of the vehicle was painted white, making a small white triangle on each side, and there was a white "6" about a foot high painted on each side.

We had not talked on the trip over. Fontana pointed to a hooch just beyond the closest two, "That's the officers' hooch, we'll put your gear in there. Our last FO isn't here anymore. I think you ought to check in with the XO. He knows you're coming." He pointed to the nearest hooch, "That's the Troop Headquarters. The CO's office and the XO and the First Sergeant are in there."

A man came out of the next nearest hooch. His boonie hat was cocked forward on his head and the front brim was folded up and pinned to the crown with brass crossed sabers Cavalry insignia. The plaster cast on his left forearm canceled the humorous effect of the hat. He was also wearing the double silver bars of a Captain on one collar and brass crossed sabers on the other. "That's Captain Headley, the CO. That hooch is his quarters." "How'd he break his arm?" "Same fight that got Foxy dusted off." "Is he OK?" "Last we heard. He got evacuated to Japan." Headley paid no attention to us as he crossed the parking lot a few meters away.

"Sir, I think that if Charlie and I met you here in about an hour, you should be all settled and through with them." "Very good." I really had no idea what was involved, but it sounded right.

Fontana and Charlie took my gear toward the officers' hooch and I went into the headquarters. The Troop XO was in the office. He was also a First Lieutenant, Dave Schmidt. He was friendly, but obviously busy. I asked about Captain Headley. Schultz assured me that Headley was the finest there was and that, if I stayed near Headley like I was supposed to, I'd be fine. He also volunteered that Headley's wound was grenade fragments from the same fight that had gotten my predecessor evacuated.

"Have you been issued any gear since Long Binh?" "No." "You did get clothes and a helmet?" "Yes." "Do you have an M16 and a flak jacket?" "No." "Come outside, I'll show you where the Troop supply room is. Tell the supply sergeant who you are and that I said you get a rifle and a flak jacket. Get a couple of extra magazines and some ammo too."

From the corner of the building he pointed to a hooch of about the same size past the end of the parking area. He pointed out another hooch near the supply room. "That's our mess hall next to the supply room. The Squadron Officers' Club is just over there across the lot. It opens about six each night, but you can get a cold Coke whenever there's somebody inside, even if it's not officially open. Listen, I've got to chase some paperwork over at Squadron. Did they put your gear somewhere?"

"Fontana said he was putting it in the Officers' Hooch over there." "Great, that's the right place. Foxtrot Oscar gets the first bunk inside the door. The other three are for the platoon leaders. I've got the room at the other end. Get settled, get your M16, yell if you've got a problem. Dinner starts at five. Officers cut the line and sit at the table in the back with utensils and glasses set out. Anybody you don't meet at dinner should be at the O club later."

Walking to the officers' hooch, I passed several enlisted men going the other way. Most were wearing t-shirts. Almost all had greasy hands. Some saluted. Just as I walked up to the door, another First Lieutenant walked out the door. He was tall and thin with round wire rim glasses. He wore rank and cavalry insignia like Captain Headley without an upturned hat. "Are you the new FO?" "Yes. Bill Watson." I put out my hand. He shook it without enthusiasm. "Gary Carlson. I'm the First Platoon Leader. This troop is a fine unit. Don't worry, here you'll be judged on your performance." The way he said it, it sounded like he expected to do the judging. "I've got to go check maintenance on my vehicles. I'll see you at dinner or the club."

Just inside the door on the right side there was a metal cot with my bags on it. It was next to a partition wall that came out from the building wall and went up three quarters of the way to the ceiling. There was a similar cot and wall on the other side of the room, with a passageway down the center of the building. Further in there were two more sets of two cots, separated by partition walls. Past the last pair of cots was a door into a larger room that was the XO's room. His room had another door on the outside. Each cubicle had a wall locker against the outside wall. I unpacked a few things into my locker, locked it with the combination lock from my duffel bag and left for the supply room.

I told the sergeant in the supply room I was the new FO and had been sent to get a rifle and flak jacket. "I think we can handle that sir. M16, flak jacket, say four magazines and a bandolier of ammunition. Do you have a poncho liner yet?" "Must not, I don't know what it is." He handed me a small, thin quilt with an almost silken feel and a very light filling. It was colored in the standard Army camouflage pattern. "I'm not sure I'd take it into the field sir, but it feels real nice whenever you get to sleep back in base camp."

He took an M16 out of a locked rack and entered its serial number in a property book with my name, rank and serial number. He put the rifle on the counter then pulled four magazines and a bandolier of ammunition out from under the counter. I checked the rifle's serial number and signed for it in the property book. From a side bin he got a flak jacket and put it on the counter. I carried the lot to the officers' hooch.

It had been at least an hour, so I locked the new gear in my locker and went back to meet Fontana and Charlie. They were waiting next to the Troop Headquarters. I asked Fontana if he knew where our Liaison

Officer was. He said no. I asked when we were going out and Fontana said he thought it was the morning after next. Fontana didn't have the old FO's maps but he had brought the latest signal instructions and code book plus a pair of binoculars.

Fontana pointed to the APC next to the headquarters hooch, "That's our track, the right seat's yours, the radio strapped to the seat is our radio." The seat, on top of the track behind the cupola, was a simple bent steel tube frame with flat bent wire springs across the frame and an undersized pad covering part of the springs. It looked like the frame and springs had been salvaged from a jeep seat. The PRC25 field radio strapped to the back of the seat had a body eighteen inches high, twelve inches wide and three inches thick. There was a similar seat on the left side of the track, but no radio strapped to it.

"Well, I've got some new equipment to get in order and the signal instructions to read tonight. I don't think we can do anything more right now. Meet me here at oh nine thirty tomorrow and we'll work on getting our maps in order."

I went back to the officers hooch and looked at the signal instructions first. They had the radio frequency for our fire direction net and the radio call signs I needed. My Artillery battalion's radio call sign was "Jackhammer." The numeric identification for the Bravo Troop FO was 23, so I was Jackhammer Two Three. The numbers assigned for my defensive targets were bravo tango two three zero one through nine. I put what I planned to take into the field into my duffel bag. The rest of my military stuff would stay in the locker. My stateside uniform was in my garment bag that I took to the lock up in the Troop supply room.

I loaded my four magazines from the boxed ammunition in the bandolier. When I finished, it was time to get to dinner. The mess hall was about half full and it was obvious that most of the unit had finished and gone. Schultz was at the officers' table with another First Lieutenant. "Watson this is Jones, the Second Platoon Leader. Watson's our new FO." Jones nodded as I sat down. Schultz made pleasant small talk. Jones didn't say much at all. They were both almost done when I sat down. They stayed a polite amount of time before excusing themselves saying they'd be at the officers' club later.

When I went to the club later, Headley was at the bar. He wasn't wearing his hat, but it was on the bar. He was easy to identify by the cast on his arm. As soon as I walked in, he motioned me over. "Are you our new FO?" "Yes sir, Lieutenant Watson." "Did you really go to Princeton and Harvard Law School?" "Yes sir." "Well, welcome aboard. You're replacing a good man. Damn, I've got an Ivy League lawyer for an FO and an MBA for a Track Commander. Have a beer."

By the end of the night I had met the last Platoon Leader, First Lieutenant Tom Mead, the Squadron Surgeon and a Captain who was the new Squadron Communications Officer. I learned that a stand down was three days of vehicle repair and rear area pleasures. I also learned that Bravo had just turned in three M48 tanks per platoon and we were going out before the tank crews returned from training with their replacement Sheridans. I knew what an M48 was, but had no idea what a Sheridan was.

Headley talked about Bear, Six Track's Track Commander. Bear had an MBA from the University of South Carolina, was highly decorated and had been recommended for a direct commission. He was also, "most definitely a damned fine trooper." As the evening wore on, it became clear that Headley thought his driver Romero was a fine trooper too. Romero had been awarded a Distinguished Service Cross shortly after joining the Troop for recovering an M48 under fire. The tank had been hit by an RPG and abandoned by its crew when the rest of the Troop backed away. Chico took it upon himself to run back to the tank under fire, climb into its driver's seat and drive it back to the Troop.

Bravo was just back from breaking up an NVA ambush near someplace called the Big Rubber. That was the fight where my predecessor was wounded. Any reference to Ryan triggered a recital that I was destined to hear many times about what a first class Forward Observer old Foxy had been. Foxy was a nickname for an Artillery forward observer derived from Foxtrot Oscar, the mnemonic for FO.

January 23

I opened my eyes about as Jones was walking out of the hooch. He pointed to the left as he walked out, "Showers down that way." There were a few stragglers showering when I arrived, but the building was empty when I finished my shower and left.

Walking toward the Troop Headquarters, I could see Headley standing next to Six Track. "Watson, come here, I want to introduce you." As I approached, he continued, "This is Bear, our TC, and Chico Romero, our driver. Lieutenant Watson is our new FO."

I shook hands with them in order. Bear was an E5 Buck Sergeant, a big white guy about six foot tall and 200 pounds. Romero was a Spec4, six inches shorter and apparently Mexican-American. Neither said much more than hello before they went back to doing something inside the track.

"Captain Headley, when are we leaving?" "Tomorrow morning. Why?" "I don't have any maps and my Recon Sergeant doesn't know where the old ones are."

"We don't keep maps in Troop supplies, but the Squadron supply room has all you'll need. It's over there." He pointed toward some buildings on the other side of the asphalt road. "Tell the supply sergeant that you need a set of maps for our area of operations." "Yessir."

I headed in the direction he had pointed and found the Squadron supply room next to the airstrip. The sergeant seemed to know exactly what I would need. He gave me two copies each of three 1:25,000 maps and one 1:100,000 map. The sergeant said that the 1:25,000 maps covered all of where the Cav normally operated and the 1:100,000 map covered almost all of the Division's area. The 1:25,000 maps were the same scale we used at Ft. Sill, about 2½ inches to the mile. Obviously, the land and terrain they showed was a lot different. It was the 1:25,000 maps that I used almost all of the time.

I got back to the Headquarters hooch about 0945. Fontana and Charlie were standing next to Six Track talking to Bear and Chico as they worked. I showed Fontana the maps and he said he thought I had all the maps the FO had before. Fontana said I would need to mark the checkpoints on the roads and the reference points. We were supposed to radio in each time we crossed a checkpoint on the road and use the reference points to report our location off road. Fontana said the reference points were all at grid line intersections on the map and locations were called in by left or right and up or down from a reference point identified by number. Left one and down one meant a klick west and a klick south of the reference point. Left one point five meant 1500 meters west and so on. I asked Fontana where the checkpoints and reference points were. He didn't know, but volunteered that the Cav used the same ones and the CO should have them on his maps.

I asked Charlie about the radio. He assured me that it was checked and ready, with a new battery installed and two spare batteries loaded in Six Track. He said a battery lasted at least a week, usually two, and that replacement batteries had always arrived the day after they were requested. I released them and started looking for the reference points and checkpoints. I got them all from Lieutenant Carlson and confirmation from Lieutenant Jones.

When I left the Artillery battalion I had received no maps, no radio instructions and no instructions for reporting location. I did get the special rules for firing near the Cambodian border. After dinner, I went to the officers' club for one slow beer then went back to the officers' hooch. I saw some rags and a bottle of rifle lubricant on Lieutenant Jones' cot and borrowed a rag and the bottle. I stripped my M16 and wiped a light coat of oil on the moving parts.

2—Welcome Aboard

January 24

Breakfast was fast and the troops all seemed quieter than the past two days. I brought my gear to Six Track after breakfast. Bear showed me where to stow it inside the track and announced that there wasn't enough room to carry a cot for me.

My uncertainty was partially relieved by the calmness of those around me. Headley seemed more disturbed about having to get up early than facing the enemy. Bear seemed unconcerned about anything. Romero, invisible from where I sat, drove the APC smoothly toward the gate. Or at least I thought it was smooth, I had never ridden on an APC before.

We left Cu Chi's main gate just after 0730. It was only a short distance to Route 1 in the town of Cu Chi where we turned right and headed northwest. Six Track was the fourth vehicle in the Troop's line of vehicles. First Platoon was leading and we were right behind Lieutenant Carlson's track. The Medic Track followed us with the rest of First Platoon after them then the other two platoons. We had seven armored personnel carriers per platoon plus Six Track and the Medic Track. The APCs looked a lot like a shoe box on treads with the front slanted back a little.

I noticed a Vietnamese in a plain green uniform riding on the Medic Track and asked Fontana, "Who's the Viet on Medic Track?" "Nam. He's a Hoi Chan. Used to be VC, but he switched over. He's our scout."

Each of the platoon leaders had a jeep seat strapped on the left rear side of his vehicle, the same place as the CO's seat, just over the radios inside the track. The drivers sat in a compartment in the left front of the hull. On the road the drivers rode with their seats high and their heads sticking well out of the hatch at the top of the compartment. The vehicle's engine was in a compartment just to the right of the driver. The Track Commander rode in an open topped cupola a little forward of the center of the top of the vehicle. The cupola mounted a .50 caliber machine gun with a wide rectangular gun shield. The bottom of the cupola was a circular hatch into the inside of the vehicle. The Track Commander usually rode sitting on the hatch cover opened to the rear with his feet dangling through the open hole. Immediately behind the cupola was the "cargo hatch" that covered most of the space between the two jeep seats on Six Track. It was almost always open, hinged to the rear. Fontana and Charlie rode sitting on the cargo hatch cover with their feet down into the vehicle. Fontana was to my left and Charlie to his left.

It was pretty easy to keep track of the checkpoints on the road and I radioed them in as we crossed them. Checkpoint 09, a road crossing. Checkpoint 17, a village. Checkpoint 08, a stream crossing. They were not in numerical order. The next was Checkpoint 07, an intersection in Trang Bang, a rather large built up area. We stayed on Route 1 past Checkpoint 19 and stopped near Checkpoint 20. It had taken just over an hour from Cu Chi. Fontana hadn't said much during the trip but had been watching to make sure that I didn't do too badly.

As soon as we stopped, Fontana pointed to a dirt walled fortification about 100 meters off the road, "That's Fire Support Base Hampton, the Cav forward Headquarters." I nodded. "Why are we stopped?" Headley looked over. "We're waiting for one of the Assistant Division Commanders. He wants to go on this trip with us."

As he spoke, a helicopter landed between Hampton and us. Two passengers got out. One was wearing a shiny black leather belt and holster that was only worn by generals. The other carried a Colt Commando, the special short version of the M16. An APC came out of the Hampton gate and stopped to pick them up. Headley spoke, "General Black will be traveling with us on Colonel McGowan's track. They'll be right behind us." Lieutenant Colonel McGowan was the Commanding Officer of the Cav Squadron.

We continued on into Go Dau Ha. At Checkpoint 05 in the center of town, we stayed on Route 1 as it turned west toward Cambodia. The road was the same as it had been all the way from Cu Chi, two lanes of blacktop. At the western edge of Go Dau Ha was a bridge over the Oriental River. West of Go Dau Ha, I didn't have any checkpoints on my map. I radioed in our location about every three klicks. I used left or right and up and down from the nearest reference point. The radio operator at the FDC took the locations without comment.

About nine clicks west of the river we turned off Route 1 into what had been rice paddies. There were no crops in the fields. We moved slowly across the paddies, toward a cluster of huts named Xom Ba Ao on the map. As we moved further away from the road, I could see where Route 1 crossed the border. On the Vietnamese side was a tan colored building and on the Cambodian side, a white colored one. There appeared to be permanent vertical barriers in the road between the two. There was no sign of people at either location and no traffic approaching from either side.

At 1120 we pulled up on line facing Xam Ba Ao from the east. As best I could tell, we were 300 meters east of the Cambodian border. Xam Ba Ao had more people about than any place we had seen since Go Dau Ha. Apparently it was a market. I could see a two-strand barbed wire fence about where I thought the border was. There was an opening in the fence near the south end of the huts that had two partially uniformed men with rifles on the Vietnamese side. There were people going through the

2—Welcome Aboard

opening both ways and the two uniformed men stopped some of them to check papers.

The General, his aide, Colonel McGowan, Lieutenant Carlson and about ten of his men with M16s dismounted and walked into the market. Headley sat still, so I did too. He made small talk between radio calls. When he was busy, I just smoked in silence. We waited for an hour or more before the General and his group walked back to the vehicles. I hadn't seen any organized reception in the market. There were enough military age men in the crowd who were not in uniform that it seemed likely that some were VC or NVA. Maybe the General was just showing that he could go anywhere.

Shortly after they returned, a helicopter landed and the General, his aide and the Squadron CO left by helicopter. We went back the way we came and by 1600 were inside Hampton. When Six Track parked, Headley announced, "We're here tonight."

Fire Support Base Hampton had a circular dirt berm pushed up by a bulldozer. There were sandbag bunkers spaced along the inside of the berm. The circle was big enough to hold the tents and bunkers that were the forward headquarters of the Cav on one side and the six self propelled 155mm howitzers and assorted bunkers and vehicles of the resident Artillery battery on the other side, with room left over for all of our Troop's vehicles parked spaced inside the wall, pointing out. The berm was about five feet tall, but the .50 caliber machine guns on the tracks parked just behind it could fire over it.

There really wasn't anything for me to do. I wandered around a bit and had dinner. After it got dark and I got sleepy, there wasn't anyone inside Six Track, so I lay down on the bench on the right side inside. It had been designed as the seat for half of the infantry squad riding into battle and was just barely wide enough to lie on and had a very thin pad on it. Eventually, I fell asleep.

3

Ap Bien Hoa

January 25

It was dark when I was shaken awake and told that we were moving out. I wasn't told anything else. Leaving Hampton, I overheard we were headed to a village near the Cambodian border that had been attacked during the night. Once we were outside Hampton, troopers started popping hand flares, keeping three or four at a time in the air over our column. The flares cut the dark, but it was still mostly opaque shadows all around us. Fontana and Charlie rode silently beside me, both holding their M16s in their laps. We went into Go Dau Ha again and over the bridge. We continued on down Route 1 toward Cambodia, the same route we had taken the day before. I didn't like moving on a big, noisy vehicle in the dark. As soon as we crossed the bridge, the hand held flares were replaced by brighter parachute flares dropped from a helicopter.

There was still no sign of the sun when we stopped three klicks beyond the bridge. When we stopped, I radioed in our location. "Jackhammer One Eight, this is Jackhammer Two Three, from Bravo Seven, right three point three, up three point zero, over." "Jackhammer Two Three, Jackhammer One Eight, from Bravo Seven, right three point three, up three point zero, out."

That radio exchange reflected some basic radio procedures. Transmissions start by identifying who is speaking then to whom the message is directed. My message was reporting to my FDC where my unit was. "Bravo Seven" was one of the map reference points. "Over" at the end of my message meant that I expected a response. Their response confirmed my message by repeating it. "Out" at the end of their message meant they did not expect a response. I doubt that anyone followed correct radio procedure all of the time but format and confirmation reduced communication errors.

The column turned left off the asphalt and headed south on a narrow dirt road at slow walking speed. Headley was on the radio almost constantly. I heard only snippets. In the half light of the flares, I could see

3—Ap Bien Hoa

two troops walking in front of the lead track, steadily swinging their mine detectors in front of them. Six Track had moved to immediately behind the lead vehicle when we turned off Route 1. Almost as soon as we turned, both sides of the dirt road were swamps with standing water and scattered clumps of vegetation. My map showed the road we were on, but as we moved away from Route 1, I had little sense of where we were on that road. I couldn't identify anything in the shadows on the sides of the road. I radioed in our position each time I thought we'd gone another klick but I wasn't confident of my estimates.

By the time we were what I estimated to be three klicks from Route 1, the sky had turned light grey. The hedgerows marking the fields away from the road were clearer. The CO decided it was light enough to see any mines that had been dug into the road. We stopped for the mine sweepers to mount the lead track then started again at a slow driving speed that was still faster than our prior walking speed.

Immediately I was smashed by the sound of an explosion and the lead track was surrounded by smoke. I snapped my head right to look at the hedgerow a hundred meters from the road, expecting a storm of automatic weapons fire or an infantry rush to complete an ambush. Nothing came. When I looked back to the track in front of us, there was little sign that anything had happened to it. I expected it to be spread out like an unfolded paper model, but it looked almost unchanged. Two of the troopers who had been riding it were on the ground peering at the broken left track and a three foot wide hole in the road under the track. Headley was on the radio reporting the damage and that we had stopped. Some of the troopers from the track behind us walked past with little apparent concern to join in inspecting the damage.

Looking around, I noticed there was only one track behind us. I asked the CO where the others were. He said they had stayed behind on Route 1 when we turned onto the dirt road, but that they were coming now. For almost an hour I had been reporting the entire Troop was where I thought I was.

In ten minutes the rest of the Troop stopped behind us. After a bit, the seven tracks of one of the platoons squeezed past us and the damaged track and Six Track fell in behind them. This time the CO assured me that all of the Troop would be together, except the damaged vehicle. A mechanic track was already on its way from Hampton to repair the damaged track. In the open and in the daylight, there wasn't much danger to the crew left behind or the mechanics coming to get them.

My concern returned to keeping the FDC advised of where we were. I had no instructions how often to call in our location when we weren't on a road with checkpoints, but every klick or so seemed right. In daylight, I could see things around us that I could identify on the map and was confident I was reporting accurate locations. I radioed in our location so often that I won't mention it much.

Not too far from where the mine exploded, the road came out of the swampy area. As soon as the adjacent fields were solid ground, we pulled off the road. Initially we stayed close to the road, paralleling it, then moved away from it to go around a small settlement. After that, we continued pointed at the next cluster of huts.

We came up on Ap Binh Hoa from the north and I radioed in that we were a klick north of the village. As soon as the FDC radio operator acknowledged my message, the Liaison Officer I had never met was on the radio, "Jackhammer Two Three, this is Jackhammer Three Five, your location is from Bravo Seven, right two point four, down one point eight, over."

He located us over 1500 meters north of where I had. I could hear helicopter noise when he transmitted. "Jackhammer Three Five, this is Jackhammer Two Three, I have the village in sight. I believe my prior location is correct, over."

"Two Three, this is Three Five, I am overhead your column. Your prior location was wrong. Break. Jackhammer One Eight, this is Jackhammer Three Five, Jackhammer Two Three is from Bravo Seven, right two point four, down one point eight, over."

"Jackhammer Three Five, Jackhammer One Eight, Jackhammer Two Three is from Bravo Seven, right two point four, down one point eight, out." Even over the radio, I could tell from his tone that the discussion was over. I checked the map and found that he had reported us near a small village that we had passed fifteen minutes before. I was worried, but wasn't really sure how accurate our position reports had to be.

As we skirted the village, I could see the next village almost 1500 meters away. Even at that distance, I could see a massive gate in the north wall of the next village, an identifying feature of Ap Bien Hoa that was shown on the map. Ap Bien Hoa was four or five times the size of the village I had mistaken for it.

We were west of the north end of the Ap Bien Hoa when I saw a corpse, face down about twenty feet from my side of the track. He was barefoot. His uniform was forest green shirt and pants. There was a green NVA sun helmet next to his head and he wore a canvas belt and a heavy canvas pack. There was no weapon in sight. He was just dead in the middle of a field with no sign of injury or fighting. We stopped ten feet from the body. All the other tracks kept moving. Fontana jumped down. He stood near the body and looked at it for a while then rolled it over on its back. There was no sign of how the man had died. Fontana checked his shirt pockets and pulled some paper out. There were no pockets in his pants.

Fontana stripped off the belt and pack, picked up the helmet and came back to the track. He held the gear up toward me. "Would you like these sir?" "You got them, don't you want them?" "No sir, I've got a helmet."

The pack was internally divided into three vertical compartments. The dead man had been the ammunition carrier for an RPG team. Fontana climbed on board, sat down on the cargo hatch next to me and unfolded the paper. It was a two page letter in Vietnamese. Inside the letter was a black and white photo, a studio portrait of a Vietnamese young woman standing next to a small waist-high table with a potted plant on it. She was wearing almost shapeless dark pants and a white blouse and held a flat conical straw hat in one hand against her leg. She looked at the camera without expression. She would never see her loved one again. Fontana folded the paper and passed it to Headley who put it in a pocket without interrupting his radio transmission.

As we approached the junction of two dirt trails west of the village, about ten small explosions erupted a hundred meters south of us. Headley looked over, "Chuck must have a sixty millimeter mortar in there targeted on the crossroads, but no way to adjust."

We kept moving to the southwest and stopped a klick west of the village, between the village and the Cambodian border three klicks further west. We had been moving in a single file column all morning, but pulled into a rough circle of vehicles when we stopped. The seven vehicles of each platoon, facing out, formed rough thirds of the perimeter. Six Track and the Medic Track parked near the center of the circle. Headley told someone on the radio that he didn't like putting the Platoon Leaders on line, but, with no tanks, needed the extra vehicles. Between us and the village to the east were open fields with some low rice dikes. To the south and west was about the same. About a hundred meters north was a line of brush that stretched off to the west.

We just sat there. I heard enough of what Headley was saying on the radio to know that there were some RFs near us. He was also concerned that the Aerorifles, apparently part of the Cav, were in or near the village. Several times we heard two rifle shots fired from the village wall. Apparently someone was sniping at us, but I never saw a bullet strike near us. After we had sat there for almost an hour, a huge crowd of civilians came out of the north gate of the village and hurried up the road to the north. About 1400 we got word that Charlie Company, 4th of the 9th Infantry would be joining us. They were south of the village. Within a few minutes we could see them walking toward us well away from the village.

As the grunts approached, Headley told the Platoon Leaders to make our circle bigger. By the time Charlie Company was getting close, each of the perimeter tracks had pulled ahead about twenty meters. Apparently

Headley passed the word that we were spending the night, because our troops started digging in. Each crew began a slit trench just a little to the right of their track. Colonel McGowan and the new Communications Officer arrived by helicopter. Headley said that we were staying the night here and went off to meet with McGowan and the Infantry CO.

When the Infantry Company walked into our circle, I found their FO and asked him how he wanted to coordinate. He smiled and said it was all mine because he couldn't reach the Artillery on his radio. His RTO was carrying the same radio I had, but didn't have a long antenna. He had only an eighteen inch antenna that looked like a heavy steel tape. My antenna was about three times that long. He went off to join his CO and we spoke no more. The Infantry had already spread themselves around the circle and were working on digging another two or three holes between each of the vehicles.

I knew that I was supposed to assess our situation and plot defensive targets for that night. The most obvious risk seemed to be the brush line immediately north of us. A few hundred meters to our west the brush line was thicker with some trees in it. I decided to pace off the distance to the nearest clump of trees in the brush line and use that as one of my targets. I was about a hundred meters toward the trees when I was stopped by a chilling sense of how alone I was. I had taken my M16 with one magazine, but I was in the middle of an open space, the Troop seemed very far away and walking up to the brush line alone a few hundred meters further out no longer seemed like a good idea. I estimated the distance to the trees and returned to our laager.

Walking back I noticed that almost all of the crews had put up a short chain link fence across the front of each track. They were RPG screens erected by driving two steel posts into the ground and wiring the fencing to the posts. The screen was supposed to detonate an incoming RPG before it hit the track. Each track carried its posts and rolled fencing strapped to the front of the track.

Some crews were already stretching the two concertina rolls of coiled barbed wire that each track also carried as part of a simple barbed wire barrier around our position. Closed, each concertina looked like a three foot diameter barbed wire donut. Each one of them could stretch into a self supporting circular barbed wire fence. A single band of concertina didn't make much of a barrier ten meters beyond the perimeter of tracks, but it would slow someone running in from the dark.

When I got back to my radio and called in my defensive targets, the FDC took the ones that I had put in some clumps of trees well to the south, but insisted that the ones I put in the brush immediately to the north had to be much further away from us, at least 900 meters. They would not take any target in or near the village. Calling in a defensive target meant me telling the FDC the map grid coordinates I wanted assigned to one of my assigned target numbers. They pre-plotted each defensive target I called in so that they could fire on it faster.

Just after 1800 a Chinook helicopter arrived with what Headley called a night kit. There were more barbed wire concertinas, apparently enough to complete a single ring all the way around our expanded laager. There were fifty sheets of PSP, pierced steel planking, for the Infantry. Each of our line tracks carried a sheet of PSP strapped to one side of the hull. A sheet was over six feet long and two feet wide. It was lightened by a pattern of holes, but was rippled on the long axis and was strong enough to hold two layers of sand bags for a roof over the two-man slit trenches the Infantry was digging. The Cav troopers were already using their PSP to put overhead cover on their slit trenches. The rest of the night kit was over a thousand sandbags for the Infantry. All of this came in a single cargo net.

As soon as the first Chinook left, another came in with a 105mm howitzer slung below. It hovered near the center of our laager low enough for the gun to be unhooked, then moved to the side and landed to let seven men off. Its departure was followed quickly by another Chinook coming in with a second howitzer slung below that was dropped off next to the first. Another seven men got off. Then came two more Chinooks each delivering a cargo net of artillery ammunition and baled sandbags. The gun crews manhandled the guns a little closer together, with one pointed north and the other pointed west.

Through all of this I stayed at Six Track. For all the bustle going on, I heard little discussion of plans or assumptions. Colonel McGowan and Headley passed by occasionally but said little to me about what was going on. Once Colonel McGowan said he was glad we had gotten a Killer Junior team. I guessed he was referring to the two howitzers.

When I saw some of the others eating, I ate part of a C-ration. By the time it got dark, Headley had gone somewhere to sleep. I stretched out next to a low rice dike a few meters from Six Track and went to sleep.

January 26

I was awakened by an explosion. I think there were four or five more with a few seconds between them. They all were less than a hundred meters south of our perimeter. As I ran the few steps to Six Track there was an explosion on the perimeter about due north and what looked like four big Fourth of July rockets flew together through the laager from the north about three feet off the ground. When I reached Six Track the north part of our perimeter erupted in machine gun fire. It was a noise that I had never imagined. Ten or so .50 caliber machine guns and an equal number of M60s created an almost continuous sound. Every third or fourth round was a tracer and the bright yellow lines wove a glow on the other side of the vehicles that I saw only as dark shapes outlined by the glow.

Headley came running over from the Medic Track putting on his flak jacket as he ran. His radio helmet was waiting on top of the track. Headley had been sleeping on a stretcher slung inside the Medic Track when the attack started.

When I checked my watch, I could barely read 0215. I radioed in that we had taken some high explosive fire, direction unknown, and ground fire from the north. My Liaison Officer radioed that he was with the Squadron XO in a chopper about five minutes from being on station. Headley was busy on his radios. Colonel McGowan arrived to talk to him. Colonel McGowan said the first helicopter fire team was two minutes out.

The volume of our fire to the north had decreased, but was still steady. The rest of the circle fired from time to time, apparently only when they thought they could see a target. When I ran to Six Track, I had gotten inside the track, standing with my head and shoulders through the cargo hatch. I couldn't see what was going on, so I climbed up into my jeep seat on top. For the next two hours I sat there contributing little to the battle that went on around me. Sometimes the noise of our firing went up, sometimes it went down. For almost two hours it never stopped entirely for more than a few seconds. We had erratic light from parachute flares and the light from the flames coming out of a track almost due north of Six Track that burned through the rest of the night.

After the initial hits I knew that what had looked like Fourth of July rockets were RPGs. They continued to pass through our laager sporadically, most well overhead. One hit the ground between Six Track and the Medic Track and skipped without exploding, still climbing at a slight angle as it passed on to the south. Two more tracks got hit during the two hours, but most of the time I didn't know how much anyone was firing at us.

On the Artillery net I could hear my Liaison Officer radioing in fire missions on targets to the north of us. He was shut off whenever helicopter gunships came on station and allowed to resume when they had expended their ordnance and left. Incoming artillery and helicopters shouldn't share the same airspace. The most visible enemy fire was bursts of green tracers climbing toward the gunships from .51 caliber machine guns. One of the enemy machine guns appeared to be inside Ap Bien Hoa and there were others to the north and west of us. The enemy machine guns didn't fire continuously because when an antiaircraft machine gun fired for too long it identified itself as the next target. In the dark, I could see the exhaust

3—Ap Bien Hoa

flames marking the rockets' flights. The helicopters fired several rockets on each firing pass. Their miniguns were six barreled, electrically powered, high speed machine guns. Our machine guns tracers came fast, but were still separate. The tracers coming out of the helicopter miniguns looked like glowing yellow water coming out of a hose.

A couple of times when there were breaks in the artillery missions for helicopters, I asked the Liaison Officer to bring the fire in closer. Some of what he fired seemed 2000 meters away. He said he couldn't fire much closer to us. Some of the helicopter rockets hit just outside our perimeter, but the artillery fire seemed to be in a different fight.

For most of the fight, I had Six Track to myself. One time Colonel McGowan came into the track through the small door in the rear ramp and radioed a report to someone. When he left, he looked up at me, "Good job, son." A while after that, the new Communications Officer came in the same door. He didn't say anything, he just smiled, handed me a cold Coke and left. By 0330 there was still fairly steady outgoing fire from the north of our perimeter but little sign of return fire.

By 0415 we were getting no incoming fire except from the north and that was almost nothing. Each shot or burst elicited an overpowering response. I heard on the Artillery net that a dust off chopper was coming in and saw a strobe light in an open space on the west side of Six Track. I couldn't see the bright light directly, but the shielding was not entirely effective and I could see a flashing glow over somebody's head.

The slick came in fast and low from the south and stopped hard just above the landing spot and dropped in. Shadows moved quickly. Four times a man supported by his arms over two other men's shoulders was hustled up and pushed on board. Then two man sized bundles were thrown on and the chopper pulled up and raced off to the south.

By 0500 all the firing had stopped. The Liaison Officer radioed that his chopper was leaving to refuel and instructed me to call in harassing fire between us and the Cambodian border. For the next hour I slowly adjusted two guns in an essentially random pattern a klick or more to the west of us. When full light arrived, I was told to shut it off and scout helicopters started flitting over the target area looking for anyone moving back to Cambodia.

At the same time, the grunts sent foot patrols into the brush to the north of the laager. They came back with three seriously wounded prisoners, a confirmed body count of fifteen, a machine gun, three AK47s and a pile of ammunition, grenades and gear. Two enemy bodies were draped over the concertina wire ten meters in front of the burned out track. The immediate report was that the POWs were seventeen-year-old kids who'd come in from Cambodia for the first time the night before.

At 0830 a general came to visit us. The troops were exhausted, They paid little attention to him as he walked about with his aide. Minutes later my Artillery battalion S3 flew in by helicopter. He was in fresh fatigues with a shiny clean Colt Commando, just like the General's aide. I saw him walk to the Killer Junior location then he came to Six Track. I got down and saluted as he approached. He did not return the salute. "Lieutenant, why didn't you take command of the guns when they arrived? Why didn't you report the guns were running out of ammunition?"

I had no idea what he was talking about. "Sir, I didn't know I was supposed to take command. I didn't know anything about their ammunition." Near the end of the attack the 105s had run out of ammunition. I not only hadn't known that they were out of ammunition, I hadn't even noticed when they were firing or not firing. He didn't take it any further than making it clear that I had damn sure better take charge next time. Apparently the guns and their crews were from one of the firing batteries in my battalion. I did not point out that battalion had not even advised me that the guns were coming, let alone instructed me to take command.

"Look at these Cavalry troops. They haven't cleaned themselves up. They aren't even standing up when the general comes by. You make sure that our Artillery troops never act like that." "Yes sir." Then he got back into his helicopter and left. He never said a word about how I had done as an FO. I knew I hadn't done much. I had stayed calm, but really hadn't known what to do and still didn't. My asshole S3 offered no guidance.

I had not noticed the Killer Junior team during the attack, but they had provided critical fire. During the first two hours of the attack they had fired 370 flechette rounds over open sights between the vehicles. A flechette round is just a huge shotgun shell. A fuse set anywhere from at the end of the muzzle to a thousand meters away blew the projectile cover off and 10,000 steel darts begin scattering.

The two bundles loaded on the helicopter in the dark were Lieutenant Jones, who was mortally wounded, and a Track Commander in the Second Platoon who was killed by an RPG round that hit him in the chest without exploding. One track had burned to an empty hulk and three other tracks were seriously damaged. The two enemy corpses on the wire meant that they had been close to penetrating our perimeter.

A resupply convoy of two Headquarters APCs, two tracked cargo carriers and another APC carrying a ground radar unit arrived at 1500. The primary load of the cargo carriers was ammunition for the Killer Junior team. The APCs brought assorted stuff and some cooks. As soon as they were unloaded, the two Headquarters APCs and cargo carriers went back the way they had come. I went over to watch the gun's ammunition being put in two partially covered holes, but saw nothing for me to do.

3—Ap Bien Hoa

When it got dark, Bear pulled up the rear ramp on Six Track and turned on the light inside the track. I sat inside to read. The radios were on speakers and the others came and went, but I just stayed and read. Bear stuck his head in the little door in the rear ramp, "Are you willing to take a radio watch sir?" "What's that?"

"An hour here in Six Track with two half hour reports from the Platoon Leaders' tracks." "Okay, when?" "From one to two. Somebody will wake you. You wake me after the platoon reports at two."

At 2100 the Radar Track radioed that they saw about ten people moving about 1500 meters from us. Headley said I should call fire in on them. "Charlie, get the radio and bring it to me at the Radar Track."

When I got to the Radar Track, I stuck my head in the back door, "What ya got?" A voice came out from in front of a screen with some green squiggles on it, "Ten gooks moving at four zero nine zero mils, fourteen hundred sixty meters out."

Charlie arrived with our radio. "Jackhammer One Eight, this is Jackhammer Two Three, fire mission, over." There was almost no delay. "Jackhammer Two Three, Jackhammer One Eight, fire mission, out."

"One Eight, this is Two Three, direction four zero niner zero, distance one four six zero, ten men in the open, battery three in effect, adjust fire, over." Because "nine" could sound like "five" on the radio, proper radio procedure was to say "niner." In the Artillery using "niner" on the radio was a point of honor. Getting a number wrong in a fire mission could kill a lot of friends.

"Two Three, One Eight, direction four zero niner zero, distance one four six zero, ten men in the open, battery three in effect, adjust fire, wait, out."

Describing the target by direction first told the FDC to start plotting from where I was, something they already knew. "Direction four zero niner zero" meant 4090 mils. A full circle, 360 degrees, is 6400 mils. Due north is 6400 mils, 1600 is east, 3200 south and 4800 west. A direction of 4090 mils is a shade north of southwest. The target was just under a mile away from us, probably sure we couldn't see them in the dark. The FDC's "wait" was a reminder that they needed to get clearance to fire. The wait lasted only a few minutes.

"Jackhammer Two Three, this is Jackhammer One Eight, on the way, over." "One Eight, Two Three, on the way, out." The FDC report of "on the way" meant that the guns, the center two when adjusting, had fired and the rounds were in the air. A few seconds and the flash of the rounds exploding was visible in the distance. The sound followed quickly.

I poked my head inside the track again, "Did you see it?" "I think so. About a hundred meters short and a hundred mils right of the target."

At one thousand meters distance, an angle of one mil is a meter wide. One hundred mils at fifteen hundred meters is one hundred fifty meters wide. The conversion isn't perfect, but it's close enough for adjusting artillery rounds. No calculation was needed to pass on the correction for shortfall.

"Jackhammer One Eight, this is Two Three, add one hundred, left one five zero, fire for effect, over." "Two Three, One Eight, add one hundred, left one five zero, fire for effect, out."

All of the adjustments I asked for were based on the direction from me to the target that I had given the FDC. This time the wait was less than thirty seconds. "Jackhammer Two Three, this is Jackhammer One Eight, on the way, over." "One Eight, Two Three, on the way, out."

Six rounds landed at about the same time followed shortly by twelve more that came as fast as each gun could load and fire two more. I yelled at the track, "How's that?" "Looks OK." "One Eight, Two Three, end of mission, over." "Two Three, One Eight, end of mission, out."

I waited for a few minutes, but they saw nothing more on the screen. Charlie and I went back to Six Track. I told Headley what happened and went back to reading. Twenty minutes later we were called again for another target 500 meters from the first. The drill was the same. This time I stayed at the Radar Track. The third target was twenty minutes later. The third time the radar operator said he could see the fire for effect rounds landing right on the target on his radar screen. I wasn't sure I believed it, but I radioed in, "radar observed rounds on target" as a report of fire effect in my "end of mission" message. After the third mission, no more movement was seen on the radar and I went to sleep against my rice dike.

January 27

Nothing happened on my radio watch except platoon status reports every half hour. I woke Bear right after the 0200 reports. I took a radio watch on the Six Track every night we were in the field after that. Like location reports, I usually won't mention it.

I woke up again about 0630. There wasn't any call, just the noise of other people moving about. I shaved and changed uniforms. The Cav troopers and the infantry grunts were mixed up getting the breakfast that the Cav cooks who spent the night with us had fixed. I got some hot pancakes and canned grapefruit juice.

At 0800, the Troop formed on line facing west. As soon as we had swept the klick immediately west of the laager, Headley started sending single platoons to check different things, hedgerows or clumps of brush and trees. When I thought we were within 700 meters of the Cambodian border, Headley pointed out an unusually large hole in the midst of some artillery impact craters. "Watson, looks like you might actually have hit something." Headley smiled. "How's that sir?" "Secondary explosion. Looks like there was more explosion than just the shell."

We had turned back toward the laager when helicopters started arriving there just before noon. I could see the two 105mm howitzers lifted out by Chinooks. Then there were two Chinooks that left with full cargo nets slung below. By the time we were close to the laager site, the traffic was Hueys picking up smaller cargo nets and some personnel. There were still three Cav tracks at the laager site and we were headed back for them when a formation of Hueys arrived, loaded up the Infantry company and disappeared to the east.

Ten minutes after we reached the laager, we were on our way out, the way we had come, without any visible concern about mines. Twenty minutes after we got back to Route 1 we were pulling into Hampton. After dinner Bear saw me near the Cav headquarters tent. "Sir, I found a cot for you. It's stowed in the track."

January 28

When I got up, I stripped to a towel sarong and flip-flop sandals and headed for a crude shower stall I had noticed. When I got back Bear said I should use the Cav laundry service. For three bucks a week I could get all my laundry done. I would give the dirty stuff to whatever headquarters track was heading to Hampton from our laager or to Cu Chi if we were in Hampton and the clean stuff would be returned to me. He suggested bundling a change of uniform with a towel for a full set. You piled it on the top half of the blouse, folded the bottom of the blouse over and tied the bundle with the blouse sleeves. I turned in two full sets to a Troop headquarters track that already had a pile of bundles inside and went to breakfast. I sent laundry in almost every day from then on.

We left Hampton at 0830. Headley said we were headed to the Little Rubber and pointed to a rubber plantation on the map about eight klicks north of Go Dau Ha. Most of the road we covered had a new asphalt surface, but we still moved slowly. The first checkpoint was Checkpoint 21, a stream crossing two klicks out of Go Dau Ha. Next was Checkpoint 04 then Checkpoint 22 in Ap Bao Dung, the first village north of Go Dau Ha.

At 0915 we pulled up to the edge of the rubber plantation along the northeast side of the road. The plantation was a neat pattern of evenly spaced rubber trees planted in rows. The space between the rows was just a little wider than an APC. A fifty meter strip next to the road was clear, with stumps showing that the trees had originally come to the edge of the road.

As the Troop was forming on line to go down the tree rows to the northeast, two platoons of Alpha Troop moved up the road behind us and joined the left side of our line. I hadn't heard their FO reporting in any checkpoints. The triangles and numbers on Alpha's tracks were red.

Six Track was behind the line in the middle of the Troop. The Medic Track followed us. We rolled forward slowly and stopped frequently. I couldn't hear what caused the stops, but I could hear Headley give the order to halt into the mike on his radio helmet then we would stop for a while. His helmet was a hard plastic helmet like pilots wear with built in earphones and a small mike in front of his mouth. He had a switch to select between a radio on the Troop frequency that he used to communicate with the Platoon Leaders and one on the Squadron frequency that the Squadron CO used to communicate with the Troops. Both radios were mounted inside the track almost directly under where he sat.

My radio was a lot simpler. It was designed for a man to carry on his back and was strapped to the back of my seat as a convenience. I had a handset similar to a telephone. When I wasn't actually using it, I kept it hooked on the front of my flak jacket so I could hear it. Sometimes I gave it to Fontana or Charlie and they clipped it on their flak jacket. We used just one frequency, the Artillery fire direction net.

Our slow progress though the Little Rubber brought us to the northeastern end of the plantation at 1200. We crossed a dirt track that marked its boundary into a fairly open area and stopped for lunch. Alpha was still on our left. When we stopped there were scattered hooches about another 200 meters on. Within a few minutes boys from the hooches were walking our way. They stopped about half way and stood for a while. Then they came another fifty meters and stopped again. Nam had seen them and went halfway out to them and called them in. They came to him and he shared some C-rations with them as they talked for a while. When they were done, he came back and the kids headed back to the hooches. Nam came back and reported to the CO that the kids said there were VC in the area, but they hadn't said how many or where. Headley said that was certainly a surprise, but despite his sarcasm radioed in the report. Nam didn't talk much, but his English was functional.

At 1300 we loaded up, each vehicle pivoted 180 degrees and we went out the way we had come in. We still traveled only a little faster than walking until we were back on the road, but we pulled into Hampton at 1405. The Alpha Troop platoons had disappeared, again with no report from their FO on the Artillery net.

3—Ap Bien Hoa

I had no idea why we had come in so early, but didn't care. Most of the troops were soon busy doing something on their vehicles or gear. I had nothing to do but read a *Stars and Stripes* and some magazines I found.

Before dinner Headley invited me to the Troop briefing. It wasn't much, Headley, Lieutenant Carlson, Lieutenant Mead, the senior sergeant from Second Platoon and me. Headley said we'd be clearing roads in the morning, then do a sweep on the other side of Ap Suoi Cao, a village seven klicks northeast of Go Dau Ha. I was at every Troop briefing after that.

The map showed a good quality road from Go Dau Ha to Ap Suoi Cao. Headley said nothing about the road, so I assumed he wasn't worried about it. The distinctive feature of the village he pointed to was the cultivated land that stretched back three klicks from the highway next to the village. The cultivated area was three klicks wide. About two klicks east of the cultivated area the map showed two separate areas of dark green that indicated woods. Headley called them the "Bo Loy" Woods. Later I learned that it was spelled Boi Loi.

After dinner, I was reading inside Six Track when Headley walked up the lowered rear ramp and sat on the other bench. He asked about my reading and made some small talk. Eventually he started talking about the fight at Ap Bien Hoa. At one point he figured Second Platoon, on the north side of the perimeter and bearing the brunt of the attack, was zero percent effective. He was considering moving another platoon to that side. Moving at night, under attack with an infantry unit mixed in, even inside our own laager, would have had a tremendous risk of confusion, even panic. At the crisis time Colonel McGowan was going from position to position to get Second Platoon and the grunts mixed in with them back into the fight. He found some tracks with no one firing the .50 caliber, probably because it was more exposed than being on the ground or in a trench. When he found one like that, he climbed into the cupola, fired a few bursts then yelled out that the machine gun was working fine now and the Track Commander should take over. Apparently it worked and in each case the machine gun was put back in the fight. At least it never was necessary to move in another platoon.

January 29

I had slept on my cot in the bunker next to Six Track. Stand to was at 0600, then shave, shower and half a breakfast. We were loaded and starting our road sweeps at 0700. Each platoon was given a separate stretch of road. Headley told me where First and Second Platoons were headed and I radioed that in to the Artillery. Six Track went with Third Platoon down the dirt road from Go Dau Ha to Ap Suoi Cao. As we passed a PF post at the edge of town, we slowed to less than ten miles an hour. "Why so slow?" "Mines. Lead track is looking for signs of digging in the road."

Twenty minutes after leaving Go Dau Ha we were almost to Checkpoint 06, a road intersection two-thirds of the way to Ap Suoi Cao. I could tell enough from the CO's radio transmissions to know that the other platoons were through with their road sweeps and catching up with us. Within minutes I could see tracks joining the end of our column.

Next to the road at Checkpoint 06 there was a small dirt fort with an impressive band of barbed wire entanglements around it. There was one RF with an M16 standing next to an opening in the wall at the end of a crooked path through the wire. We speeded up a little and soon were where the road ran into Highway 19 at Ap Suoi Cao. At the intersection we turned south for a short distance past the edge of the village and turned left. This turn to the east off Highway 19 just south of Ap Suoi Cao was one that we would make over and over.

After the turn off Highway 19, the column moved east in an area at least 300 meters wide immediately south of the village fields was flat with almost no vegetation. We headed in faster than we had moved on the road. In the fields, I could see a few kids, each with a water buffalo, headed away from the village. The end of the easy ride came at 0925. The vegetation on the south side of the strip had gotten gradually taller and closer to us. It wasn't solid, it was irregular clumps as tall or taller than my head seated on the track. Almost all of the clumps had room for a track or two to pass between, but they were dense enough that you couldn't see very far into them.

The Troop shifted into a line formation. We headed into the brush almost like we had headed into the rubber plantation, but none of the tracks could move in a straight line. They snaked through the brush trying to stay close to on line. We moved slowly when we moved and stopped often. Many of the troops had dismounted and looked carefully at each clump of brush we passed. If anyone saw something that merited further review, we stopped. Otherwise the tracks just moved at walking speed.

Once we were well into the brush, I couldn't see much of anything. We hadn't gone far enough to be really lost, but I couldn't see a thing that I could use to locate us on the map. About the third time we stopped, I stood up on top of the track and could see over a lot of the brush. I could see back to the village and forward into a large open space not too far beyond where we were stopped. Then it struck me that it might not be a good idea to be the only head in clear sight above the brush and sat down.

We pulled out of the band of brush at 1030. On the other side was a large relatively open area stretching off to the east. To the north I could see dense green brush with scattered trees that corresponded to the woods shown on the map. The map showed the area south of the woods as rice fields. There was a grid of rice dikes, but no sign of cultivation. There appeared to be some hooches and hedgerows well to the east, some hooches on the south edge of the fallow fields and patches of brush and hedgerow scattered throughout the fields. We spent an hour poking into the closest brush patches, then stopped for lunch. I opened a C-ration can of meat but couldn't eat all of it. A can of peaches was better. Immediately after lunch I was thirsty again.

During lunch Colonel McGowan's chopper landed then took off again as soon as he got off. Headley went over to meet him and they talked a little. Colonel McGowan visited several of the tracks then his chopper came back and he left. After lunch we did another two hours of the same thing. I wasn't sure exactly where we were, but I could estimate direction and distance to the west end of the Woods and that was good enough to start a fire mission and be sure the first rounds wouldn't hit us. Headley ended our day's work by heading back to Highway 19.

We turned into Hampton at 1420. Six Track pulled into the same spot as the night before. After dinner Headley went to Squadron headquarters and I tagged along. There was a homemade chair with a trooper in it getting a haircut. I'd given no thought to haircuts, but decided I needed one. My cut was about as complex as what the Marines give a new recruit, just a little longer. I got a haircut every time we came back to Hampton if it had been more than a couple of weeks since my last.

January 30

I was awakened at 0600 by increased activity. I finished my morning drill and dropped off my bundle of dirty laundry by 0700. First and Second Platoon left at 0715 for road sweeps to Trang Bang and Ap Suoi Cao. Third Platoon stayed at Hampton. When the two platoons were back, Headley, the Platoon Leaders and I were called to Squadron headquarters. Colonel McGowan pointed to a map and began.

"You're going back to the market up against the Cambodian border. Jerry, you pick a good spot near there about a klick back from the border for your night position. We have choppers laid on for extra PSP and sandbags for bunkers and you'll get enough extra concertina for a second circle around your laager. Make sure the troops use the extra PSP and sandbags for better bunkers. You're also getting a Killer Junior team. Any questions?" Headley spoke, "No sir." "Stay here until 1000. Use the time to double check your combat loads."

I radioed my FDC to confirm that my radio frequency was the same where we were headed. I didn't ask where our fire would come from. We were going to be about fourteen klicks from Hampton, close to the range limit of the 155s at Hampton. We left Hampton at 1000, went through Go Dau Ha, across the bridge and west on Route 1. When we moved off Route 1 and got to near the cluster of huts at Xom Ba Ao, Headley had the Troop form on line fifty meters from the huts facing toward the border.

"Foxy, we're going to sit here for a while. I'm letting about half our people go into the market. Do you want to go in?" "Yessir. Fontana, you stay here on the radio. Charlie you can go in. Take your rifle." "Recall is a green star cluster."

Charlie and I joined the group dismounting and walking toward the huts. The "market" was thirty or so outside stalls along a narrow street. They had a strange mix of black market PX goods and local goods. The stall that fascinated me displayed bolts of cloth. The old woman who appeared to be the shopkeeper sat on the back of the waist high platform that displayed the goods. In addition to the cloth, she had one small roll of strip lace an inch wide. I picked it up to look at it and she said something to me. I smiled and nodded my head. She spoke again. I still had no idea what she was saying. I reached for my wallet and asked, "How much?"

She smiled and nodded. I took out a five dollar MPC. "Is that enough?" She smiled and nodded. I pointed at the lace then at me. Next I pointed at the money then at her. She smiled and nodded. I gave her the MPC, put the lace in my pocket and walked back to Six Track. I didn't know if she would end up complaining about foreigners stealing from her or laughing about the Yankee rube she snookered.

At Six Track I released Fontana to go in. At 1300 Headley popped a green star cluster and about thirty men headed back from the market. When they were all climbing aboard, Headley radioed each Platoon Leader to confirm that everyone was back. When the head count was confirmed, he called the Platoon Leaders to Six Track.

"When we move out, I'll lead. I'm going about 600 meters northeast. Where I stop is the center of our position. About ten meters between tracks. Platoon Leaders on line. First Platoon parks first, take the western third of the perimeter. Third take the north end around to the east. Second take the rest. Make sure your people use the extra PSP that's coming. Put the extra concertina five feet outside our normal wire. Put the Claymores between the two concertinas."

Six Track started moving before the platoon leaders were back to their tracks. It was just a short move. We stopped in about the middle of a field pointing southwest back at the market. The Medic Track parked about ten meters behind us pointing the other way. The platoons were soon forming

3—Ap Bien Hoa

up around us. There was some moving of vehicles at the Platoon Leaders' instructions, but the rough circle of evenly spaced vehicles formed fairly quickly and the crews began immediately putting up RPG screens in front of each track. A Chinook with our extra supplies came promptly.

"Captain, where do you want the Killer Junior?" "One gun on each side of Six Track."

"They need to keep them both together." "OK. The village is to the south side. Put them on the north side."

"When are they coming in?" "They're a few minutes out."

"Let me put out the smoke for where they land." "Can do. Two guys from Third Platoon are doing the unhooking."

I went to where we wanted the guns and watched Headley until he pointed at me and yelled. A Chinook with a 105 slung under it came into view as I tossed the smoke grenade in front of me. Immediately it headed for the smoke. The sergeant from Third Platoon stood near the smoke and pointed both arms at the chopper. The pilot slowed and came in low toward the sergeant. The sergeant signaled the pilot to settle slowly until the gun was on the ground. As soon as the sling was slack he signaled the pilot to hover and the other man ran under the helicopter and unhooked the sling from the hook in the center of the chopper's belly then ran back to the sergeant. The sergeant gave an all clear signal and the pilot rose a little, slipped to the side and landed long enough for the gun's crew to get off with their personal gear. The chopper was away quickly and almost out of sight by the time Headley yelled again and I popped smoke again.

The same drill was repeated for the second gun and crew. A third Chinook arrived with a cargo net full of ammunition. As soon as they landed the crews pointed one gun north and the other west. Then they began digging four holes, one on each side of the two guns. They collected PSP and sandbags from the piles brought in earlier and started filling sandbags and stacking the ammunition in the holes. They worked continuously until they had two small sandbag bunker for each gun filled with ammunition that was accessible on the side toward the gun.

While they worked, I found the sergeant in charge and introduced myself as the Troop's FO and asked if he needed anything. He said he didn't.

January 31

We were up at the normal hour, but there was no rush getting packed. The outer wire came down first and the extra concertinas were stacked inside the perimeter. Then the regular concertina was loaded back on the tracks, the RPG screens were taken down and stowed and finally the sandbags were emptied and stowed and the PSP hung back on the side of the track or stacked with the extra concertina.

At 0930 First and Third Platoons went off with Lieutenant Carlson in charge to sweep the open fields to the north of our laager. We stayed with Second Platoon and the guns at the laager. The 105 crews rigged their guns to be lifted and stacked all of their ammo back on one of the cargo nets.

The first Chinook showed up just after 1100. The loading drill was just the reverse of the unloading drill. The last load was out by 1145. The CO then called the two platoons back and we had lunch. While we ate, the CO's radios were on speakers. At 1300 a message came in from Squadron that Division had given the Cav the mission of screening Go Dau Ha against night attacks from the north and east. We were called back to Hampton.

We pulled into Hampton at 1410. It took us almost an hour because there was heavy civilian traffic on some stretches of the road and particularly in Go Dau Ha itself.

4

Little Rubber

The Troop, with an added Radar Track, left Hampton at 1705. Our trip was through Go Dau Ha then a klick north on Route 22. A right turn took us into a big empty field where we laagered 400 meters from the road. There was broad strip of empty land that headed off northeasterly from our laager. Almost all the ground in the area was flat, but there was a trickle of a creek in the middle of the hint of a valley. In the distance there were hedgerows on each side of the valley. The Radar Track took a position in the circle so that its radar scan was up the center of the valley.

It was about dark when I noticed three troops opening the concertina wire and heading out. Bear was looking the same way. "Where are they going?" "That's Third Platoon's LP. They'll go out about fifty meters and spend the night outside the wire." "Each platoon do that every night?" "Most nights, except in Hampton." No one had told me and I hadn't noticed them going out before.

The first radar report was radioed to Six Track at 2030. They thought they spotted four to six people 600 meters north of us. Then they saw nothing. At 2045 the thought they saw four to six people less than a hundred meters to our north. Headley ordered flares and machine gun fire. In a few minutes, flares popped and two or three M60s fired in that direction. Nobody saw anything in the light and Headley ordered ceasefire.

I was about to turn in for the night at 2215 when another call came in from the Radar Track. The CO's radios were on speakers. They had readings that looked like four to six people again, moving around on the left edge of the valley about 1500 meters away from us. Headley spoke, "Foxy, you go shoot them."

I unstrapped my radio, got my map and walked over to the Radar Track. The Sergeant in charge saw me coming and stepped out of the back of the track. "Sir, we've got four to six people milling around at two hundred mils, fifteen hundred seventy meters out." "OK, I'll call that in and we'll confirm it as soon as we get clearance. Somebody warn the LPs."

I radioed in a fire mission with that direction and distance for battery three in effect. I added "at my command" so that they wouldn't fire until I told them to. Then I asked to be advised when we had clearance. It took almost half an hour to get clearance. When it came, I stuck my head in the back of the track. There were three of them in the dark staring at the small green screen. "I've got clearance to fire. They still in the same place?" "Yessir, they haven't moved except around in circles."

"Jackhammer One Eight, this is Jackhammer Two Three, fire for effect, over." "Jackhammer Two Three, this is Jackhammer One Eight, fire for effect, out." About a minute later they radioed "on the way." The flashes a mile away came quickly, then the sounds of eighteen rounds exploding.

"What do you see now?" "Nobody moving above ground!" I radioed in "end of mission" and waited outside the track. Fifteen minutes later the radar picked up two or three people moving in the same place. I called in another twelve rounds. This time the fire came a lot faster. After that there wasn't any more movement. I strapped my radio back, put up my cot and went to sleep.

February 1

At 0700 Second and Third Platoons left on road sweeps to Checkpoint 22 and Trang Bang. First Platoon, Six Track, the Medic Track and the Radar Track left for Hampton. As we pulled in, Alpha Troop was leaving in their red marked vehicles. I asked Headley, "Why is Alpha red?" "A, B, C, red, white and blue. Just like the flag. Easy to remember. Alpha's red, we're white and Charlie's blue. Headquarters tracks are marked in Cavalry yellow"

Alpha had an FO who had been out about as long as I had. Their Six Track passed us going out and I saw him standing in the back of the track with his head and shoulders sticking up out of the cargo hatch. He looked like a spooked rabbit.

When Second and Third Platoons finished their road sweeps we all assembled just outside Go Dau Ha on the Ap Suoi Cao road. At Ap Suoi Cao we turned north on Highway 19. Four klicks up the road we reached Checkpoint A at the south end of Long Cong, a long skinny village on both sides of the road.

At Checkpoint A we turned left into the rice paddies heading southwest. The paddies were fields of scattered weeds separated by rice dikes. We moved slowly on line and stopped whenever anyone thought they saw something, but there wasn't much. We moved along the edge of a big cemetery for a while, but didn't go into it.

After chow we turned south away from the cemetery and started stopping to check abandoned hooches. With stops, it took us an hour to move 600 meters south from the cemetery to an intersection of two dirt tracks. On my map the tracks were marked with dotted lines, the lowest quality of road or trail shown on the map. At the intersection the dismounts found a recently filled hole. It contained three fresh bodies in green shirts and shorts. That was enough to call for an extended search of the area. About an hour later somebody found a hole with an AK47 and some papers in it. Less than an hour after that one of the platoons found a small tunnel and pulled a .50 caliber machine gun out of it. There wasn't any tripod for it, but the VC having the shooting part of a .50 caliber wasn't a happy thought.

After finding nothing more, the Troop headed directly back toward Checkpoint A. We were still on line moving at the speed of a fast walk, but we did the four klicks back to Highway 19 without stopping. We retraced our route back to Hampton, pulling in at 1640. We dropped off the .50 caliber machine gun, fueled up the tracks and had dinner. The Cav S1 set up a pay table next to the chow line. Fontana, Charlie and I had to wait for our pay from the Artillery Battalion. At dinner I got a quick introduction to Mike Gramm, the new Second Platoon Leader.

We left Hampton a little before 1800, with a Radar Track added. Within fifteen minutes we were pulling into our laager for the night, within a hundred meters of where we had spent the night before. I was about to turn in for the night at 2130 when a call came in over the speaker on Headley's radio from the Radar Track. They had spotted four to six personnel moving around on the left edge of the valley about 2400 meters out and wanted to engage them. Headley pointed at me, "Foxy, same same last night." This time it only took ten minutes for the firing clearance. No one had moved from the original location and I fired eighteen rounds at the radar plot. This time no movement was detected after impact.

February 2

Stand to was just before 0600. Breakfast was waiting at Hampton.

After breakfast, we waited. Apparently something was going on, but nobody told me what. About 1030 Headley came back from some meeting and said that Bravo had been officially designated a reaction force. A few minutes later, we were told that Alpha Troop had flushed six VC a klick north of last night's radar target and was in contact with an unknown force. I turned on my radio and listened on the Artillery net. Alpha's FO wasn't calling in any fire or reporting anything. After a while, I went over to the Cav headquarters and listened to their Squadron net with the

Troop's officers. It wasn't clear to me exactly what was going on, but Alpha was in a fight and Charlie Troop was moving to their support.

It was well into the afternoon when we were told to get ready to move out. We went through Go Dau Ha and north up Route 22 to the south end of Ap Bao Dong, then stopped along the left side the road.

It wasn't too long until Vietnamese civilians were coming up to the tracks, some to sell something, others just out of curiosity. One of them was pedaling a tricycle with bicycle size wheels. He had ice for sale out of a cooler mounted between the back wheels. U.S. troops weren't supposed to use Vietnamese ice because the water used to make it wasn't properly purified.

Headley didn't like the civilians so close. He radioed the Platoon Leaders to clear the civilians away from the vehicles. Nothing happened. He radioed again. Still nothing happened. He could see civilians next to many of the vehicles behind us. He tore off his radio helmet and yelled back down the column, "Keep the fucking zips away from the tracks!"

After Headley yelled at them, the troops on the tracks closest to us waved away any civilians near them. Many of the troops yelled "dee dee mao" which we believed meant "go away." The civilians drifted away. I remembered the movie at Long Binh about being polite to the Vietnamese. It wasn't all that easy in the field. Headley went back to his radio. I looked back down the column and saw the Track Commander of the last vehicle in line waving the tricycle over to buy some ice.

While we waited, a convoy of twenty trucks carrying Vietnamese troops arrived from the south. They unloaded four trucks at a time across the road from us. They were a lot sharper looking than any Vietnamese troops I'd seen before. They all wore camouflage fatigues, boots and helmets with camouflage cloth covers. They appeared to be armed about the same as U.S. infantry and moved briskly. As soon as they got off the trucks they moved off in tactical formations to the northeast toward the sound of the scattered firing. Headley said they were ARVN Marines.

All the while I sat, smoked and listened to the Artillery net. I could tell that Alpha and Charlie were in contact, but neither FO was reporting much. Headley was listening to his radio most of the time and didn't say much, either on the radio or to the rest of us. About 1720 I heard Headley telling the Platoon Leaders to move out. He looked at me and pointed forward about the same time the column started moving. We pulled ahead to an intersection with a dirt road and turned right. As soon as we were outside the village we got off the road and drove alongside it for a klick through open fields to the beginning of an area of scattered hooches. We snaked through them then stopped in a clear area next to the road. We were only a few hundred meters from the radar targets of the night before.

4—Little Rubber

When we stopped, the Troop formed a tight circle with the line tracks facing out. Headley said we were supposed to wait here. The occasional firing was closer now, but still not very intense.

We stayed only a few minutes before getting orders to move to join Alpha Troop. We formed on line and headed east very slowly. That was supposed to bring us up on Alpha's right flank. Apparently Headley was being guided by Colonel McGowan overhead. There had been no firing for quite a while, but joining a unit in proximity with the enemy is still a delicate task.

We took almost twenty minutes to go five hundred meters and come to a stop. Headley looked over, "We're married up with Alpha on our left flank. Don't know where Charlie Troop is exactly." I could see all of the tracks of the platoon directly in front of us, but scattered vegetation and hooches hid most of the tracks of the two flanking platoons. For an hour we sat there. Headley was busy on the radio, but we were doing nothing. Charlie was sitting closest to me on the back of the cargo hatch with our radio handset clipped on the front of his flak jacket, monitoring the net. There was still nothing of note being reported on the Artillery radio net. While we sat, dusk arrived.

About 1900 Headley got an order from someone and he, in turn, ordered the platoons forward. Our speed was quite deliberate. In a few minutes I got confirmation on our location when we crossed a road that ran almost due north up to the Little Rubber. We were 1500 meters from where we had found the bodies and machine gun yesterday. We continued east, almost creeping.

Fifteen minutes after starting, we were approaching a north-south hedgerow three hundred meters beyond the one lane road. The Platoon Leader's track in front of us had moved a little to the right and we were twenty meters behind the line tracks when they started to climb over the low dirt dike with brush and bamboo on top. It was dark enough that I couldn't see much color. Just after they started to climb the dike two of the tracks were hit by RPGs. One was just to the right of the track in front of Six Track. The other was three tracks further to the right. After the explosions, a silence followed. Then I heard scattered small arms fire, not coming from us. Headley was on the radio as soon as the tracks were hit and apparently cleared firing. The Troop opened up with all machine guns firing forward, long bursts close together. The noise was at least twice as loud as the opening fire at Ap Bien Hoa. This time all of the Troop was firing. I didn't know if Alpha was firing, but assumed they were. Soon our fire slowed a little.

The line tracks that weren't hit backed away from the hedgerow a few meters and concentrated their fire grazing the top of the dike. While they were backing off, a track to our left was hit with an RPG. I yelled for my radio and got no response. When I turned to look, Charlie and Fontana were gone. I grabbed the handset's coiled cord where it connected to the radio. I let it slip through my hand as I pulled, then it was gone. I checked again holding it directly in front of my face. The cord was attached to the radio, but there was no handset at the end of the cord, just some broken wires. While it was sinking in that I couldn't use my radio, one of the tracks that had been hit exploded. All three of the tracks that had been hit were now burning and casting flickering light on the dike and bamboo in front of us. I noticed our cupola was empty. Bear was gone too. I was still thinking about what I was going to do about my radio when two men supporting a third between them passed my side of the track.

It was Bear and Charlie holding up Fontana. When the first two tracks were hit, all three had jumped off to help wounded. Charlie had taken my handset with him. Fontana had been shot climbing onto the track hit closest to us. Bear said later that Fontana had been shot by someone who had crawled under the other damaged track and was firing his rifle between the road wheels. Nobody with Fontana had a rifle with them. Shortly after they grabbed Fontana, the track the shooter was under blew up. With luck, the explosion killed him.

Bear and Charlie took Fontana toward the rear to be evacuated. Headley had gone somewhere before I knew he was leaving. It was just me and Chico. I couldn't see him, but assumed he was there. The Troop was continuing to fire at a reduced but steady rate. I had no idea if they had targets, or were just firing to keep heads down on the other side. I had no way to repair my radio and not enough reason to demand one of the Cav radios.

As I sat there staring at it, the space immediately in front of us between a burning track and the next track to its left seemed awfully wide and no one was firing into it. I got into the cupola, put an ammo belt into the .50 caliber, pulled the cocking handle twice and started pushing the thumb trigger between the handles to fire three and four round bursts between the tracks in front of us into the hedgerow beyond them. I had never fired a .50 caliber before.

After a few bursts, the gun wouldn't fire when I pushed the trigger. I pulled the cocking handle and it fired a few more bursts before it stopped again. Again the cocking handle, a few bursts and a stop. There was a bottle of M16 lubricant inside the cupola. I put some oil inside the receiver of the .50 caliber and it went a little longer between stoppages. When I opened the second box of ammo, I just squirted oil on the ammo and that worked a lot better. It was terrible field procedure. If we had been interrupted, the oiled ammunition would have collected dust and crap that

4—Little Rubber

would have seriously jammed the gun. We had plenty of ammunition and I wasn't worried about saving a half used open box. I was finishing a fourth box of ammunition when Headley ran past. "Foxy, cut that shit out! Don't shoot between tracks!"

About then Bear and Charlie came back. I gave Bear back the cupola and got in my seat with my M16 ready. As soon as Bear was settled, Six Track followed the way Headley had gone. He was next to the Platoon Leader's track for the right flank platoon. By now it was completely dark.

We picked up Headley and started back toward behind the center of the Troop's line, all of the line tracks started backing up slowly, still firing. Six Track, the Medic Track and the platoon leader's tracks turned their backs on the line and moved forward in advance of the line tracks that were backing out. After retiring a hundred meters, the line tracks stopped firing, turned and passed us on line. Now we were all headed back the way we had come. We crossed the dirt road again and stopped in the field on the other side. It was roughly square with light brush boundaries.

Bravo formed the south half of a laager, Alpha the north. The field was too small for a circle, the formation was more like an octagon, seven tracks in a row almost up against the brush sides, with two or three tracks clipping the corners. Charlie Troop was somewhere else.

While we setting up, the Alpha CO came over to Six Track, "Jerry, your FO's got to fire anything we need tonight, mine's not worth a damn." "I think he can do that, can't you, Foxy." "I need a handset for my radio. My RTO tore it off." "You can have his, he doesn't know what to do with it. I'll send it over."

He and Headley talked some more then he went back to his troop. A few minutes later a trooper brought me a handset and cord. I plugged it in and radioed in our position. The Alpha FO was replaced within a week. I still wonder if he was truly incompetent or just faked it to get out of the field.

Fifteen minutes after we pulled into position, word was passed that ARVN Marines were coming into the perimeter from the west. They marched in with little noise and distributed themselves silently on the east side of the perimeter.

Air strikes in the contact area began about 2230, first some marking rockets from a spotter plane, then six jet loads of bombs and napalm. We could hear the planes and explosions and feel the shock from the bombs and even a little heat from the napalm, but most of it seemed much further away than the hedgerow where our tracks had been hit. Just before midnight we were told that ARVN marines to our south were moving into the contact area.

February 3

The ARVN Marines inside our perimeter moved out to the east about 0100. Within fifteen minutes Headley said the Marine advisors reported they were in the contact area with no sign of any remaining enemy.

At 0830 we moved back across the 500 meters to join the ARVN Marines. We didn't find much except the blackened hulks of the three tracks we had left behind. Alpha recovered a wounded trooper who had been left behind when they pulled back. He said that when the Cav pulled back, it was women and children who collected the enemy dead and policed up gear and ammunition. At 0930 the CO got a report that the ARVN Marines had found thirty dead VC, taken one prisoner and captured a 75mm recoilless rifle, a .50 caliber machine gun, a Chicom .51 caliber machine gun, an M60 machine gun and a Browning Automatic Rifle.

The last of the ARVN Marines marched back toward Ap Bao Dong about 1100. We left just before noon and were back inside Hampton by 1230. Most of the troops ate lunch, did some repair and resupply work then took a nap. I had lunch and went immediately to the nap.

I was back up by 1500. When I arrived at the Cav headquarters Colonel McGowan introduced me to Captain Thomas, my new Liaison Officer. The old one, the one who had called in our artillery fire at Ap Bien Hoa, had rotated home. I never met him, I never knew his name, he was just Jackhammer Three Five. Now Thomas was Jackhammer Three Five.

We ate an early supper and left Hampton just after 1700. By 1730 we were setting up our laager north of Go Dau Ha, in sight of where we had been two nights before. The night passed without incident.

February 4

In the morning we went to Hampton for breakfast. We spent the whole day in Hampton. No one told me why we had the day off, but I didn't complain.

In the late afternoon Headley brought a new First Lieutenant, Tom Nelson, to Six Track. Mead had left for Cu Chi earlier in the day and Nelson was the new Third Platoon Leader.

After supper we left Hampton about 1720. Ten minutes later we were pulling into our field north of Go Dau Ha. At 2100 four 60mm mortar rounds landed a quarter mile north of our laager. They must have been meant for us, but whoever was firing was probably as far away as a 60mm mortar could fire. If they had been close enough to see us, they would have fired slower and adjusted. No one had heard the muzzle pops. Radar had nothing.

An hour after the mortar rounds landed, I was called to the Radar Track. They had spotted three or four individuals walking south at 1455 mils, 1350 meters from us. I had a defensive target called in at 1600 mils, due east, a klick out.

"Where's the nearest LP?" "We were told there is one due east, fifty meters out, sir." "OK. No sweat. Have somebody radio them not to worry, we remember where they are."

I called in a fire mission based on my defensive target adjusted to where they appeared to be headed. After clearance, I called for firing as soon as the radar crew said they were about to arrive. After half an hour without movement on the radar, I strapped the radio back to my seat and turned in.

February 5

By 0640 all three platoons were out on road sweeps. All were back in Hampton by 0820 for breakfast. We spent the rest of the day standing by for something that didn't happen. The troops had maintenance and minor repairs to do while they waited. I had nothing to do except hang around the Cav Headquarters, Captain Thomas was on the ground for part of the day and I asked about my team's pay.

We left Hampton at 1615 with a cook's truck and went to Ap Suoi Cao. We went south to the Highway 19 turn and pulled in to laager in the field east of the highway. I called in defensive targets a klick east, west and south of where we were. There was no north target because it would have been too close to Ap Suoi Cao.

The school solution for defensive targets was what I had tried to do at Ap Bien Hoa, evaluate likely enemy approach routes and integrate my targets with the unit's defensive fire plan. The fire plan for our laagers was tracks parked in a circle shooting out. Rarely did attack seem more likely from one direction than another. I decided the most likely use for my defensive targets was as a reference point for calling in initial fire and opted for putting them in the same place as often as possible to simplify remembering where they were in the middle of the night. My standard pattern was one target north, one east, one south and one west, all one klick out. If one of those targets was too close to something I couldn't shoot at, I just left it out. I called in defensive targets every night we spent in the field. I'll only mention them if there's something worth mentioning.

February 6

In the morning Second Platoon and Third Platoons cleared Highway 19 between Trang Bang and Checkpoint 25. First Platoon stayed in the laager. The Troop outposted the part of Highway 19 we had cleared until the convoy had passed both ways. The convoy went past headed north about 1030. After that we just sat.

In bits and pieces during the day, Headley explained a lot about the convoys. The Division had three large permanent base camps. The Division's main base and the Second Brigade headquarters were at Cu Chi, as I knew. The Third Brigade headquarters was at Dau Tieng. The First Brigade headquarters was at Tay Ninh West, located, unsurprisingly, just west of Tay Ninh City. Tay Ninh West was also home to one brigade of the 1st Air Cavalry Division.

Every day a supply convoy came north up Route 1 from the supply dumps in the Saigon area. Part of the convoy would peel off at Cu Chi and the rest would keep going, part headed for Tay Ninh West and part for Dau Tieng. From Cu Chi to Trang Bang, there was no alternative to Route 1. South of Trang Bang there were few promising ambush sites on Route 1. North of Trang Bang, the opportunities for ambush increased.

Part of the security for the convoy was varying its route north of Trang Bang. There weren't too many options to get from Trang Bang to the two base camps, but there were some. If there was any intelligence to indicate an ambush attempt, the route was chosen to avoid the ambush. If there wasn't any intelligence, it was just a matter of trying not to be too predictable. Whatever convoy route was chosen for the day, all of the possible routes were checked for mines each morning. All of the Troop's road sweeps were part of that; clearing the roads the convoy might take.

All of the different routes were fairly close together, so what good was switching the routes? Any serious attempt at a convoy ambush needed a fairly large number of troops, say at least fifty men, with some heavy weapons and mines. The NVA could not wait until they could tell what route the convoy was taking that day then move to ambush it. Besides the risk of being observed moving, their command structure wasn't that flexible. At a minimum they had to move to their ambush site the night before. More likely, to be sure of getting all of the men and equipment in place, two nights before. This need to position their men and equipment in advance was why we sometimes got intelligence of where an ambush was planned.

The convoy passed going back at 1500 and First Platoon went in to spend the night at Hampton. Second and Third Platoons assembled to laager near last night's site. After a few minutes, a cooks truck, a cargo carrier with fuel and a repaired APC pulled in. Headley called the varying group of vehicles that came out to join our laager most nights our "trains."

The evening chopper was bringing Fontana's replacement, PFC Dave Johnson. Charlie was a Spec4 now so he became my Recon Sergeant. I got word the chopper was coming and went to greet him. There was a jumble of gear being delivered, but only one man got off.

"Johnson?" "Yes sir." "I'm Lieutenant Watson, the FO. I hear you're joining us." He shook my hand, "Yessir."

He was another blonde kid, a little taller than Fontana, about six foot. "We're on Six Track. This way. Do you have any FO team training?" "No sir, just AIT." "Can you run a Prick 25?" "Yessir." "Well, that's most of the job. Charlie's our Recon Sergeant. Charlie! This is Johnson, our new RTO. Stow his gear and show him around."

February 7

After the morning road sweeps, the Troop outposted from Trang Bang to Checkpoint 25 again. Six Track and the Medic Track stayed with one of the outposts near Ap Suoi Cao until the convoy passed in the morning. Then Headley took Six Track and the Medic Track to visit the whole string of outposts up to Checkpoint 25. We went back to the outpost we started from until the convoy passed on its way back.

About 1530 Six Track and the Medic Track moved south to an open space next to Checkpoint 12 and First and Second Platoons came in to laager around us. Third Platoon headed in to spend the night at Hampton and passed a repaired APC and our dinner in a cargo carrier coming the other way to join us.

February 8

The morning road sweeps were about over when Headley announced that the Troop's Sheridans were passing through Go Dau Ha on their way to join us. Third Platoon came up from Trang Bang and the rest of the Troop fell in behind them as they passed. The Sheridans were waiting for us at Checkpoint 18. Three Sheridans joined each platoon. Getting the Sheridans didn't bring the platoons to their full strength of ten vehicles. Each platoon usually had at least one track out of the field for some repair or the other.

Compared to the APCs, the Sheridans sparkled with newness. They weren't really tanks. Technically they were "Armored Reconnaissance /

Armored Assault Vehicles." They had aluminum armor like the APCs, but they had a turret with a big gun. They certainly looked a lot more dangerous than our APCs. Each of the Sheridans had a shiny white band about two feet long painted on the middle of its main gun as Bravo Troop identifier. Headley had told me the Sheridan's gun had been designed to launch a guided anti-tank missile as well as firing conventional ammunition. We didn't get any anti-tank missiles and all of the fancy gear for the missiles had been stripped off.

One of Third Platoon's new Sheridans led as we continued north on Highway 19. Third Platoon Leader's 30 Track was the fourth vehicle in the column with Six Track next behind. Just south of Checkpoint 25, 30 Track hit a mine. The three vehicles in front of 30 Track had passed over the mine without setting it off or seeing it.

The mine had broken the right track and blew off two road wheels. Lieutenant Nelson moved his second radio to another track. As soon as his radio was moved, we were on our way again. An M88 was on its way from Hampton to recover the damaged track and its crew was in little danger on the road in the daytime.

We went past Checkpoint 25 up Highway 19 for a klick to the northeast. Then we did a slow cross country sweep on line to the southeast through light brush next to the Upper Boi Loi Woods. Four or five klicks later we went through a fairly open area that separated the fields behind Ap Suoi Cao from the western end of the Lower Boi Loi Woods. We stopped a few times, but didn't find anything.

We stopped for lunch at 1230, directly behind Ap Suoi Cao. We started moving again at 1340 and swept an area of light brush back to Highway 19 south of the village. Then it was back to the field north of Go Dau Ha to laager with Second and Third Platoons. When our trains and Radar Track arrived, First Platoon left to garrison Hampton for the night.

February 9

We joined First Platoon at Hampton. After breakfast we headed across Go Dau Ha bridge toward Cambodia. I now had the checkpoints for this stretch of Route 1. We stayed on Route 1 to about three klicks short of the Cambodian border. We headed on line in a generally northwesterly direction across the empty fields to a klick from the Cambodian border. I could see the market at Xom Ba Ao. We didn't have anyone down on foot, but moved slowly and stopped frequently. Each time we stopped, our dismounts got off and investigated whatever it was that made us stop.

After lunch, we began a counter-clockwise sweep of a large oval

A Bravo Troop Sheridan in crew training with the identifying white band on its gun barrel but no vehicle number yet (National Archives photo CC54081).

pointed away from the border. There were many occupied hooches inside the oval and we passed close to some of them. Nobody waved and the kids just stared silently as we passed. We didn't stop at any of the hooches. There was no overt hostility, but our reception was a lot cooler than we got in other populated areas. By 1500 we had completed our loop around the oval and went back to Route 1 without stopping and reached Hampton by 1640. After an early dinner we left Hampton and within minutes we were pulling into the field north of Go Dau Ha to spend an undisturbed night there on radar picket duty.

A while after we arrived a trooper came over to Six Track. I was sitting on top. "Do you smoke sir?" "Yes, why?" "Would you like a carton of Pall Malls? We just opened an SP pack and nobody wants them."

An "SP" was a Sundries Pack, an Army issue of stuff it was assumed troops in the field couldn't get, like cigarettes and toothpaste. "Sure, I like Pall Malls." "You ought to tell everybody. You'll get lots." He handed me the carton and left. He was right, except I didn't have to tell anyone.

Apparently he did. From then on I got the Pall Malls almost every time a Sundries Pack was opened that had Pall Malls inside. The Marlboros, Winstons and mentholated brands were coveted by many, but the Pall Malls were mine.

February 10

First Platoon and Second Platoon cleared road while Third Platoon, Six Track, the Medic Track, the Radar Track and our trains went to Hampton. The sweeping platoons finished quickly and returned to Hampton to finish the breakfast the rest of the Troop had started. By the time they pulled in, I was coming out of the shower.

We left of Hampton at 0900 for Ap Suoi Cao. By 1000 we were on line sweeping light brush a klick east of the southern end of the village. Half an hour into the western end of the generally open area south of the Boi Loi Woods we found several oxcart trails. There were other signs of recent activity in the area and our search found a bunker complex in some brush, complete with seeds from recently eaten watermelons, some cooking utensils and Vietnamese newspapers less than a week old. The bunkers were just large foxholes with partial overhead cover made of small logs covered with dirt.

The bunkers were crushed by driving a track over them. Sometimes just running one tread over the bunker collapsed whatever roof it had and partially filled the hole. Sometimes it was necessary to make a sharp turn over the bunker. When the bunkers were all crushed, we continued south with dismounts down. We moved at a slow walking pace, but found no reason to stop until we approached a single hooch near the southern edge of the open area. When we stopped the right end of our line was next to the hooch and the rest of our line of vehicles stretched off to the east. Six Track was behind the center of the line. As soon as we stopped, Headley yelled at Nam and pointed to the right end of our line. Nam jumped down from the Medic Track and walked toward the right end.

A few minutes after Nam disappeared in front of the tracks near the hooch Headley told Chico to drive down to the right end. When we got there I could see Lieutenant Nelson, Nam, four or five troopers and a Vietnamese man and woman in what looked like a big garden on the other side of the hooch. Most of the garden was just recently turned bare soil. There were some small plants growing near the far edge. The man was bareheaded, wearing black shorts and a black short sleeve shirt. He had short grey hair and thin, gnarled legs. He was furiously digging away with a heavy bladed hoe. Everyone else, including the woman, just watched.

4—Little Rubber

The man's digging exposed patches of black plastic. After a bit Lieutenant Nelson signaled the man to stop and the troopers found the edge of the plastic and lifted it up. Underneath, with only a little dirt spilled on them were almost white bags of rice laid in a row. One of the bags had a USAID logo on it.

The man was put back to work and Headley reported the find to Squadron. Before we were done, three rows of buried fifty pound bags of rice were uncovered, about a hundred bags. Each row had a continuous sheet of plastic under it, another sheet over it and six inches of dirt or so on top of the plastic. When it was clear how it was buried, the Third Platoon troops moving the bags sometimes just peeled back the plastic without waiting for the dirt to be pulled off. Whenever there wasn't a trooper in the way, the old man hoed steadily to pull the dirt off.

Headley stared at the man for a while. "Poor bastard. The VC probably made him work all last night to bury the stuff and now we're making him dig it up." The old man may have been a VC sympathizer, but even if he wasn't, he didn't have much choice. There are a few families scattered in the space south of the Woods and no government troops near enough to protect them from the VC and NVA units in the area. They had the option to leave, but resisting the VC was not an option if they stayed.

Just before what proved to be the last bag of rice was uncovered, a slick landed behind us just long enough to throw off two cargo nets. The troops working on loading the rice spread out the two nets on the ground, close together, but not overlapping. As soon as the nets were ready, about half of the rice was piled in the center of each net. Once the piles were ready, the corners of the net were pulled over the pile and three of the straps hooked to a heavy ring that was permanently attached to the fourth.

When Headley reported the first Chinook inbound, Nelson did the honors with smoke and hand signals. One of his troopers did the hooking. The second Chinook arrived and left quickly. It was exciting to see the Chinooks snatch away the heavy piles of rice, but their prompt departure was still welcome. While they hovered they kicked up serious wind and debris.

When the Chinooks were gone, we loaded up and left the old man and woman without comment. We went to Highway 19 and on to Hampton. We had an early dinner on arrival and were headed back out at 1730. First Platoon went to spend the night guarding Go Dau Ha bridge and the rest of the Troop went back to the field north of town with our Radar Track.

5

First Boi Loi

February 11

 Third Platoon left to sweep to Checkpoint 22 at 0540. Second Platoon, Six Track, the Medic Track and the Radar Track went directly to Hampton. First Platoon pulled in from the bridge behind us. Third Platoon joined us fifteen minutes later.

 The Troop left Hampton at 0730 to clear the road to Ap Suoi Cao, then north on Highway 19 to pick up some RFs. At the south end of Xom Bao Don we pulled up next to the RF compound. It was surrounded by a wire fence and most of the buildings were sandbag bunkers. It looked like a miniature version of Long Binh.

 Troops started moving out to join us. The first group out was twenty-five men, led by a U.S. Second Lieutenant, about half U.S. and half Vietnamese. Headley said they were part of the Combined Reconnaissance Intelligence Platoon from the 2nd Battalion, 22nd Infantry. The CRIPs were created by adding local Vietnamese intelligence officers and police to the battalion's reconnaissance platoon. It was supposed to increase the recon platoon's intelligence gathering capacity and add U.S. military muscle to the intelligence the locals already had.

 Forty more RFs followed the CRIPs. They all wore fatigues that were greener than ours and cut tighter. Some wore the shirt tucked, others wore it out. A few wore black leather boots. Most wore what looked like high topped black tennis shoes. One or two wore sandals. About half wore helmets or helmet liners, the other half wore cloth caps.

 The senior Vietnamese officer and a U.S. advisor got on Six Track. The CRIP platoon leader, his RTO and his senior Vietnamese NCO got on the Medic Track. The rest of the CRIPs mounted the lead platoon's vehicles. The RFs were distributed to the other two platoons.

 Loading took a while, but by 0930 we turned around and headed back to Ap Suoi Cao. By 1030 we were behind the village, 500 meters from the western end of the Lower Boi Loi Woods. The lead Sheridan stopped and

5—First Boi Loi

the Troop lined up on either side of it. Once the Troop was redeployed, we moved slowly toward the southern edge of the Woods, stopping just before entering the dense brush of the Woods. Once the tracks stopped, the RFs and the CRIPs dismounted and pushed ten or twenty meters into the brush on foot.

When they were done, they came back and remounted. The tracks turned right, then paralleled the Woods well past the end of our prior search. We stopped, each track turned left, approached the edge of the Woods and stopped. It was the same drill again, dismount, search and remount. We repeated the whole cycle a third time. I had no idea why we searched some parts of the edge of the Woods and not others.

After the third search it was about noon. We moved 500 meters south of the Boi Loi Woods, formed a half circle facing the Woods and had lunch. None of the Vietnamese appeared to be carrying food. Headley offered the Vietnamese officer on Six Track the choice of C-rations from an unopened case. He couldn't offer from the open case because someone might already have taken part of a ration and left the rest behind. For the rest of the Vietnamese, the track crews were probably giving each of their allies a couple of ration cans that the crew didn't want. I had no idea what the Vietnamese troops thought, but they seemed happy as they ate. Charlie said the RFs usually got two ration cans, opened one and kept the other for later. I wondered if they knew what can they were opening or if it was just a surprise when they opened the can and saw what was inside.

After lunch we went back to the edge of the Woods and repeated the same drill. About 1400 the RFs found a complex of seven bunkers. Two of them had booby traps that were blown in place. After that find, we moved the tracks twenty or thirty meters into the brush and our dismounts joined the search. Several shallow holes filled with bagged rice were found. By the time all the rice was collected, we had about 3000 pounds in fifty pound bags. We were able to load about 2000 pounds on our tracks. The rest was spread on the ground and doused with diesel fuel.

As we were about to pull out somebody found a hole with twenty Chicom mines in it. A block of C4 with a long fuse was put next to them and lit as we left. We stopped a hundred meters from the edge of the brush to wait for an appropriately big bang. When it came, we moved to Highway 19 and back to the RF compound. The RFs seemed a lot happier unloading with the rice than they had been in the morning.

Whenever we found enemy ammunition, explosives or booby traps or our own artillery duds we put some C4 on them with a long fuse and blew them up behind us. I won't mention that drill anymore unless there's something interesting about it.

We laagered southwest of Ap Suoi Cao. Shortly after we arrived our trains joined us. After they arrived a message was relayed to me over the Cav radio that an Artillery pay officer was coming out. His chopper was already on approach so I went outside our circle to pop smoke. The Huey landed and I recognized my S1 getting off. As soon as he was clear of the chopper's door, it lifted off. His head snapped around, apparently surprised it was leaving.

"Welcome to Bravo Troop." "Where's your team? Why aren't you ready?" "Charlie and Johnson are over by Six Track." I pointed the way and he bustled past toward the Track. Charlie must have heard it was a pay call because he saluted as the S1 walked up. Nobody saluted in the field, but saluting the pay officer was deeply ingrained.

"No saluting, no saluting, just sign here. What's your name?" Charlie replied with full formality.

The S1 looked at his book, "OK here's your money." He started stuffing MPC certificates in Charlie's hand. When he was done, Charlie started to salute again, as was standard drill for pay call, but stopped himself before his hand was up to his shoulder.

"Where's the other man?" Johnson went through the same drill but didn't have any trouble remembering not to salute.

"Watson, here's yours. Sign the book. Where's the helicopter?" I took the money and counted it slowly, while thinking how worthless he was. After counting the money, I signed the pay book.

Chico was on the Cav radios. "Chico, give me a smoke grenade and call the chopper back." I caught the grenade Chico tossed and handed it to the S1. "When Specialist Romero tells you to, walk outside the circle over there and throw the smoke grenade when you see the helicopter."

"Outside the circle?" "Yes, ten meters outside the circle, and throw the grenade another ten meters out." I turned and walked away. I was pointed toward Carlson's track, so I walked over to it as if I had some reason to go.

When Chico gave the word, the S1 almost ran to about five meters outside the circle and threw the smoke grenade a few meters further on. There was no chopper in sight when he threw it. The smoke was almost burned out when the chopper came in view, but there was enough for them to spot. It landed, he got on, they left. That was our last excitement that night.

February 12

As usual, the cooks had a breakfast ready as the troops not on watch woke up. In the daylight, keeping watch wasn't all that big a deal, but there was always supposed to be at least one person on watch for each perimeter

5—First Boi Loi

vehicle, up behind the .50 caliber. Each Sheridan had a .50 caliber machine gun mounted on the tank commander's hatch with a rectangular shield like an M113. There was no cupola on a Sheridan, but the hatch cover on the Sheridan was two half circles that folded to the sides and could be locked in an almost vertical position. The opened hatch covers gave almost as much protection as the cupola on an APC.

I followed what had become my standard morning drill. I brushed my teeth and shaved, then rinsed the razor and blade. Next I stripped naked and put on a pair of shower clogs. I put a jerry can of water on edge on top of the track sticking out a little bit from the side of the vehicle with the opening down and opened the small cap near the edge of the larger screw cap that was used for filling. I bent down to get under the stream of water, got wet and put the small cap back on. Then I soaped up, put the soap away and rinsed off the same way.

For grunts who had to carry their water, water was precious. We were never short. We had a full water trailer delivered to the Troop most nights, either pulled by a vehicle or slung under a helicopter. I took that field shower almost every morning. When we went into Hampton, I used the shower there that was luxurious compared to showering under a jerry can.

After my field shower, I opened a laundry package and toweled off with the clean olive drab towel inside. Then I put on the full change of clothes in the package and made a bundle of the clothes I had taken off and the towel I had just used. The laundry was processed and returned just as Bear had said. The weekly laundry fee was about the only thing I paid for in the field. I never met the people who did the laundry, I just paid whoever on the Cav trains asked for money whenever they asked.

The full morning drill in the field was the same almost every day. About 0800 the Troop and our trains went south of Ap Suoi Cao to Highway 19. When we got to Checkpoint 18 our trains turned toward Hampton and the Troop continued on north to the RF compound at Xom Bao Don. This time it was only RFs, about eighty of them. As soon as they were on board, we retraced our path back toward the Woods. By 1030 the Troop's vehicles were on line just outside the southern edge of the Lower Boi Loi Woods near the western end and the RFs were walking into the brush.

This time we didn't wait for them to return. We didn't put down our own dismounts, but the vehicles pushed into the brush and stayed just behind the RFs. The edge of the Woods was almost solid brush. There were scattered trees standing above the brush further in, but most of what showed as a forest on the map was just dense brush, about track high. For a while I could still see the open space behind us, but as soon as we moved into the Woods we were wrapped in hot, damp, still air that seemed part of the brush. Everywhere was hot and humid, but in the Woods it was worse.

The RFs found some spaces and cracks between or under bushes to move through. The tracks moved on almost drunken paths to avoid trees or the densest parts of the brush, but every zig or zag involved pushing some brush down or aside.

When the RFs found something worth checking, the whole line stopped while they checked it out. Almost immediately we found several old fighting positions and some newer bunkers that we collapsed. We found some cooking gear, a small bag of rice and a bicycle. We also found lots of dud U.S. artillery rounds. Apparently the gooks collected duds that we were afraid to move. We passed enough artillery craters to know not all of the rounds were duds. Some of the craters were fresh and raw, others were weathered and partially revegetated.

The open space behind us disappeared from view. Sitting on top of the track I could see over the nearby brush, but I couldn't see much except sky beyond a hundred meters. There was nothing in sight that marked the open space behind us as soon as we were 300 meters in. Even if I couldn't see anything to tell me exactly where we were any more, we had to be close to the open space we'd left. While I tried to reason with the green morass, my mouth got dryer and water didn't help. Long drags on a Pall Mall cut my thirst better than half a canteen of water.

Within half an hour of becoming immersed, a large clear space came into view in front of us. The Lower Boi Loi Woods looked a little like a pork chop with the tail pointed at Ap Suoi Cao. The clearing was a rough circle about 200 meters in diameter in the middle of the tail. We reached the southwestern edge of the clearing at 1200 and found a bunker with a freshly cut melon and some warm rice in it. There were six foxholes nearby and a half finished bunker with a shovel left behind in it. There was an east to west trail that crossed the clearing that had signs of recent use.

We stopped for lunch in the clearing. We were back at searching the brush on the western edge of the clearing by 1230. The RFs found some used bandages and bloody rags on the ground and about 3000 pounds of bagged rice stacked under freshly cut brush. There were seven bunkers in the immediate vicinity, including one containing cooking utensils, an RPG launcher and four coils of rope. We kept the RPG and the rope, but Headley decided not to carry the rice out. The bags were cut open and the rice spread in the brush or mixed with dirt to fill in the bunkers.

After the rice was trashed we headed north out of the clearing and got sucked into the green. We forced our erratic path north another klick then broke out of the heavy brush into a hundred meter wide strip that separated the Lower from the Upper Boi Loi Woods. The strip had more low brush than clear land and an intermittent stream meandered through its center, but you could see far enough to not feel trapped. Most of the Troop were out in the open when we stopped. The RFs had found some blood trails and another 500 pounds of bagged rice. This time we loaded the rice, then mounted the RFs and headed toward Ap Suoi Cao down the open strip. It was only a few hundred meters on until we reached essentially open space and our release from the Woods was complete.

Twenty minutes after breaking into the open we were at Checkpoint 18 headed north. While we were dropping off the RFs at the Xom Bao Don compound with the rice, Headley got an unusual flurry of radio messages. "Foxy, Division says there's a US plane down two klicks inside Cambodia, about a klick south of Route 1. There are aircraft firing suppression around it, but they say they can see the NVA moving in. Do your maps cover the area?"

The 1:25,000 map that I was using for the Boi Loi Woods didn't come anywhere near Cambodia. Apparently Charlie already knew that because he was inside the track, handing up the RPG pack I had converted to a map case. "Yessir, the one to hundred thousand does, but that's probably outside the range of 155s at Hampton. The last time we were that far away my radio didn't work very well."

"Well, right now we're the ground reaction force. If they decide to helicopter somebody in to save the crew, we go in to bring everybody out."

We were headed south and almost back to Ap Suoi Cao when we got word that Cambodia was a no go. When we got to Checkpoint 18, instead of turning to go to Hampton to wait for a trip to Cambodia, we continued on south of Ap Suoi Cao then east to laager near the eastern end of the village fields.

February 13

At the morning briefing Headley said today would be a lot like yesterday, and it was. We went to the RF compound. After picking up some RFs, we went back the same way and on line into the Boi Loi Woods. This time we went into the body of the pork chop. The green closed up against the side of the tracks and rarely let go. The RFs drifted from in front of the tracks to immediately behind. Part of the drift was forced by stretches of brush too thick to walk through, but probably part of it was that being behind a track seemed safer than being in front of it. Sitting on top, I could see many nearby APCs and Sheridans, but I could see the ground only when we passed near a crater. We passed two bomb craters big enough to show a lot of ground.

At 1010 one of the tracks got high centered. Something was pushing up against the bottom of the body hard enough that the treads lost traction. It took almost half an hour to maneuver two other vehicles to where they could pull it free. While we were sitting, waiting and hoping no one was crawling up on us, the dismounts found a bunker complex and nine damaged bicycles. One bunker with a bloody dirt floor was big enough to be a hospital room.

By noon we were near the middle of the main body of the Lower Boi Loi Woods and found a group of bunkers containing twelve metal barrels of clothes. There were also an undamaged bicycle, an RPG round and a cloth bag of M60 ammunition. We ate lunch while the bunkers were being checked.

We took a fairly direct route from there to the south edge of the Woods. Once we were out into the fields and light brush things seemed a lot better. In the open we moved at a steady pace to Highway 19 then road speed to the RF compound. We let the RFs off about 1630. They were enriched by all of the clothes that we had found and the undamaged bicycle. We went back to laager between Ap Suoi Cao and the Woods. By 1730 we were enjoying the dinner brought out from Hampton.

February 14

After breakfast First and Second Platoons left for Highway 19 to drop our trains then on to pick up RFs at Xom Bao Don. Six Track, the Medic Track and Third Platoon waited until they came back about 0900. As they arrived, Squadron passed on a message from Division to stand fast because we might be needed to reinforce Patrol Base Diamond. Diamond was next to Ap Bien Hoa, almost on the site of our January fight. After a half hour delay, we were released and headed toward a klick-wide brush donut south of the Woods. Alpha and Charlie Troops had both had found rice there. So much rice was found that the Cav named the donut the Country Store.

We searched an arc on the northwest side of the Country Store. Our dismounts found fresh sandal prints throughout the area. Within minutes they had 2200 pounds of rice in fifty pound bags, in a complex of over forty fresh bunkers and small tunnels. We also found about fifty pounds of clothes, an AK47 magazine and a 155mm dud artillery round. The rice was loaded one or two bags on each APC.

We left the Country Store at 1500 for Highway 19 and on to Xom Bao Don to drop the RFs and the rice. We were back to Hampton by 1730.

February 15

The platoons' morning road sweeps were north to Checkpoint 22, south to Trang Bang and across to Ap Suoi Cao. Today's trip to the southwestern edge of the Country Store was without any RFs. We found two bunkers much larger than we usually found in the area, eight by fourteen feet and six feet deep with overhead cover. Eighteen smaller bunkers were nearby. After blowing up the big bunkers and caving in the little ones, we stopped for lunch and were back on the move about noon. Three hundred meters on we found another cluster of bunkers that were collapsed by the tracks.

At 1415 we received some long distance rifle fire about the same time there was heavier firing in the distance. After a flurry of radio conversations, Headley said Charlie Troop was in contact about 700 meters to our northeast. Apparently the enemy was on or near the northeastern extremity of the Country Store. We moved out of the brush promptly and stopped five hundred meters south of the brush. Charlie Troop's fight went on long enough for artillery and gunships, but we were not called to assist them and the firing was over in less than half an hour.

By 1600 we were headed back across the open area toward Ap Suoi Cao. It took twenty minutes to reach our laager a klick east of Highway 19 and a klick south of the village. Twenty minutes after that we saw the head of Charlie Troop's column, a Sheridan, on a dirt cart track five hundred meters north of our laager headed toward Highway 19. The rest of the Troop wasn't too far behind, but the lead Sheridan was alone, showing off, doing twenty-five or thirty miles an hour down a dirt trail raising a rooster tail of dust behind it. Half of our Troop stopped and stared at it. The Sheridan had almost reached Highway 19 when it blew up. I was looking at it when it blew. I saw a flash cloud of dust around the vehicle then I heard the sound of the explosion. There was a brief delay and then a really big explosion and a bright orange flame flared straight up from the turret. Most of Charlie Troop stopped well away from the burning vehicle. The fire stopped after a few minutes of irregular muffled explosions. A dust off helicopter arrived about the same time the fire was no longer visible. Two of the Sheridan's crew were killed. The other two were seriously injured, but somehow were able to get out.

When Charlie Troop left to spend the night in Hampton, First Platoon was sent to set up an outpost around the smoldering Sheridan hulk. The rest of the Troop stayed where we were in a smaller perimeter.

February 16

As soon as Second Platoon had eaten and packed their gear, they replaced First Platoon around the hulk and First Platoon came back to eat. Once it was light, there was little concern that the enemy would bother what was left of the Sheridan, but some of the villagers were curious and drifting toward it. The platoon around the hulk was mostly to keep them from disturbing anything before our experts arrived to look at it. Headley said a big-deal evaluation team was flying in to check it out.

A Cav M88 arrived about 0830 behind a mechanized infantry road sweep team coming up from Trang Bang. The armored recovery vehicle stopped at the hulk while the sweep team continued to Checkpoint 18 then turned around and left. The M88 made our APCs look small. It was like an armored motor home on tracks with a huge A-frame lifting boom folded back on its rear deck.

After a bit we could see a couple of tracks come to join the M88. They were followed by a slick dropping off two guys. Second Platoon radioed that they were the hot shot investigators and had started photographing the hulk as soon as they arrived. About 1015 a heavy load semi-trailer truck came up from the south with a one track escort. About that time Second Platoon was released to rejoin us. As we pulled away from our laager about 1030, the truck appeared to be maneuvering to turn around. I assume that the M88 used its boom to lift the Sheridan hulk onto the trailer to take it somewhere for investigation. Our Sheridan crews bitched for days that the mine that toasted the Sheridan would only have blown a roadwheel off an M48.

Aside from our late start, our sweep was like the day before. We went into a small finger of brush that pointed toward the Country Store on the southern edge of the Boi Loi Woods. Then we crossed over to the northern end of the County Store and searched some more brush. While that search was going on one of the APCs threw a track turning in the brush.

While we were waiting for the track to be reassembled, the dismounts at the left end of the line found a bunker cluster in an area we had passed through the day before. There were no bunkers there then. The new bunkers were little more than big foxholes with minimal overhead cover, but they had been slept in the night before. When the track with the thrown tread could move again we headed east. Two hundred meters on we found twelve fighting positions on the edge of the clearing in the middle of the Country Store.

Headley passed the reports of the bunkers on to Colonel McGowan overhead who radioed he was coming in. Headley yelled to the track nearest the center of the clearing to pop smoke. I heard Headley confirm yellow smoke on the radio and a LOH landed almost immediately. Colonel

McGowan got out and walked over to Six Track. McGowan asked where the stuff was and the CO pointed to the brush at the edge of the clearing while he was talking on the radio to someone. McGowan was bare headed, wasn't wearing a flak jacket and had no weapon. He just started walking into the brush alone. I grabbed my M16, jumped down and followed him.

The brush wasn't terribly thick. It probably looked almost solid from the air, but on the ground the bases of the bushes were far enough apart that the space between was like a web of trails. As I hurried after Colonel McGowan, it seemed clear that the area had been walked through by a lot of people recently. When I caught up with him he was stopped and looking at an area with a collection of mostly trash scattered about. I saw an RPG round on the ground next to the base of one of the bushes and picked it up. I was standing with the round about chest high in one hand when I realized what a stupid thing I had done. Fortunately for me, it had been left behind by someone departing in haste rather than someone fishing for dumb lieutenants. I showed it to Colonel McGowan. "Fine son, bring it back to the tracks with you."

Some more Cav troopers came up and started checking the area carefully. I followed Colonel McGowan back to Six Track. "Watson, are you a career officer?" "Two year career, sir." He paused, then walked away without comment.

When we had finished our search of the area about 1500, Colonel McGowan called his helicopter back and left. All together we found one recently buried NVA soldier, two Chicom grenades, five 60mm mortar rounds, three RPG rounds, four 81mm mortar rounds, a Chicom mine, a 25 pound shaped charge, a partially burned AK47, four AK47 magazines, a saw and a VC training manual for woman soldiers.

Almost immediately after we left a Sheridan hit a mine that blew off two road wheels on the left side. A small fire started inside the vehicle, but was quickly extinguished by its fire suppression system. The lens on the searchlight mounted over the main gun was shattered and the gunner who was riding on top of the turret had some minor frag wounds. He was shook up, but wasn't dusted off. As soon as the damage was assessed and it was clear that the tread could not be remounted, the front of the damaged Sheridan was connected to the back of another Sheridan by crossed steel cables. The cables were about ten feet long and had eyelets at each end that fit the four towing hooks near the corners of all of the Troop's vehicles.

When we headed toward Ap Suoi Cao the platoon with the damaged Sheridan brought up the rear. The towing Sheridan had enough power to pull the disabled vehicle, but strained to keep up with the column. We were laagered two klicks behind Ap Suoi Cao by 1800. The damaged Sheridan was towed into a position on the perimeter.

February 17

We waited for an M88 to come for the Sheridan. It arrived at 0920 with a one track escort. Riding on the track and the back of the recovery vehicle was a team of LRPs from the Division's Long Range Patrol Company. We waited while the mechanics on the recovery vehicle rigged the Sheridan to tow it back to Cu Chi to repair. It was almost 1030 when our trains, the M88 and its escort and the damaged Sheridan were ready to head to Highway 19. As they left, the Troop headed north.

About 900 meters north of our laager we turned east toward the part of the Boi Loi Woods closest to the village. We stopped at 1130 after driving just a little into the Woods and dropped all of our dismounts and the LRPs. They all milled around for a while until the LRPs had figured where they wanted to take cover, then our dismounts got back on and the Troop headed on northeast on line further into the Woods. In the dense brush, the LRPs were invisible as soon as we had moved a few meters. It was a frightening lesson in how hard it would be for us to see any gooks in the Woods who didn't want to be seen.

If anybody had been close, they might have noticed that the LRPs wore heavy packs and carried lots of gear and our dismounts didn't, even if they didn't notice that more people got off than got back on. Still, a stay-behind insertion was a lot less conspicuous than the LRPs walking in alone or a helicopter landing.

We never really got too far away from the LRPs because we swept in a curve to the right instead of straight away from them and kept finding things to stop for. One cigarette and 300 meters on we stopped for the first time at five old bunkers and some fresh fighting positions with a U.S. grenade and an unopened can of .50 caliber ammunition. Our dismounts took the ammunition and set a small charge on the grenade. Another cigarette and 400 meters on we found twelve foxholes around a bunker with overhead cover. There was a latrine off to the side. The area was decorated with fresh sandal prints, but the only stuff left behind was in the latrine.

Another hundred meters and another cigarette on, about 1310, we found a bunker with six foxholes around it and a 155mm dud. Further on we found seven interconnected bunkers with a pan of warm rice and thirty-five 60mm mortar rounds left behind. From there it was across the paddies and light brush to spend the night within a few hundred meters of our prior laager. A cook's truck, a cargo carrier with fuel, a headquarters track and a repaired Sheridan arrived shortly after we did.

Four times that night, movement was spotted 500 or 600 meters from our laager and fired at. I was up for the first two ready to fire artillery that wasn't needed. The second two just woke me up. When I realized it was only a few rifles or a single machine gun I knew I wasn't needed.

February 18

Headley said that the Commanding General of II Field Forces, our Division Commanding General's boss, was en route to see a demonstration of our Sheridans. The Cav was the first unit to get Sheridans in Vietnam. Officially, it was called field testing. At 0800 we moved north and stopped in a tight laager formation a klick west of the end of the strip of open land between the Upper and Lower Boi Loi Woods.

For the Troop's officers the General's visit was a big deal. Making a good impression, etc. For me it was a rest.

At 1000 the General's pilot called for smoke. The Huey landed and a general and two other officers got off. The pilot stayed on the ground and shut down his engine. No one else landed, but there were two other helicopters loitering in the air not too far away. I stayed at Six Track, but the CO was responsible for meeting the General and had started walking out from the circle of tracks as the chopper was landing. Headley saluted the General and took him to the nearest Sheridan. The General climbed up and talked to the crew. He did the same thing again with the next Sheridan. He exchanged greetings with the crews of the APCs he passed, but only took time with the Sheridans. After he had inspected two Sheridans close up, Headley led the General to the side of the formation closest to the Woods. A Sheridan on that side drove out thirty meters and turned back with its main gun pointed at the General.

They wanted to demonstrate the Sheridan's turret stabilization system and center pivot turn capacity simultaneously. The turret stabilization system kept the gun pointed in the same direction regardless of how the vehicle turned. If the gun was pointed north when the stabilizer was engaged, the turret automatically turned as the vehicle turned to keep the gun pointed north. The Sheridan had been designed to pivot on its own center by moving one tread forward and the other backward at the same time. It could spin in place without moving forward, back or sideways. The beginning of the demonstration was impressive, the chassis of the vehicle started slowly rotating under the turret that pointed at the General without moving at all. The Sheridan got almost all the way around, but then something in the bustle rack welded to the back of the turret got jammed up against something on the chassis and the turret started turning with the vehicle. The driver had increased the speed of the pivot, so the vehicle and turret were spinning pretty fast with a jammed turret.

The Sheridan stopped as soon as the Track Commander could tell the driver to stop. That was the end of the demonstration. The General said a few words to Headley and the Platoon Leaders while the demonstration Sheridan's crew unjammed the turret and restowed their gear in the bustle rack. One of the General's aides signaled the helicopter pilot to start the engine. By the time the General finished his conversation and walked back to the helicopter, its engine was warm enough to take off as soon as the General got on board. When Headley mounted Six Track, he only spoke of the demonstration once, "Shit."

After the General left we didn't head into the Woods proper, we moved in the scattered brush 1500 meters north of where we had demonstrated the Sheridan. It was a transition area between generally open fields to the west and the Upper Boi Loi Woods to the east. We stopped at 1120 and put down dismounts for a careful search. Most of the time the tracks were stopped. After the dismounts had searched an area, the tracks would pull forward twenty meters and stop again.

We found a cluster of six bunkers and seven foxholes within two hundred meters of where we started. There was some old food left behind and some fresh shit. We also found a cigarette lighter, a World War II German pistol, a hundred M60 rounds and 400 AK47 rounds. I don't know who got the cigarette lighter and the pistol, but I doubt either made it to the rear.

By 1430 we were moving away from the Upper Boi Loi Woods closely paralleling the unused part of Highway 26 that ran to Highway 19 at Xom Bao Don. From Xom Bao Don it was a road trip back to Hampton at 1540.

February 19

After breakfast Third Platoon swept north to Checkpoint 22 and Second Platoon south to Trang Bang. About 0730 we left Hampton with First Platoon leading the Troop clearing the road to Ap Suoi Cao. By 0815 we were a klick behind the village and found enough sandal prints crossing a dirt track to indicate a platoon size unit had crossed headed north the night before. There was nothing else in the immediate area.

At 1000 we were approaching the edge of the Lower Boi Loi Woods at the western end of the strip separating the Upper and Lower Woods. We moved into the Lower Boi Loi Woods on line with the left end of the line right at the northern edge and the right end as far into the Woods as the line stretched. We were embraced as tightly by the brush and dead air as our other days in the Woods, but I could see the edge of the Woods and that made it easier to take. The thick brush kept the tracks from traveling right next to each other, but the urge for safety meant the tracks drifted left and converged. Headley spent most of his time on the radio insisting that the Platoon Leaders maintain proper spacing between their vehicles as we moved slowly forward.

Two hundred meters into our sweep we found 33 one hundred pound bags of rice. Headley decided to carry eight out and scatter the rest on the ground. Another hundred meters on a Second Platoon Sheridan hit a mine. The mine blew off a road wheel and busted the left tread. The loader had been riding outside on the left side of the turret and got a fragment wound bad enough for a dust off. By the time Second Platoon had dragged the damaged Sheridan into the strip between the Woods, a dust off chopper arrived for the wounded loader. Second Platoon made a rough circle in the open strip and was left behind with the damaged Sheridan while the rest of the Troop continued.

Six hundred meters further on we found another 3200 pounds of rice that Headley decided to load on the tracks. When it was loaded, we turned around and started back the way we had come. Just after we turned, we took a few sniper rounds from the west. We couldn't fire back toward Second Platoon except to stop a serious assault, so we stopped and formed a rough perimeter. At 1300, after about ten minutes without any further fire, we moved into the area where it sounded like the sniping had come from. We found several fresh foxholes, but nothing else. Headley ordered the Troop to move directly to the open strip then toward Second Platoon.

When we got back to Second Platoon, Third Platoon continued on out while Six Track, the Medic Track and First Platoon waited for Second Platoon to finish rigging the damaged Sheridan to be towed out by another Sheridan. Headley said that Third Platoon was going on to pick up an M88 at Checkpoint 18 and escort it back to get the damaged Sheridan. As soon as the towing cables were rigged, we moved west near the middle of the open strip. As the space got wider I felt a lot better. We paralleled the edge of the Lower Boi Loi Woods about a hundred meters out as it curved to the south. When we reached the western end of the Woods we stopped and Headley sent First Platoon toward the Woods on line. They stopped up against the brush and the LRP team that we had dropped there two days before walked out and mounted the vehicles.

Third Platoon and the recovery vehicle met us a klick away from the Woods. With a recovery vehicle to tow the Sheridan we could travel at normal speed. We were tucked into Hampton by 1645.

As soon as Six Track was parked up against the berm everybody else moved away from the track, but Bear started packing all his gear in his duffel bag. "What's up?" "I'm going in. Chico's taking over Six Track." "Good luck, Bear." "Same to you Foxy."

Bear got on the evening chopper that came a few minutes later.

Shortly after Bear left, I was introduced to Marino, a black haired skinny white kid who was our new driver.

February 20

When the road sweeps to Trang Bang and Checkpoint 22 were done, Third Platoon led the Troop across to Ap Suoi Cao. By 0850 we were within a klick from the western end of the Lower Boi Loi Woods approaching from the southwest. When we got a little closer, we switched to on line and moved into the Woods and pivoted right. The drill was the same as yesterday, except it was the right end of our line that stayed at the edge of the Woods.

We found four bunkers in the brush almost immediately, but nothing in or around them. Six hundred meters further on at 1000, we found twelve old bunkers with some webgear and documents. Another three hundred meters and we found five damaged bunkers decorated with medical leftovers and bloody bandages. Another two hundred meters on we found about 900 pounds of rice on the ground next to bags that looked like they were destroyed by artillery fire. We turned north and reached the edge of a small clearing at 1130 where we stopped for lunch.

After lunch Headley told the Platoon Leaders that a helicopter had reported something unusual in the fields behind Ap Suoi Cao and we were going to check it out. We moved south on line about as fast as we could move in the Woods. When we broke out, we continued south, then west past the western end of the Woods, then north. At 1250 we arrived at the location the helicopter had called in and found two new foxholes, each lined with a vertical piece of concrete sewer pipe.

One platoon was put to work getting the pipe out of the ground and the other two searching the area. The two pieces of pipe were half dug out then pulled out with towing cables. It took considerable effort, but each piece was eventually broken up by driving a track over it. Two hours of searching the area found two pounds of coffee, two cartons of Cambodian cigarettes, a small bag of rice, a canteen and assorted food, some clothing, two copies of *Stars and Stripes*, an RPG round and an SKS rifle with a silencer. The foxholes were within a klick of our normal route from Highway 19 to the Woods and the area where we had laagered several times. At that distance, without a scope, the shots would have been mostly luck, but, if the silencer worked, we wouldn't have known anyone was shooting at us until somebody or something was hit.

We pulled into our laager for the night at 1645, a klick west of the west end of the Boi Loi Woods. When I radioed in my defensive targets I fired in the east one right on the edge of the Woods. That was where a sniper, mortar or second wave of an attack was most likely to be if something happened later. If anybody was there watching us, the adjusting rounds encouraged them to leave.

An APC and a repaired Sheridan plus a Troop Headquarters track, a cargo carrier with diesel fuel and another cargo carrier with our cooks and dinner came out at 1700. The repaired vehicles joined their platoons and the cargo carrier with the diesel tank started around the circle topping off the tracks. The cooks set up for dinner and the headquarters guys started doing whatever they came for.

February 21

We began our day moving north from our laager then turned east on line through the light brush next to the edge of the Upper Boi Loi Woods. We didn't have dismounts down but moved slowly through the brush. It took twenty minutes to get to the edge of the Woods. The edge of the Woods wasn't a crisp line, but there was a clear increase in the density and size of the brush plus some scattered trees about where the edge of the Woods was shown on the map. The brush in the Upper Boi Loi Woods seemed denser than its lower namesake and there were more trees. The erratic twisting and turning of the individual tracks resulted in a ragged line moving slowly.

Ten minutes into the Woods the tension was broken by three incoming RPGs and scattered automatic weapons fire. One of the RPGs hit an APC. The Troop's eruption in response was immediate. Seconds after our machine guns started new notes were added to the symphony, the Sheridans firing their main guns. Each of them fired three flechette rounds as fast as they could load and fire. The Sheridan flechette round was smaller than the one for the 105mm howitzer, only six thousand steel darts. The seven Sheridans then with us each firing three flechette rounds meant 126,000 steel darts swept our front within seconds after the first incoming fire. The darts didn't spread out immediately and didn't travel very far through the brush, but an area beginning ten or twenty meters in front our line was almost immediately cleansed of any enemy above ground.

After the initial mad minute the intensity of the Troop's machine gun fire reduced and Sheridan main gun firing was sporadic. Headley checked the status of the platoons and updated his initial report of contact to Squadron. There was no sign of return enemy fire. Headley confirmed that only the one APC had been hit. It had not caught fire, but the driver and track commander were dead. We had two others wounded badly enough to need evacuation. Headley yelled at me that gunships and a dust off had been scrambled, but I started a fire mission hoping for clearance before the gunships arrived.

"Jackhammer One Eight, this is Jackhammer Two Three, fire mission, over." The reply was emotionless, "Jackhammer Two Three, this is Jackhammer One Eight, fire mission, out."

"Jackhammer One Eight, Two Three, grid x-ray tango four niner five three three five, direction zero eight hundred, enemy position, battery two in effect, over." "Jackhammer Two Three, this is Jackhammer One Eight, grid x-ray tango four niner five three three five, direction zero eight hundred, enemy position, battery two in effect, wait, out."

Starting the fire mission request with "grid" meant that the FDC should put the first rounds on a point identified by the grid on our maps. Everywhere we went was in the x-ray tango, or "XT," grid. The first three digits were the east to west position. Grid line 49 was a north to south line a klick west of grid line 50. "Four niner five" meant five hundred meters east of grid line 49, half way to grid line 50. The next three digits were the north to south position. Grid line 33 was an east to west grid line a klick south of grid line 34. "Three three five" meant five hundred meters north of grid line 33, again half way. With a six digit grid location I was estimating to the nearest hundred meters, but that was close enough to start. We were moving a little north of east when we were hit and the enemy automatic weapons sounded off to our right front before our return fire masked the sound of enemy fire, so I had called for fire on a grid location to our northeast, at least five hundred meters away.

While I waited for clearance and the first rounds, I noticed that the brush in front of us was markedly thinner. The flechettes had stripped most of the leaves off the bushes.

Clearance came fast in the Woods. "Jackhammer Two Three, this is Jackhammer One Eight, on the way, over." "One Eight, Two Three, on the way, out."

When the two adjusting rounds landed, they were in the right direction and far enough away. "Jackhammer One Eight, this is Two Three, fire for effect, over." "Two Three, this is One Eight, fire for effect, out." "On the way" came a few seconds later.

After the rounds landed, but before I could respond, the FDC was back on the radio. "Jackhammer Two Three, this is Jackhammer One Eight, we must suspend firing for gunships coming on station, over." "One Eight, Two Three, suspending fire for gunships, out."

When the gunships arrived overhead a line track in each platoon popped smoke. The team of two Cobras began rocket and minigun runs across the front of the Troop, about forty or fifty meters in front of our line. The two wounded had been loaded in the Medic Track and the two killed in the Third Platoon mortar track. They moved fifty meters back to the edge of a cluster of craters that made a clearing big enough for a slick to land. All four were dusted off while the first team of gunships was working out. A second team of gunships followed the first.

While the gunships were alternating firing runs across our front, Headley said that Charlie Troop was coming up on our right flank. We couldn't see them coming in from where Six Track was, but, because the Troop didn't fire with helicopters flying across our front, we could hear the noise of Charlie Troop moving up in the short quiet periods between gunship passes. They linked up with our right flank track at 1010.

The second gunship team had expended all its ordnance about the same time that Charlie linked up and both troops began a steady machine gun fire as soon as the last helicopter cleared the area in front of us. Captain Thomas was now overhead in with the Squadron CO, flying somewhere out of the line of shell flight from the battery firing in our support. He radioed that he was taking over my fire mission.

Captain Thomas called in only a few more salvos until he was shut off because a Forward Air Controller had arrived overhead to spot for incoming fighter bombers. Between 1045 and 1230 we got four pairs. Each pair had a mixed load of bombs and napalm. The FAC knew where we were and fired white phosphorus rockets to mark the targets for each pass. All of the bombing runs went from right to left across our front. Each pair started with the first aircraft dropping two tanks of napalm, then the second aircraft with napalm, then the first aircraft with two bombs then the second aircraft with two bombs. The napalm was about a hundred meters out. There was a hot flash on your face about the same time you saw the fire ball spreading. The bombs went in at least three hundred meters out. With the bombs, the flash and shock wave arrived just before the sound and rumble in the ground.

Between aircraft departures and arrivals, Captain Thomas got in some more artillery fire, but not very much. I sat with my M16 across my lap and smoked while I listened to Captain Thomas calling in fire. Through the air strikes there was practically no firing by either Troop. It was hard to believe that anyone in the target area would have peeked out of a hole if they were in one or that they wouldn't get into a hole if they weren't. When the last air strike was complete, the Troop began a steady fire again and we moved slowly forward. Our dismounts were down, usually walking next to a line track and checking out any holes they passed. Unless the hole was a simple foxhole that they could see the bottom of, checking out a hole meant throwing a grenade in it and looking in after the explosion. By 1320 we had swept three hundred meters forward from our start line after the air strikes and seen no sign of any remaining enemy. Headley ordered a cease fire and the dismounts began a more systematic check of the area we had passed through. The area that Bravo had swept had one cluster of 22 bunkers around an L shaped tunnel with one large underground room at the end of the tunnel. The room showed signs of recent use, but all they found was an RPG round.

The search of the contact area was over about 1430 and both Troops moved out of the Woods on line, retracing the way we had come in. When we were into the light brush on the edge of the Woods, Charlie Troop headed south into the fields east of Ap Suoi Cao and we moved north to the unused portion of Highway 26 and paralleled it to Xom Bao Don. From there it was a road trip to Hampton.

February 22

First Platoon's morning sweep was to Checkpoint 22 and back. Second Platoon cleared to Trang Bang, then up Highway 19 to Checkpoint 18, then closed the triangle back through Go Dau Ha to Hampton. Six Track stayed in Hampton with the Third Platoon.

Headley was at Squadron Headquarters when Second Platoon came in and he didn't come back until almost an hour later. As he climbed up into his seat he said, "Looks like an easy day," putting on his radio helmet. We started out of Hampton. We went to Ap Suoi Cao, turned north on Highway 19 and turned east off the road just north of the Ap Suoi Cao fields. We spent the morning swanning about in very scattered low brush. On the map, we were in a light green, moderate vegetation area. On the ground, we were sweeping a parking lot.

At the lunch break, Headley gave me personal news, "Foxy, today's my last day." "I didn't know you were that short." "I'm not. I've got a few weeks to go. I'm going in to Cu Chi, on Squadron staff. The new CO is Mike Jackson. He was Charlie Troop's XO. Takes over in Hampton tonight." After lunch we spent another three hours carefully checking nothing.

We were back in Hampton by 1630. Headley packed his gear as soon as we parked then went over to the Squadron Headquarters. Half an hour later he came back with First Lieutenant Jackson. He introduced me, "Mike, this is Lieutenant Watson. He's a first class FO." I shook Jackson's hand, "Welcome aboard sir."

Lieutenant Jackson nodded. Jackson was about the same size as Headley, but looked tighter wound. Jackson was introduced to the rest of the Six Track crew, then Headley picked up his gear and went back to Headquarters. Jackson had already met the Platoon Leaders. He busied himself checking his radios and gear and stowing his personal gear. Headley was on the evening chopper back to Cu Chi. As soon as the evening chopper left, Jackson radioed the Platoon Leaders to come to a briefing at Six Track. He gave a standard taking-command speech: he'd heard what a fine unit Bravo was and all policies and procedures remained the same until he ordered a change. After that he went through the road clearing assignments for tomorrow then broke up the meeting. Jackson said nothing about his rank, but he clearly outranked the Platoon Leaders and probably was close to being promoted to Captain.

6

Second Boi Loi

February 23

Everyone was rousted up at 0145. There was a report of a ground attack on Go Dau Ha bridge and First Platoon was ordered to reinforce. They moved out promptly and arrived at the position on the east side of the bridge at 0220. They had no problem getting there and there was no incoming fire when they arrived. After they had been in place with no problems for a while, I went back to sleep.

I was shaken awake again at 0415 and told to report to the Cav Headquarters. First Platoon thought they had an artillery target about a klick west of their position, across the river and just north of Route 1. I was told that the gooks were attacking a company of the Second Wolfhounds in Patrol Base Diamond. I heard nothing more about an artillery target, but I heard First Platoon reporting on the Headquarters radio that they had spotted antiaircraft machine guns that appeared to be firing at helicopters over Diamond. The guns they saw were south of the bridge, so they were probably east of Ap Bien Hoa.

I was still at Cav Headquarters when Jackson got the word that Bravo was being sent to Diamond. It was still dark and not a pleasant thought. I didn't have a lot to do to get ready. Make sure my flashlight and radio worked and that I had the right map ready. Charlie and Johnson were doing the same without instruction, We waited a while for Alpha Troop to start one of their platoons to the bridge. We left Hampton at 0510.

There wasn't much worry about Route 1 because it was hard surfaced and difficult to mine on short notice, but we did move a lot slower than during the day—time to give the crew of the lead vehicle a chance to see the road in the light of the intermittent flares. We didn't have any illumination support initially. I suspect the artillery and helicopters were absorbed with Diamond. We relied on hand flares. At the center of Go Dau Ha we turned to cross the bridge. First Platoon stayed where they were when we passed, waiting for the Alpha platoon that was supposed to arrive soon.

6—Second Boi Loi

We kept up our slow drive down Route 1 on the other side of the bridge and ten minutes later we were at the same left turn we had taken to go to Ap Bien Hoa in January. I radioed in our position at the intersection.

While we were putting down mine sweeping teams on the dirt road to the south, Jackson said that First Platoon had been relieved at the bridge and should be joining the tail of our column in minutes. On the road we had already swept they would move a lot faster. Once we turned on to the dirt road and were moving at walking speed, Jackson gave orders to turn on the Sheridans' search lights. The lead vehicle was a Sheridan and it lit straight down the road. The following Sheridans in the column lit alternating sides of the road. They moved their turrets to sweep the fields as we moved. The light from a Sheridan's searchlight was still an eerie light, but it was a lot better than our last trip down the same road in the dark. The Sheridans pushed the darkness way back and everywhere the light went, it was backed by a really big shotgun.

About three klicks south of Route 1 the sweep team found a mud wall about a foot and a half high across the road. The column stopped while it was checked carefully. They found no sign of metal in or near it or wires leading from it. After they blessed it, the column rolled over it without incident, or at least part of the column, rolled over it. Part of the column hadn't crossed the wall when we stopped another hundred meters on, because the sweep team found a recently filled hole in the road. The mine detectors indicated metal in it. The sweep team confirmed it was a mine and we pulled back so they could blow it. It made a large crater, but didn't block the road and we passed on. The sun was almost fully up by then and we only used mine sweeping teams for another two hundred meters or so. By then the field next to the road was dry enough to move across and we pulled off the road and began moving cross country parallel to the road.

By 0730 we were a klick and a half north of Ap Bien Hoa and started southwest cross country. I couldn't see any signs of fighting. I could hear sporadic rifle or machine gun fire, but nothing continuous or heavy. Diamond's circular dirt berm and observation tower were visible as we approached, but we never got closer than 500 meters. Jackson told me that Bravo Troop was now under the operational control of the 2nd Battalion of the 27th Infantry.

The fighting was pretty much over. They had a few gooks isolated and pinned down close in and wanted to finish those off themselves. They asked us to sweep the flat lands toward the Cambodian border hunting up their body count. We moved up onto line and started west. There were enough enemy bodies in the fields to stop and check that we didn't move all that fast. We also got one prisoner. Jackson sent the platoons to search separately. We sat still in the middle for a while until Jackson ordered us off at high speed to join the platoon that had gone west toward Cambodia.

"Watson, they're chasing a gook straggler who refuses to surrender." We were fifty meters away from a group of tracks when one of them fired a single long burst from a .50 caliber. By the time we got to where they had stopped, they were checking the body. The track commander who had shot him said that they had spooked him out of a clump of brush and he just kept running. He wasn't carrying any visible weapon, so they just followed him, not very far behind. They kept yelling "chieu hoi" at him, asking him to surrender. Once he stopped, panting and looked back at the track where it had stopped, then he pointed toward Cambodia and started running again. They followed. The next time he ran out of steam and stopped he pulled out a grenade from somewhere. The machine gun fire we heard dropped him before he threw it. He died immediately. He may have been stupid enough to think he could just say sorry and go back to Cambodia or just very brave to keep running. He certainly was very stupid when he pulled out the grenade.

Shortly after that the Troop parked in a blocking position well west of Diamond and the infantry began a foot sweep toward us. Diamond was only about a two hour walk from the Cambodian border. It may have looked like an easy attack to the NVA. Get rested up, pass out ammo, stroll over toward Diamond after dark, attack it for three or four hours and stroll back to Cambodia before it gets light. But it wasn't easy: Diamond was bait. The first NVA attack on Diamond had cost them about eighty dead, this one about a hundred.

The sweep toward us didn't stir up anything and we were released at 1445. We left immediately for Route 1, passed through Go Dau Ha at 1630 and laagered behind Ap Suoi Cao at 1700. It was a quiet night for us, but at 1930 we got word that Cu Chi was on yellow alert. I was asleep when the alert was raised to red at 2230 and Jackson received warning orders that Bravo was the reaction force if Cu Chi was heavily attacked. At 2300 two Cav tracks that were in Cu Chi for repairs were sent to reinforce the main gate and Cav troopers in the rear area were assembled and moved to reinforce the bunker line behind the Cav area. No attack came.

February 24

By 0830 we were back through Go Dau Ha and about half way to Cambodia down Route 1. We spent the next six hours finding nothing in the open fields immediately north of Route 1. At the end of our looking, we went back through Go Dau Ha to laager behind Ap Sui Cao, less than a klick from where we had spent the night before.

February 25

When fed and packed, we headed off to the north, while our trains went toward Ap Suoi Cao to wait for a cleared road back to Hampton. We found many footprints, also headed north, on a trail near where the unused part of Highway 26 entered the Upper Boi Loi Woods. We moved into the Woods about 0800 and spent over five hours crashing about. We found 45 bunkers and a day-old NVA corpse. Half the bunkers had been used within the last 24 hours. At the end of the day one of the APCs busted a drive sprocket near an unexploded bomb. Someone was carrying a spare sprocket and when it was replaced we called it a day and cleared the Woods by 1330.

Our laager for the night, without First Platoon, was in an open field just west of Highway 19 two klicks south of Ap Suoi Cao. First Platoon outposted the culvert at Checkpoint B where a stream crossed under Highway 19. The culvert wasn't very big, but apparently someone thought it had become important. When First Platoon got there they relieved an Alpha Troop platoon that had been guarding the culvert all day.

February 26

I was awakened at 0450 with the news that the Cav headquarters had reported that Cu Chi was being mortared. By the time I joined Jackson in Six Track, it was clear that there was a ground assault on Cu Chi. Division again alerted Bravo Troop to be ready to react if needed. "Delta Troop just asked the CO where they should fly their choppers. Some choppers have been blown on the ground in Cu Chi. It doesn't sound good."

Our call never came. Morning stand to was at 0530. At 0610 there was a report over the Squadron radio net that the attack had gone through the Cav area at Cu Chi. Three dead gooks were found between two perimeter bunkers near the Cav area and three Cav troopers had been wounded. A couple of Cav hooches had been hit by RPGs.

About 0650 First Platoon went past us headed north clearing the road to Checkpoint 18 then on to Go Dau Ha. They were assigned to guard Go Dau Ha bridge. For the rest of us, the day was spent clearing the rest of Highway 19 between Trang Bang and Xom Bao Don and outposting the six klicks south of Ap Suoi Cao. Second Platoon found Viet Cong propaganda leaflets on stakes alongside the road south of Checkpoint B. The convoy went past us headed north at 1030.

After the convoy passed, Jackson took Six Track and the Medic Track to join the outpost that included the Second Platoon Leader's track. Gramm had kept some of the propaganda posters. They were hand printed in English, but whoever had copied them didn't fully understand what they were copying.

"STOP THE WARG.I'S DON' TFIGHT THE VIETNAMESE PEOPLE WHO ARE STRUGGLING FOR PEACE, INDEPENDENGE AND FREEDOM!"
"PEACE IN VIETNAM BRING AMERICAN JROOPS HOME."

The return convoy started past us at 1520. As soon as the convoy cleared, Second Platoon relieved First Platoon at the bridge. Then First Platoon joined Third Platoon and us in a laager in a field just west of Highway 19 a little north of where we spent last night. Six Cav troopers came back on the evening chopper. It was a much higher than usual number of returnees. Apparently the attack on Cu Chi had helped speed their recovery from whatever had sent them to the rear.

That night we got more radio reports on the attack on Cu Chi last night. The gooks had been headed for the main helicopter pad on the other side of the Cav area. They blew up five Chinook helicopters. Most of them died trying to get in through the wire and most of the rest died trying to get back out. Aside from the helicopters and the shock of having the enemy inside the wire, there was not much damage to Cu Chi.

February 27

Morning road sweeps from Trang Bang to Xom Bao Don began at 0700. When they were done, we outposted Highway 19 again. The northbound convoy went by at 1000 and came back southbound at 1430. Second Platoon was released from Go Dau Ha bridge at 1600. We met them at Checkpoint 18 and laagered three klicks behind Ap Suoi Cao. Just before 1730 we were ordered to move to FSB Wood. That was put on hold almost immediately and at 1800 we were ordered to come to Hampton. We packed, left and were in Hampton by 1840. We'd already eaten in the field, but there were the shower and outhouse to enjoy.

February 28

Road clearing was south to Trang Bang, across to Checkpoint 18, and north to Checkpoint 22. When everybody was done, the Troop assembled at Ap Suoi Cao. Like so many previous days, we headed east past the southern edge of the village. At 0845 we turned north, passing about a klick west of the western end of the Lower Boi Loi Woods. As the brush got thicker, Jackson ordered the Troop on line. Six Track was behind Third Platoon in the center of the line. We moved slowly, but had no dismounts down. We reached the edge of the Upper Boi Loi Woods at 0930, very near our fight on the 21st.

We were a hundred meters or so short of reaching the track of Highway 26 through the Woods when, at 0945, we took some small arms fire from our right front. A mad minute of machine gun fire in response came as soon as Jackson cleared fire. The machine guns were joined by three or four salvos of flechette rounds from the Sheridans. The Medic Track took off to the right. Someone in Second Platoon had been hit in the initial enemy small arms fire. While Jackson called for a dust off and gunships, I radioed in a fire mission behind where the shots had come from. Because I was calling fire in on the other side of a road that I knew we had not crossed, I could start a little closer to where I thought we were than usual.

The first flurry of firing subsided and slower outgoing fire was maintained for a while. A little after 1000 Jackson gave the word to move forward slowly with dismounts down. Almost as soon as we started moving, three RPGs came in from three different places to our front. That triggered another mad minute.

"Jackhammer Two Three, this is Jackhammer One Eight, we cannot clear fire, negative air"—the message ended in a burst of static. "Jackhammer One Eight, Two Three, say again all after cannot clear fire, over."

"Say again" was Artillery language. "Repeat" was a firing command; the simplest, fastest one. "Repeat" meant fire the same thing you last fired; same point of impact, same ammunition, same number of rounds. Saying "repeat" on the radio by mistake could get a lot of rounds fired somewhere that might not be right any more. So, when you only wanted someone to repeat a message or part of it, you said "say again." "Say again all after" was a short cut when part of a message had been clear.

"Two Three, this is One Eight, I say again, cannot clear fire, negative air clearance, over." "Jackhammer One Eight, Two Three, negative air clearance, out."

Helicopter gunship runs began a few minutes after my firing clearance was denied. Then the Medic Track took off again, this time almost straight ahead. By the time it got there the medics had nothing to do. An RPG had gone off on top of a track. The APC wasn't seriously damaged, but the kid on it who was hit by the projectile was dead. After our firing slowed again, Jackson ordered a slow advance, with steady firing as we moved. I couldn't hear exactly what was happening, but the sound of firing was punctuated with grenades going off in holes. We moved very slowly, but by 1045 we had moved thirty meters or so and the platoons reported the recovery of seven enemy bodies, an AK47 and a loaded RPG launcher.

Jackson said that Charlie Troop was being sent our way and would be coming up behind us, about the same way we came in. Just after 1100 a two aircraft air strike went in across our front. The closeness of the first napalm drops was confirmed by the heat on our faces. The second run bombs were dropped further away, but still close enough to feel their shock waves. Between explosions, Jackson radioed that we had four wounded that needed dust off.

After the aircraft cleared, we resumed a slow but steady machine gun fire and started slowly forward again through the shredded brush. As soon as we started moving, I heard Captain Thomas on the radio. I recognized his voice and knew from the background noise that he was calling from a helicopter even before he got to his call sign, "Jackhammer One Eight, this is Jackhammer Three Five, get clearance on Jackhammer Two Three's mission, grid x-ray tango four eight six three three seven, direction three hundred, I will adjust, over."

His message was acknowledged. Clearance came almost immediately, all they needed to check was air space. Captain Thomas fired for effect where the first rounds landed then started working volleys across our front, probably about five hundred meters out. The chopper he was in was being flown for Colonel McGowan's convenience, generally flying in a loop to keep us in sight, but out of the flight path of the artillery shells. Sometimes Thomas didn't see the shells hit and just called in a "repeat." The main task of the artillery fire today was to prevent large scale enemy movement and precise location wasn't necessary for that.

By 1145 the platoons reported another eight enemy bodies, a Russian radio and a prisoner. The prisoner was badly wounded and the Medic Track went for him as soon as he was reported. Nam was riding on the Medic Track and questioned the prisoner. The prisoner said there were seventy people in the area we were trying to move through. The dismounts were still finding bunkers while the Troop put out steady machine gun fire and advanced at a bare crawl. I couldn't hear any enemy return fire, but there must have been some because we got another wounded trooper at 1220.

The FDC suspend Captain Thomas' firing for a second airstrike like

Opposite, top and bottom: Two views of Six Track. The .50 caliber machine gun has been dismounted. On the front view the hole from the RPG hit on February 28 is near the center of the front of the track. On the side view the forward observer's seat is visible on the right side (author's collection).

the first. Two runs of napalm about a hundred meters in front of us, then two runs of high explosives further north. Before the first run the line tracks marked their location with smoke and the FAC used that as a reference to mark aiming points for the F100s with white phosphorus rockets. While the air strike was going in our firing was shut off. Platoon status reports during the air strike included two new enemy bodies and four more AK47s. After one radio exchange Jackson announced personal news. "Squadron says I just got my orders for Captain." Chico must have heard. He passed out warm Cokes and we raised our cans in salute to his promotion.

The air strikes and our celebration were over by 1230 and we resumed suppressive fire and crawling forward. Captain Thomas was off station with Colonel McGowan to refuel the chopper. "Jackhammer One Eight, this is Jackhammer Two Three, do we have clearance to resume firing? Over." "Two Three, this is One Eight, we have clearance to resume firing. Who will adjust? Over."

"One Eight, this is Two Three, I will adjust, repeat, over." "Two Three, this is One Eight, repeat, out."

The last rounds were still far enough away to be safe and I started moving the twelve round salvos across our front again. We were moving slowly, but I did have to move the rounds out a couple of times to keep them far enough away from us. At 1245 Second Platoon took two RPGs, one from our right flank and the other from our right rear. Jackson called for our third dust off. We got a report that Charlie Troop was taking rifle fire as they came up behind us. We were assured that they had tight fire discipline because we were so close. At 1300 we were still crawling forward and I was calling in battery volleys every few minutes well in front of us. The next discrete event was fifteen minutes later when a Sheridan in Second Platoon claimed that a grenade had been thrown at it from behind.

Second Platoon reported sporadic rifle fire from the right rear just as they broke into a clear space on our right flank. Third Platoon pulled another enemy body out of a hole. Second Platoon had reached a field just south of Highway 26. The field was fifty meters wide between the edge of the wooded area and a hedgerow that ran along the edge of the road. Jackson had the Troop pivot a little to the east so our line paralleled the road and instructed me to move the artillery fire to cover the right flank. I couldn't bring it in close enough to really cover the flank, but I could make it hard for anyone to come to the assistance of whoever was already there. We pulled ahead so that the line tracks were just a few meters behind the hedgerow. I couldn't see all of the Troop because there were light hedgerows that ran perpendicular to the road. They had very low dikes and only a little brush on top, but they were enough to prevent seeing the vehicles on the other side. The space between the hedgerows that I could see held Third Platoon and a little of First Platoon to the left.

We paused for the next air strike. The road in front of us was a great control line. It was easy to tell the air controller where we were and even a jet running in at high speed could see the road. Before the jets came in, there were several gunships ready to rocket and hose with miniguns. The artillery was shut off again to clear the air for the choppers. Just as the gunship runs were beginning, one of the platoons reported finding three 57mm recoilless rifle rounds. If the gooks had a 57mm, it would be more of a problem than just RPGs. While the gunships were making their strafing runs, Colonel McGowan landed in a LOH just a little behind Six Track. As soon as he got off, the pilot pulled out hard. Colonel McGowan came to Six Track and talked to Jackson a few minutes then his chopper came back for him at the same spot. As soon as McGowan left, Jackson ordered Marino to cross over the hedgerow on our left to meet with Lieutenant Carlson. On the way back, he stopped to talk with Lieutenant Nelson. Then we headed toward the hedgerow that had been on our right to get to Second Platoon and Lieutenant Gramm.

We were ten meters from the hedgerow when an RPG hit Six Track in front. I don't know if I was blown off or jumped. My M16 had been in my lap and I still had it when I hit the ground. It took two or three seconds on the ground to realize that I hadn't been hurt. I was on the right side of the track and could hear air strikes going in, but I couldn't see anyone. Then I saw Charlie and Johnson on the ground behind the track. As we were climbing back on Six Track, Third Platoon's Sergeant Ramos' Sheridan, 35, passed close on our left side and stopped just in front of us. His gunner and loader were down inside the turret, but Ramos was riding up behind his .50 caliber. When they stopped he opened a hand flare, held it horizontal in his left fist and launched it generally in the direction of the hedgerow we were approaching when we were hit. He did the same thing four more times. If it hadn't been so brave, it would have been funny. He couldn't fire his main gun or his 50 without serious risk to our people on the other side of the hedgerow so he was firing flares to keep the RPG crew's heads down. A direct hit by a flare probably would have hurt, but they weren't designed to be aimed. Apparently the RPG team didn't know that, or didn't know that he couldn't fire his other weapons, or had already pulled out.

The RPG had hit Six Track's front, almost in the center. The blast angled across the driver's compartment and burned and broke Marino's leg. Still, Marino climbed out and ran a fair distance before he collapsed.

I don't know what happened to the man who fired the RPG that hit us. Shortly after we got back on Six Track, some dismounts followed 35 and grenaded a couple of holes in the hedgerow. Then they and 35 left and went back to where they had come from. Chico got into the driver's compartment and reported that he could drive the track but not at full power. Charlie moved into the cupola. Jackson walked up and told me to stay on Six Track and put the artillery fire on our right flank. Then he moved to an undamaged track. Chico drove us back to about the center of the formation, twenty meters behind the line tracks. I fired volleys between gunship runs. Whenever the gunships weren't to our front, the Troop fired a steady suppressing fire. About 1520 the intensity of fire on the right flank increased a great deal.

At 1530 artillery fire was suspended for fighter bombers on station. Captain Thomas radioed me that the air strike would go in as soon as we moved out. The Troop moved to our left rear, away from the heavy firing on our right flank and almost directly toward the nearest light brush. Six Track sounded like it was straining to keep up.

The tracks fired sporadic suppressing fire to the right side of the column. I fired a burst of M16 fire into each clump of brush near our right side as we passed about the first 200 meters out. There was no one in our way on the way out. Later, some of the troops claimed they saw men with RPGs in the woods running parallel to us. They were on the left side of the column and we couldn't shoot at them because of the risk to Charlie Troop. If there were gooks trying to catch up, none did.

Within minutes of our pulling out, air strikes began with the napalm going in about where we had just left. As soon as we were two hundred meters out of the Woods, the Troop stopped in a rough laager. A slick landed inside the laager almost immediately to dust off Marino, Lieutenant Gramm, a couple of other wounded and Sergeant Evans' body. Charlie Troop arrived from the south, formed a screen on the Woods side of our laager and started unloading boxes of machine gun ammunition and Sheridan main gun rounds. It wasn't anywhere near a full load, but several of our tracks were nearly out of ammo and Charlie brought enough to assure a couple of boxes of ammo for each machine gun and four or five more rounds for each Sheridan gun.

We pulled away from Charlie toward Ap Suoi Cao about 1740. Jackson stayed on his new track. Six Track was towed by another APC. We were at Checkpoint 18 about 1820 and in Hampton at 1905. Dinner was ready when we arrived, but I wasn't very hungry.

I went to the FDC of the Battery at Hampton and confirmed that they had been the battery firing in our support all day. The Battery CO was nearby. "Sir, I'm Lieutenant Watson, FO for Bravo Troop. I'd like to tell your gun crews what they did for us today." "Excellent. Sergeant Palmer, escort Lieutenant Watson to the guns. Start with one and go in order. Matthews, phone number one section to fall out for a visitor."

6—Second Boi Loi

The Battery was equipped with self propelled 155mm howitzers that look a little like tanks, but have a bulkier shape and much lighter armor. Each was parked inside a low circular sandbag wall with an opening just a bit wider than necessary to drive the gun in or out. The crew lived in a bunker next to their gun position. The first gun section was standing in a loose group next to their bunker when the Sergeant and I arrived. "Gentlemen, I'm the FO for Bravo Troop. I think you fired a few rounds for us today." Most of them looked at their feet, one man said, "yessir."

"I know you really can't tell what you're doing for us when you fire. When a fight like today starts, we're stuck deep in the woods and alone. A Cav Troop is heavily armed and we get other help, but it's the Artillery that's always there and always ready. When you put that hard rain on the gooks, we know we're not really alone. After a day like today, I'm proud to be in the Artillery. Your rounds keep whoever we're fighting from getting reinforced, keep them from maneuvering and keep them from getting away. We recovered more than twenty-five enemy bodies today. Most of them died because they were frozen in place by your rounds. We don't know how many more were directly killed by the rounds you fired. Thank you."

Some of the section nodded; a couple said, "thank you, sir." My escort asked the section chief to telephone the second section we were coming. I gave about the same speech to each gun section and each responded about the same. Six Track was repaired before we went to sleep.

March 1

Most of Bravo had the day off. Not really a day off, but restocking and maintenance instead of another day in the Woods.

Our intelligence report was that we had fought a company of the 88th NVA Regiment yesterday. Jackson said that when Six Track was hit, he'd climbed on Sergeant Evans' Sheridan and gotten connected to the Troop radio net just in time to hear Carlson report him dead. Immediately after announcing his survival, Jackson was blown off the Sheridan by the RPG that killed Evans. It was after being blown off two tracks that he spoke to me and took over Carlson's track. I hadn't even noticed that Evans' Sheridan was in the vicinity.

From time to time during the day I noticed unusual activity in the Artillery Battery area. Why became clear at 1130 when Third Platoon was detailed to escort the Battery to FSB Wood a little past Xom Boa Don on Highway 19. They left at 1300. Half of the Platoon led the Battery and half followed. The move went without incident and Third Platoon was back at 1520. Mike Gramm, the Second Platoon Leader, hadn't been seriously wounded but he left on an afternoon chopper to Cu Chi rotating home. After lunch Chico introduced a Spec4 named Baker as Six Track's new driver. He had moved over from driving an APC in Third Platoon. There was a Cav pay call at dinner.

7

Long Trench

March 2

Second Platoon got a second day to recover. The rest of us were headed for what Jackson later said Colonel McGowan called "a ride in the sun." We left Hampton by 0720 and were two klicks east of Ap Suoi Cao by 0830. We continued east, swinging south of the Country Store. A klick east of the Country Store we formed on line facing east toward scattered hedgerows around what appeared to be abandoned hooches. They were part of a band of intermittent hedgerows and hooches about 800 meters wide on the west side of Road 6A. Road 6A ran northerly out of Trang Bang past the eastern end of the Lower Boi Loi Woods. Jackson said that Road 6A was assumed to be mined. There were many gaps in the band we could have passed through, but today we were checking the hedgerows.

An APC on the left end of the line hit a mine before we reached the first hedgerow. The mine broke its tread and blew off one road wheel. The only casualty was a trooper on the back of the track whose split lip merited a routine dust off. While the track crew was replacing the road wheel and repairing the tread, of the rest of the Troop did a detailed search of the area. The search found a fresh dirt mound that was the grave of a recently killed Vietnamese male wrapped in a U.S. poncho liner.

By 1100 the track was repaired and we turned right to sweep south on line down the band of hedgerows. Within 500 meters, we found a cluster of bunkers and foxholes. There was an unexploded 155mm artillery round near one of the bunkers. When the dud blew behind us we stopped for lunch.

After lunch we continued to the south checking anything that seemed interesting. About 1400 we came to a hedgerow running north south. On the east side of the hedgerow there were scattered bushes about six feet high and ten or so feet apart. The west side was mostly open. Third Platoon, on the left of our line, got the brushy area. First Platoon was on the clear side with Six Track and the Medic Track. The hedgerow wasn't all that much, but as soon as it was between us, I couldn't see Third Platoon anymore. We were only a few meters on when there were four quick explosions from the other side of the hedgerow. The tracks on the other side immediately responded with full volume machine gun fire. First Platoon didn't fire at all. No one had fired at us and we couldn't see where the friendlies were. I wasn't sure what was happening, but I wanted rounds on the ground somewhere. I radioed in a fire mission about a klick south of us.

The volume of fire was substantially lower when Jackson yelled, "Foxy, Nelson's track and another are hit and burning. Nelson is dead. I'm pulling Third Platoon out to this side." "Yessir. I've asked for fire a klick south." He went back to his radios. Most of what I heard was telling the acting Third Platoon Leader to make sure that he brought out all his wounded and all the movable vehicles. In between he called for dust offs, advised Squadron of what he knew and asked for gunships.

The fire on the other side of the hedgerow lessened a little as the Third Platoon backed off and then hurried through the hedgerow to get to our side. By the time Third Platoon was coming through the hedgerow, First Platoon had moved thirty meters away from the hedgerow and further south, It was on line facing the hedgerow south of where Third Platoon had been when the enemy had opened fire. After the initial four RPG rounds there had been no sound of enemy fire. As soon as Third Platoon was out, moving to join the left end of our new line, and Jackson had confirmed that Third Platoon had all of its live people out, we opened up at the hedgerow, .50 calibers and flechette rounds. The brush hadn't been very heavy to start with and it started disappearing. Almost as soon as there was a decline in the intensity of the firing, Jackson got word that the first gunship team was approaching and main gun and .50 caliber fire were suspended. M60 and rifle fire continued, but was noticeably quieter.

I'd never gotten clearance for my fire mission to the south and now we were pointed east instead of south. With gunships starting their firing runs, there was no reason to continue the mission so I radioed in "end of mission."

The rockets looked like they were going in just on the other side of the hedgerow to the south of where Third Platoon had been hit. While the gun runs were going in, a dust off landed behind Six Track and took out four seriously wounded. Third Platoon had left two APCs on the other side of the hedgerow. Another APC and a Sheridan had taken RPG hits but were driven out. While the gunships were making firing runs, there were two loud explosions on the other side of the hedgerow.

When the dust off was safely away, Colonel McGowan's LOH landed behind us long enough for him to get off. Colonel McGowan walked to

7—Long Trench

Jackson's side of Six Track, spoke to him for a little while then walked off toward Third Platoon. Colonel McGowan wore a steel pot, but no flak jacket. Nelson had been one of McGowan's students at West Point. I didn't see it, but as soon as the last helicopter gunship run was done, Colonel McGowan went through the brush. I don't know if anyone went with him, but he came back with Nelson's body. Third Platoon had brought out their two other bodies. While this was going on there was an eerie silence. Enough of the hedgerow had been shot away that we could see the fresh dirt spoil of a trench that had been dug just behind the brush.

As soon as Colonel McGowan was back we got word that an air strike was standing by and we backed off to a hundred meters west of the trench. This time it was just napalm. The two jets made two passes each from south to north, dropping two tanks of napalm each pass, I don't think any of the napalm went directly on the trench. During the air strikes, Colonel McGowan's LOH came in low from the west, landed and took him away.

After the air strike, Jackson ordered the Sheridans to fire explosive rounds at the trench. Usually the Sheridans only fired flechette rounds, but they also carried a few explosive rounds. They were shape charges designed as anti-tank rounds. We could now see the trench clearly. The troops watched the Sheridans firing at the trench and cheered for hits. During the firing, I noticed that Jackson's left arm was bandaged and that there were fresh blood stains on his sleeve. I don't know when he was wounded or how. He called in another dust off for four or five lightly wounded men. Once the dust off was away, Colonel McGowan's LOH landed for Jackson.

Lieutenant Carlson moved over to Six Track as acting CO. Both platoons were being run by sergeants. Neither was the regular Platoon Sergeant, just the senior E6 left in the platoon. Third Platoon was severely depleted. After Carlson took over, we sat and waited for a while. There were lots of helicopters overhead in the area and Carlson's radio conversations appeared to be mostly about where other people thought the gooks were or were headed to.

At 1815 a single enemy soldier climbed out of the trench, put up his hands and started walking toward us. I didn't see him until he had walked several meters toward us. The whole Troop watched in silence. He walked very slowly. After he had walked fifty meters his arms slid down, as if he couldn't hold them up anymore. He was carrying no weapon or gear. As soon as he got close enough to see his face, you could see he was exhausted. When he was a few meters from a track, two troopers with M16s walked out and stopped and searched him then gave him some water. He was so completely alone, defeated and helpless that they didn't tie his hands. His two guards brought him behind the line of tracks, seated him, gave him a cigarette and Nam talked to him. After a few minutes, Nam reported to Carlson that the prisoner said that when the fight started there had been eight men in the trench, but the prisoner didn't think anybody else was left.

Carlson passed on the prisoner's information and conferred with whoever was overhead. An LOH swooped in, picked up the prisoner and disappeared. About 1830 we started rolling forward without firing. We stopped right up against the trench and dismounts went down into it and found an RPG launcher. They kept poking around, but didn't find anything more. If there had been seven more men there, dead or alive, they were gone.

At 1900 a few rounds of rifle fire came in from our right flank. I think someone at Squadron decided it was too late for us to be chasing snipers, We loaded our dismounts and moved west across the open area back toward Ap Suoi Cao. We came up on Charlie Troop a klick and a half to the west sitting in a circle. They had been covering our rear and waiting to come in if needed. They waved as we passed then followed us west. We continued on to Highway 19 and on toward Go Dau Ha. We hit the edge of Go Dau Ha about 2030 and were in Hampton a few minutes later. Our ride in the sun was over.

March 3

There wasn't any stand to. The troops had to pull watches through the night like every other night, but they got to sleep pretty much as late as they wanted otherwise. The Troop spent most of the day in Hampton doing maintenance and reloading the vehicles with ammunition. I think a few replacements showed up, but we were way under strength and the troops were tired.

During the day Carlson called the acting platoon leaders and me together and told us that we were going to be pulling road duty for a while. Usually that was a safer job than crashing about in the brush. However, he also shared an intelligence report that Division expected the convoy to be ambushed soon and we might have to fight a well entrenched ambush force.

We left Hampton at 1540 and crossed to Ap Suoi Cao. We went south from Checkpoint 18 and the Second and Third Platoons with Six Track, the Medic Track and the cook's truck pulled into a field on the west side of Highway 19 two klicks south of the village. First Platoon continued on south to spend the night guarding the culvert at Checkpoint B.

March 4

The Troop cleared and outposted Highway 19 between Trang Bang and Xom Bao Dom. Six Track and the Medic Track joined one of the outposts near Trang Bang. We stayed next to the road until the convoy passed going back to Cu Chi then the Troop laagered on the east side of Highway 19 a klick south of Ap Suoi Cao.

After the troops had finished digging their bunkers, Carlson asked me to join him in inspecting the laager. He walked up to the front of the nearest track and checked the RPG screen, concertina and claymores. Then he got into the bunker the crew had dug next to the vehicle. It was far too shallow. He reminded the crew why the bunker had to be deep enough for a man to stand up in and shoot. He told them to deepen it to the proper depth, then he went on to the next track. I just followed him, stood nearby and listened while he talked to the crew. By the time he had done that three times, the next crew he came to was still digging their hole, a hole that looked suspiciously like overhead cover had been recently removed. When as it looked like the whole Troop was busy digging bunkers of the correct depth, Carlson stopped his inspection. I'm not sure why he had me come with him. I think it was to increase the weight of his inspection. I was the only other officer left with the Troop.

Our trains came in with a track coming back from repair. The evening hash and trash helicopter flight brought new Signal Operating Instructions to go into effect at midnight. My Artillery call sign was changed to "Crusher." I became Crusher 45 and the FDC Crusher 36.

March 5

The day's task was the same again, clear the road between Trang Bang and Xom Bao Don and outpost the road until the convoy had passed both ways. When the convoy was done for the day, we went back to Hampton. First Platoon was detailed to outpost Go Dau Ha bridge after dinner. When I heard that First Platoon was going there for the night, I suggested to Carlson that I go with them. The rest of the Troop at Hampton was in very little danger of being attacked and had Captain Thomas to call in artillery if needed, not to mention the officers of the battery at Hampton. The platoon at the bridge would be under-strength, without an officer and alone. Carlson agreed.

I rode to the bridge with the acting Platoon Leader, Sergeant Peterson. He was the senior E6 left in the platoon. He wasn't much older than most of his troops. He probably only had three years' service. We crossed the bridge, then pulled off the road to the right side and into a small flat area next to the bridge. There were some rooms built into the bridge's brick work. We had been told that there was a unit of U.S. Seabees at the bridge. When we arrived, one of them came out and talked with Sergeant Peterson for a while. He must have known that the Army didn't allow troops in the field to drink beer, because he didn't offer to share his Bud.

The platoon set up in a semicircle with our back to the brick wall on the side of the bridge approach. As soon as the tracks were in place, Sergeant Peterson called all the Track Commanders over. The platoon was short two tracks and a Sheridan and only about four people for each of the remaining seven vehicles.

When the Track Commanders came over, there was one other staff sergeant, now acting platoon sergeant, two buck sergeants and three Spec4s. I stood close enough to listen, but didn't take part in the meeting. Peterson explained how he wanted their defense setup. The Track Commanders listened quietly until he was done. There was no question that they would do what he said, but they were more his friends than his command. When he got through, they started talking about the pounding the Troop had taken and how under-strength the platoon was and how First Platoon always seemed to get the worst duty. They didn't complain about any specific event or officer, but they appeared to be convinced that something wasn't going the way it should. Peterson didn't say much, but a couple of times agreed that the Troop had gotten hammered over the past few days. The discussion didn't last long.

When the last Track Commander moved off I approached Peterson, "Sergeant, do you have a minute?" "Yes sir."

"You need to be careful about letting your briefing become a bitch session. I don't think you should punish a man just for complaining, but you can't agree with them. If there are problems, you can't fix them tonight and listening to each other complain may make them feel worse than they did to start with. If they think you agree, then it's almost officially OK." He stared at me for a while then said, "I hadn't thought of that. I guess you're right." Somebody else might have been sarcastic; he meant it. The night passed without event.

March 6

First Platoon got to Hampton in time for the tail end of breakfast. The other two platoons cleared the road between Trang Bang and the Little Rubber. When they were back, we all left Hampton for Ap Suoi Cao.

7—Long Trench

Carlson said we were going back to where Thomson was killed. We followed the same route getting there as before.

The site of our battle was marked by the burned out hulks of the two APCs we left behind. Most of the vegetation in the vicinity of the trench had been stripped away. We crossed the trench on line and stopped on the east side. A watch was left on each vehicle, but the rest of the troops got down and walked through the area, almost like tourists. The people on watch ate while they waited their turn to look around.

Almost all of the top of Lieutenant Thomson's track was gone along with most of the front and rear of the vehicle. The left side of the vehicle was standing essentially intact over the left tread. The right side of the vehicle was still in one piece, but looked like it had fallen off the treads somehow. The vehicle's floor was covered with debris and cooled puddles of melted aluminum. Lieutenant Thomson's track was only five meters from the trench. The other track was ten meters further away from the trench, on line with Thomson's track and in about the same condition.

Colonel McGowan came in by helicopter and joined the troops. He greeted many of them by name. In a few minutes he left. We began moving again after 1500 and swept with no particular rush to the east. We had dismounts down and moved at a slow walking pace and stopped often. The platoons were so under strength that they only had about one dismount per vehicle. Most of them just walked along beside their track. We swept east to cross Road 6A and turned south in the light brush on the other side of the road.

The 6A lived up to its reputation when the track closest to the road hit a mine. The driver injured his head and a dismount was wounded by the explosion. They were dusted off promptly and we left west toward Ap Suoi Cao as soon as they were gone. We laagered at 1830 just south of the village and about a klick from Highway 19. A headquarters track, a repaired track and two tracked cargo carriers with fuel, dinner and sundries arrived almost as soon as we did.

After dinner I radioed in to ask about my team's pay. Half an hour later a message came back that we should come in and collect pay in Cu Chi at battalion headquarters. That seemed like nonsense to me, but Charlie and Johnson were entitled to their pay. I told Charlie he was going in tomorrow morning.

Carlson was called to his radio at 2130. Charlie Troop was reporting on the Squadron net that one of their platoons spending the night next to the culvert at Checkpoint B was taking fire. They were about three klicks to our south. We hadn't heard the firing at them, but when Charlie Troop's platoon opened up in return, we heard that and saw the parachute flares they popped. Initial reports were only of incoming small arms fire, but within fifteen minutes they were reporting steady RPG fire. By then a helicopter gun team was over them and we could see the tracers and rockets going down in the dark sky to our south.

Once Squadron confirmed that Bravo was monitoring, they said no more to us. The acting Platoon Leaders had drifted over to Six Track when the first report of the contact was passed to them. As soon as it was clear that the attack was serious, they went back to their tracks to ready their troops. Our wire, Claymore mines and RPG screens were left in place because we had no orders to move and we could be next. Charlie Troop reported a Sheridan hit and burning at 2200. Most of the radio traffic on the Squadron net was coordinating gunships and a flare ship that was overhead by then. The Artillery net was silent. There was no FO with the platoon. Reports of additional RPG hits increased our concern for our comrades and our own anxiety that we would be called to their aid in the dark. They were still taking scattered fire when the first dust off went in at 2230 to take out three seriously wounded and one killed. Landing a chopper at night in the middle of a platoon sized circle must have been tight.

As midnight approached the gunships stopped, the flares stopped and the sound of firing trickled off. We heard their report on the radio; one killed, twelve wounded and six vehicles hit. The Sheridan was a total loss, two APCs were towable and the other three were still operational. They had taken automatic weapons fire, rifle grenades and fifteen to twenty RPGs. If the platoon had been at full strength, thirteen casualties was a quarter of the men. If they had all ten vehicles, only four vehicles were not hit. I was relieved we hadn't been called in. Going in at night way under strength without experienced Platoon Leaders would have been horrible.

March 7

Jackson came back on the morning chopper. He had a dressing on his left forearm, but apparently was none the worse for it. Carlson returned to First Platoon. The chopper had stopped at the Charlie Troop platoon first and Jackson said it was not a pretty sight. Charlie went in for his pay with the trains. We just stayed where we were. I didn't hear any orders, but I suspect we were being kept close just in case the gooks had a daytime surprise for Charlie Troop's platoon and the teams sent to recover the damaged and destroyed vehicles.

We finally moved out of laager at 1000 and spent the day sweeping open areas south of the Woods. The area we swept probably had been selected for us to find nothing. At 1630 we a laagered a couple of klicks behind Ap Suoi Cao. Charlie came back with the cooks and supplies.

When my evening work was done, I wandered around inside the laager and paused at a little distance to watch a sergeant passing out some supplies to a group of troops sent to pick up their platoon's share. As he was dividing the supplies he was talking, "I love the Army, everybody's equal, kikes, beaners, wops, niggers, pollacks, everybody gets treated the same." His audience was mixed. I thought to myself, "shit, what do I do now." Then I noticed that all of the troops were nodding their heads in agreement. I doubt they all loved the Army, but apparently they agreed about equal treatment.

For our nighttime enjoyment, Squadron passed on a Division intelligence report that a reliable civilian had reported seeing 1000 to 1500 NVA regulars moving north into the Boi Loi Woods during the night of March 5. They were carrying thirty wounded with them. Division thought they were from the 88th NVA Regiment.

March 8

Morning came without a visit from the 88th. We left our laager toward Highway 19 at 0710. First Platoon went south toward Trang Bang. Six Track went north with Second and Third Platoons. Johnson stayed with the trains at Checkpoint 18 to go in for his pay. We cleared the road from Ap Suoi Cao to Xom Bao Don traveling at fairly high speed. At Xom Bao Don we turned left on Highway 26. At the far edge of the village, Second Platoon put down two men with mine detectors and followed them at walking speed. Third Platoon pulled off the road to leapfrog ahead before they put down mine sweepers on the road. Thirty minutes or so later First Platoon came up behind us and leapfrogged Third Platoon to finish our sweep to Checkpoint 36.

We were done an hour before the convoy was scheduled to arrive. Each of the platoons was given a stretch of the road between Trang Bang and Checkpoint 36 to outpost. Six Track and the Medic track joined a Third Platoon outpost just south of Ap Suoi Cao. Nothing happened all day. The lead of the convoy headed north passed about half an hour after we arrived. It passed going back about 1500.

When the tail of the returning convoy passed, Jackson called the platoons north of Ap Suoi Cao down to join us. When they arrived they kept moving and we joined the end of the column. We went south to Checkpoint B and pulled off the Highway to an open area just across the highway from where the Charlie Troop platoon had been attacked two nights before. Part of Third Platoon had arrived first and started the laager. First and Second Platoons and the rest of Third Platoon completed the circle.

As usual, Six Track and the Medic Track parked near the center of the circle. A headquarters track with cooks, a cargo carrier and a repaired APC arrived to join us almost as soon as we had completed the circle. Johnson was not with them.

March 9

Johnson arrived on the morning chopper. I saw him getting off and met him a little away from Six Track. "Why are you late?" "There wasn't room for me on the night chopper run last night. I spent the night in the Cav rear area."

"I told you to come back on the supply tracks." "Yessir." "Mount up, we're about to leave." As soon as the chopper left, our morning drill was the same as the day before. Our day changed after the morning convoy passed.

Jackson got a call that Alpha Troop was taking scattered small arms fire near the Country Store and we were going in to back them up. All the outposts assembled at the turn off Highway 19 south of Ap Suoi Cao. From there it was a standard trip east. I got a general idea of where Alpha was by watching the helicopters in the sky south of the Woods. Occasionally one would swoop down toward the Country Store. As we passed south of the southern end of the Country Store, we could hear scattered machine gun fire. They were not engaging anyone with full firepower. We moved a little closer and set up a circular perimeter, ready to move and covering their rear.

While we were sitting there waiting, a volley of artillery rounds came in noticeably close and there was a little "plop" in the dust outside our perimeter. One of the platoon leaders radioed to the CO that they had gotten some fragments in his platoon area. Then another volley of rounds landed and "plop, plop," two fragments. Another volley of rounds came in a little bit closer and about seven fragments landed well inside our perimeter. I got on the radio to Captain Thomas to tell him that we were getting peppered. He acknowledged my message about the same time the next volley landed and "ZING!" and a very live shard went past, arriving almost as fast as the sound of the shells exploding. When I reported the last one he agreed to move the rounds away from us a bit.

We sat there without incident for another hour and the sounds of fighting slowly petered out. Jackson ordered a delayed lunch with instructions for the troops to stay on their vehicles and ready to move if called. The call never came. About 1400 we were released and moved to laager south of Ap Suoi Cao, within a klick of Highway 19. The evening chopper brought mail and two new Platoon Leaders. Joe Nowak got Second Platoon. Paul Evans got Third Platoon.

March 10

Our mission was the same road clearing and outposting as the last two days. As soon as the lead First Platoon track moved onto Highway 26 after a leapfrog, it hit a mine. When Jackson heard on the radio, Six Track and the Medic Track pulled off the road and headed toward First Platoon. When we got to the damaged track, there was another APC with it, but the rest of the platoon was already over a hundred meters further down the road following their mine sweepers.

The driver of the damaged track hit his head when the mine went off and was dusted off. The mine crater under the left tread was over four feet in diameter and almost three feet deep. The damaged APC was towed off the road and Jackson reported in that the undamaged part of the road was wide enough to allow the convoy to pass.

Close behind the end of the morning convoy were a Cav mechanic's track and an M88. The mechanics decided not to repair the vehicle there. The M88 pulled the track back on the road and easily towed it away. Six Track and the Medic Track followed them back toward Checkpoint 18. We stopped with a Second Platoon outpost near there while the recovery team and damaged track continued on to Hampton. When the returning convoy passed in the afternoon, Jackson called in the outposts and we set up our laager near last night's.

March 11

I was summoned to Six Track about 0100. Jackson and Carlson were listening to the Squadron radio net on a speaker. "Alpha's under attack next to Checkpoint 36. They seem to be doing OK, but we're on call if it gets bad."

Nowak and Evans arrived and we listened to the rest of the reports from Alpha on the Squadron net. Most of the radio traffic was about coordinating gunship runs. The most vivid transmission was a gunship pilot reporting that he had caught a group of NVA running down the road away from Alpha in his spotlight and was making a firing run on them. NVA running down a road in a group was an unusually attractive target and indicated a collapse of discipline. At 0240 Alpha reported they had received no incoming fire for some time and we were told we were not likely to be needed. I went back to bed.

I was up again at 0545 and we were beginning to clear the road by 0715. The road drill was the same as the last few days. First Platoon ended its sweep at Checkpoint 36, the far end of the final leapfrog, but moved away as soon as its objective was reached. Alpha was still near the crossroads at Checkpoint 36 collecting enemy bodies and gear from its fight.

Later, Colonel McGowan landed to visit the outpost Six Track was with and told us what happened to Alpha. Just after midnight one of Alpha's listening post down Road 239 had reported movement on the road. The LP was called in and the laager went on full alert. A Sheridan spotted a column of troops marching toward them down the road in close order with its infrared system. They saw the column stop and a small group step forward to confer. They either didn't know Alpha was there or didn't understand how well our night vision gear worked.

Alpha opened fire as soon as their CO decided that the group that had stepped forward was a command group. The first flechette round leveled the command group. All of the column that survived the first volley of Sheridan fire broke and ran. It may have been this group that the chopper had spotted in his search light running down the road. There was scattered fire at Alpha, even a few RPGs, but nothing serious.

In the morning Alpha found 38 bodies and took three prisoners. The dead included a battalion commander and a company commander. One of the prisoners was the XO of 5th Company, 2nd Battalion, 10th Regiment, 1st NVA Division. Alpha had no casualties and recovered a 57mm recoilless rifle, three light machine guns, two RPG launchers, a rifle, a radio, piles of ammunition and gear and one cross cut saw. They also found several copies of a pamphlet in Vietnamese that was an evaluation of our Sheridans. Apparently the pamphlet had not adequately described the capacity of the Sheridan's infrared gear or the impact of its flechette rounds.

We did nothing that day but sit by the road and wait. After the convoy passed, returning in the afternoon we laagered south of Ap Suoi Cao in the same area as the nights before. At evening briefing Jackson announced we were going into Cu Chi for a three day stand down tomorrow afternoon with the return convoy.

March 12

Road clearing and outposting were the same as they had been for several days and completed without incident. When the convoy passed

7—Long Trench

headed south, the Troop rolled up behind it. Once we passed Trang Bang, I was calling in checkpoints I hadn't mentioned since we came out in January.

In the town of Cu Chi, we turned left toward the Cu Chi base camp main gate. Jackson radioed the Platoon Leaders to order all weapons cleared and report back. Once he got all the reports back he ordered it done again. We passed through the gate about 1750. The last thing Jackson did on the radio was to announce a memorial service at the Squadron chapel tomorrow at 1000, attendance voluntary.

That night Bear was behind the bar at the Officers' Club. He was about to go back to the U.S. for his commissioning and Officers' Basic Course, in the Infantry. He'd asked for Armor, but apparently the Infantry was killing off its lieutenants faster. I could imagine his training class, a crowd of Second Lieutenants fresh out of college and Bear with an MBA, a Distinguished Service Cross, two Silver Stars and a few Bronze Stars.

March 13

Carlson was leaving when I arrived for breakfast. "Foxy, you'll be getting an award at the ceremony tomorrow. Be sure to wear a clean uniform."

The 3/4 Cav chapel was little different than the office buildings and living hooches in the area. About fifty men and all of the officers showed up for the memorial service. We gathered near the chapel. When it was time, Jackson organized a two line formation facing the building.

"At ease. We don't talk much about the friends we have lost. The nine fallen brothers we remember today died doing their duty, serving our country and meeting our obligations to each other. They were men of honor and we must never forget that." He paused briefly. "First rank follow me, second rank, follow the first rank. Hats off at the door." He had spoken loudly enough to be heard, but it wasn't his "command voice." As we filed silently into the chapel, we passed nine empty pairs of polished jungle boots facing out from the end of the chapel. The Squadron Chaplain was standing by the side of the door away from the boots and quietly greeted the men as they filed in.

The chapel door was in the center of the end of the building. Inside there were backless benches on both sides of a narrow center aisle. In the center at the far end of the room was a small lectern with a simple cross on a draped cloth. The troops followed the Army's standard seating drill, the first person in goes to the seat furthest from the entrance and everyone following fills in immediately behind him in the order they come in. When all the seats were full, the rest stood behind the last benches. When the last man was in, the Chaplain came in and walked to his pulpit. His service was only a little longer than the CO's speech. He praised their bravery and sacrifice and added God's recognition. He ended by having us recite the Lord's Prayer then blessed the assembly and walked down the aisle and out the door. He waited outside the door and shook each man's hand as we walked out. Once out the door the troops walked quietly off alone or in twos and threes.

Stand down involved work for the Troop, but for me, almost nothing. They did vehicle maintenance and repair. I only had a radio and it was working fine. Gossip and bar chatter was that Bravo had been inflicting more casualties than any other unit our size in the Division. Word was the Commanding General thought the 3/4 Cavalry was the best fighting unit in the Division and that Colonel McGowan said Bravo was his best Troop. I don't know if either of them actually thought or said that, but it seemed right to me.

We were supposed to have about fifty men for each platoon in the field. We got some reinforcements just before we came in, but for a couple of days running just before the reinforcements arrived, we had less than thirty men per platoon. We'd lost a large number of troops to light wounds who weren't replaced, just kept in the rear until healed. We had a formation before dinner including all the people who still had a few days of convalescence left, and it looked almost like a full formation.

When I joined Six Track there were five other people on it. Now, a month and a half later, only Chico and Charlie remained from that original five.

March 14

The award ceremony was just before supper. The first awards were a Distinguished Service Cross and three Silver Stars. Carlson was the first in the Bronze Star group and I was next after him, standing to his left. The awards were given out by Colonel McGowan. He moved through the formation efficiently, but had something personal to say with each award.

I got two Bronze Stars for our actions on January 26 and February 2. The first citation said that on the 26th I sat on top of the APC for three hours under continuous fire assisting the aerial observers. On the 2nd it was for taking over "an exposed position" to engage the enemy. I think that was firing Six Track's .50 caliber until Headley yelled at me to stop. The citations told more colorful stories than I remembered, but I was still proud to be recognized. Charlie got a Bronze Star for recovering casualties under fire on February 2.

LTC McGowan congratulating the author at the Bravo Troop award ceremony on March 14. 1LT Carlson is to the author's right (author's collection).

March 15

After dinner the Officers' Club was a bit more subdued than the nights before. Fewer beers and quieter talk. When all of the Troop's officers had come in and were standing together at the bar, Carlson handed me a small package. "From all of us, Foxy." It was one of the crossed sabers brass collar insignia they all wore. Where the sabers crossed there was a small 4 on top, for 4th Regiment, and 3 below, for 3rd Squadron. I put them on my collar over the black embroidered crossed cannons.

8

Cau Khoi Rubber

March 16

Six Track was next to the Troop office, just like last time. We were out the Cu Chi main gate at exactly 0736. One of the MPs processing the long line of Vietnamese workers saluted as we passed. We stopped in Trang Bang at 0830. One platoon swept Highway 19 north from Trang Bang to Checkpoint 18 then came back. We were ordered to wait until the convoy had passed.

The head of the convoy went past on Highway 19 about half an hour later and we followed the convoy. At Xom Bao Don we took Highway 26 to Checkpoint 36. We got there at 1130 and pulled off the road to the south. We moved a klick or so away from the road, changed to a line formation and swept cross country southeast parallel to the highway. We moved slowly, stopping to check brush or a hole or a hedgerow as they came, but had no apparent objective. We stopped for lunch at noon then continued on as before.

Within an hour, we could see the returning convoy passing on the highway. Once it was all passed, we moved back to the highway and followed it back to Xom Bao Don. This time we turned northeast on Highway 19. "We're going to spend the night at Fire Support Base Wood Foxy."

Wood was on the north side of Highway 19 about five klicks northeast of Checkpoint 25. It was almost a copy of Hampton. The Artillery Battery usually at Hampton was inside on the east side and what had been a battalion headquarters complex on the other side. I think there had been a mechanized infantry battalion headquarters in Wood before we came. Our cooks were there when we arrived. There was a sit down outhouse and water in a shower.

March 17

Jackson called the Platoon Leaders over at 0545. Second Platoon was to open Highway 19 north to Checkpoint K at the west end of the bridge over the Saigon River into Dau Tieng. After clearing to Checkpoint K, Second Platoon would outpost the eastern edge of the Ben Cui Rubber. First Platoon was to sweep back to Checkpoint 25 then outpost the highway from there to four klicks north of Wood. Third Platoon was to follow First Platoon down to Checkpoint 25 then continue on, clearing Highway 19 through Ap Suoi Cao down to Checkpoint B. Third Platoon would wait for the convoy there and lead the Dau Tieng serials to Checkpoint K. The platoons left at 0650. Six Track and the Medic Track waited in Wood. Jackson worked his radio keeping track of the platoons. After giving my FDC a radio report on our platoons' routes, I read and waited.

At 0835 a radio report came in that a Second Platoon track had hit a mine in the road at the southern edge of the Ben Cui Rubber. There weren't any casualties. They just pulled the track off the road, left another track with it and made it their first outpost.

Fifteen minutes later, the radio report was that a Second Platoon Sheridan had hit a mine in the road two hundred meters short of Checkpoint K. No casualties, but a busted track and a road wheel blown off. Again, the damaged vehicle was pulled off the road as part of an outpost. When the report of the damaged Sheridan came, Jackson decided to go look at it. Six Track and the Medic Track headed north up Highway 19 toward the Ben Cui Rubber. When we got to the rubber, we passed three two-vehicle Second Platoon outposts. The fourth outpost, near Checkpoint K, consisted of the damaged Sheridan, a line track and the platoon leader's track. Jackson inspected the damage and called for headquarters mechanics to be sent following the convoy.

Third Platoon passed us and pulled off the road right next to Checkpoint K about 1120. A stream of trucks was right behind them. After the convoy passed it wasn't too long until an M88 arrived. It pulled the Sheridan back up on the road and towed it off to the south. Jackson got a warning when the convoy was about to leave Dau Tieng and alerted Third Platoon. At 1330 he told them to move out and they headed back the way they had come. There were only a few minutes between their departure and the arrival of the Commando armored car leading the first serial of trucks.

When the tail of the convoy passed, the outpost we were with followed and Six Track and the Medic Track followed them. The rest of Second Platoon fell in behind as we passed. We got to FSB Wood at 1430 and pulled in. The First Platoon outposts headed back to Wood as the convoy's tail passed them. Third Platoon led the convoy all the way to Checkpoint B, then pulled off the road to wait for the convoy to pass. Once the convoy cleared Checkpoint B, they headed back to Wood, arriving at 1620.

March 18

Today, like the next few days, the platoons cleared the road triangle of Highway 26, Road 239 and Highway 19, connecting Checkpoints 25, 36 and K. The rest of the day was quiet. At the end of the day Second Platoon went to Wood. The rest of the Troop went to a hard site near the center of the Ben Cui Rubber in a large open field on the west side of Road 239. The hard site was a circular dirt berm, a lot smaller than an FSB, with two entrance gaps. There were no bunkers or barbed wire, but it was a better fortification that a temporary laager.

When we pulled in, I asked Jackson to have Six Track parked pointed north. He did, but asked me why after we stopped. "I want to use the track to identify my defensive targets. I'm going to put my target number one, one klick in front, target number two one klick right, target number three one klick behind and target number four one klick left. I've been putting the targets out north, east, south and west most nights already. If Six Track is always parked pointed north, I'll know my targets from the vehicle." Jackson nodded, "Makes sense."

When we set up for the night, the platoon leader's tracks were up against the berm with the line tracks. Six Track was near the center, pointed north. The Medic Track and the trains were parked behind the line vehicles.

March 19

Wake up was at 0545. The road sweeps were about the same as yesterday. At 0710 First Platoon's lead track hit a mine in Road 239 about a klick short of Checkpoint 36. Three of crew were injured, two needed urgent dust off. Just after their dust off, they found another mine in the road, this one two hundred meters from the intersection with Highway 26.

By 0930 all the road sweeps were done. First Platoon waited at Checkpoint 36 to lead the Dau Tieng serial up Road 239 to Checkpoint K. Third Platoon outposted a two klick stretch of Road 239 inside the Ben Cui Rubber. Second Platoon outposted the stretch of Highway 19 along the eastern edge of the rubber. Six Track and the Medic Track joined a Third Platoon outpost on Road 239. The rubber trees next to Road 239 had been cut down at least twenty meters on each side of the road. There were stumps, but most of the trunks were gone.

After we were settled, Jackson put his radios on speakers, got a reclining lawn chair out of Six Track, took off his fatigue blouse and reclined for a sun bathing snooze. There was a second chair that the rest of the crew rotated through. I sat on top to read and dismounted to stretch my legs occasionally. We were warned by radio at 1100 that the convoy was approaching. Fifteen minutes later First Platoon passed our outpost at road speed, followed shortly by the convoy. As he passed, Carlson radioed a comment about our tough duty in lawn chairs.

The Dau Tieng serials returned at 1330. First Platoon led them down Highway 19, past Second Platoon's outposts and FSB Wood then pulled off the road near Xom Bao Don to wait for them to pass. When all of the convoy had passed the Second Platoon outposts, Jackson called Second Platoon to join us. With Second and Third Platoons we swept the rubber back to the hard site in a little over an hour. Six Track was parked pointing north the same place as last night. Our trains had already been started toward us and arrived from Checkpoint 36 half an hour after we pulled in. First Platoon checked into FSB Wood at 1440.

March 20

Road clearing and outposting was the same as yesterday with the jobs rotated. Six Track and the Medic Track joined a Second Platoon outpost in the Rubber. At lunchtime Chico produced a cast iron frying pan and a small portable stove. Charlie helped him pour four cans of PX Mexican food into the skillet. Chico liberally doused the contents with Tabasco sauce. "I'm making a special Mexican lunch. You want some sir?" "Thanks, no." I hadn't gotten any of the food and didn't feel right taking any. "I'd like some of the sauce for the C-rats though."

After a while Chico, Jackson, Charlie, Baker and Johnson were eating the hot meal with relish and considerable commentary. My C-rations were a bit more exciting with the Tabasco sauce added. The rest of the day's program was the same pattern as yesterday.

March 21

Another rotate and repeat day. At 0940 the trains took off and we joined First Platoon outposting Road 239 in the rubber. As soon as we stopped, Jackson got out his lawn chair.

Just after Chico started cooking a repeat lunch, Colonel McGowan's LOH landed long enough for him to get off. Colonel McGowan walked straight to Chico. "Son, I hear you're serving the best lunch in the Division." Chico beamed, "Yes sir! Would you like some?"

While Colonel McGowan went to talk to the next track over, Chico augmented the mixture with a can of C-ration beans and weenies plus a liberal additional sprinkling of Tabasco. When Chico declared the mixture ready, Colonel McGowan saw paper plates being passed out and returned. The Colonel ate with appropriate gusto, complimented the chef, called for his chopper and left.

After the convoy was gone on its way back, we began a sweep with First and Third Platoons. This time we went out of the rubber and swept a brushy area north of Road 239 and a little west of the rubber. We pulled into the hard site at 1620. Second Platoon had checked into Wood two hours before.

March 22

Another repeat day. The convoy came and went. At 1345 we started sweeping a part of the rubber south of the hard site with Second and Third Platoons. First Platoon reported that it was back inside Wood at 1510. We were back inside the hard site by 1600.

March 23

Wake up was at 0600 and the rotated road sweeps began at 0645. Today the convoy went up Highway 19 on the way in and came down Road 239 on the way back. The convoy passed the Second Platoon outposts we were with in the middle of the rubber at 1440 and Jackson called First Platoon to join us. We swept east through the rubber plantation toward Highway 19, got near it, pivoted the line and headed back to the hard site through the rubber trees.

I had just stretched out on my cot to sleep when there was single loud explosion somewhere to our southwest. Jackson was inside Six Track when I arrived. "The line tracks say it sounded like a big artillery round on the road toward Checkpoint 36. Find out if they are firing anything."

I climbed up through the cargo hatch and turned on my radio. "Crusher Three Six this is Crusher Four Five, over." "Crusher Four Five this is Crusher Three Six out."

"Three Six this is Four Five. We have possible artillery fire impacting at four six hundred mils from my position. Is anyone firing in our area? Over." "Four Five this is Three Six. Wait one." A minute or two passed.

"Crusher Four Five this is Crusher Three Six. No friendly fire in your vicinity. Over." "Three Six this is Four Five. Roger. No friendly fire in our vicinity. Out." I reported no artillery fire to Jackson. We heard nothing further and our troops picked up nothing in their night vision gear. After twenty minutes without developments, I went back to my cot.

March 24

Someone shook me and pointed to Six Track just after midnight. First Platoon thought they had spotted people moving about 400 meters southeast. Jackson was about to order firing at them and wanted me to get illumination. I radioed in a fire mission for illumination rounds immediately and Jackson radioed Carlson to fire at the movement with four M60s and M79s as soon as Carlson could get it coordinated. There was a short delay then they opened up for less than thirty seconds and stopped. After a thirty second wait they repeated the firing burst again. The first artillery illumination round didn't arrive until two or three minutes after they fired for the last time. The parachute flare popped high overhead and behind the reported movement, I called in a minor adjustment and asked for another. The second popped before the first burned out and for a time there was a very bright, metallic light. There was no sign of any enemy in the stark shadows and I didn't call for a third round. Jackson confirmed that he didn't want any more and I canceled the mission and went to bed again.

During the morning road sweeps Second Platoon reported that a culvert at Checkpoint 26, had been blown. The result was a ten foot crater in the road six feet deep. As soon as that report was in, Third Platoon reported a similar culvert demolition at Checkpoint X on Highway 19. Their hole was about the same size. The two blown culverts were eight klicks apart, but both were for the same tiny stream. Fording the stream at both places was no problem for us, but was not an option for the convoy. An engineer team with a replacement culvert and a couple of dump trucks of gravel was scheduled for each location.

By 0900 the road sweeps were done, our trains headed out to Checkpoint 36 and we moved to join First Platoon outposting Road 239 through the middle of the rubber. Second Platoon began leading the convoy at Checkpoint 12 just before 1000. We never got any report about how or when the engineers arrived, but the Dau Tieng part of the convoy passed over the damage without reported difficulty, so it must have been fixed before they got there. Second Platoon picked up the returning convoy at 1320. After the convoy cleared, the rest of the Troop swept part of the rubber without incident. Second Platoon checked into FSB Wood at 1450. Ten minutes later the rest of the Troop was back in the hard site.

March 25

Morning sweeps were routine except First Platoon discovered a mine within a hundred meters of Checkpoint 36. Six Track and the Medic Track joined Third Platoon in the middle of the rubber.

First Platoon brought the Dau Tieng portion of the convoy to Checkpoint K without incident and, after the convoy returned, escorted it to Checkpoint 12. Shortly after First Platoon dropped off leading the convoy, the convoy took some fire near Checkpoint B. The serial fired at didn't halt, but the following serials stopped before getting to where the shooting had occurred. Alpha Troop was somewhere close and was ordered to screen the convoy and engage the enemy troops. Our laager with Second and Third Platoons that night was moved to a field next to Checkpoint 36. We were there by 1610. First Platoon was at FSB Wood at 1620.

March 26

At 0730 we left our trains at the laager and began a sweep of Road 239 back to the repaired culvert at Checkpoint 26. First Platoon was responsible for clearing the road from FSB Wood to Xom Bao Don then up Highway 26 to Checkpoint 36 where we had spent the night. I think Charlie Troop was responsible for sweeping the rest of the roads into Dau Tieng that we had been clearing for several days.

We got to Checkpoint 26 at 0815 and began a two platoon cross country sweep generally to the southeast. We stopped for lunch about 1230. After lunch, we pivoted and moved deeper in the brush then swept back the way we'd come. We got to a fairly open field 300 meters southwest of the culvert at Checkpoint 26 at 1515 and started setting up our laager. As we pulled in, Jackson asked me if I wanted to park facing north. "Yes sir, every time unless there's a reason not to."

First Platoon was called in off the road and joined us, bringing in our trains, at 1545. It was the first time all three platoons had been together for eight nights.

March 27

At 0645 First Platoon drove to Road 239 and started to Checkpoint K. Second Platoon headed to Checkpoint 36. We stayed with Third Platoon in the laager. When Second Platoon reported that the road was clear to Checkpoint 36, Jackson called them back and released the trains to go to Checkpoint 36 and wait for the road back to Hampton to be cleared. We moved with Third Platoon to a spot on Road 239 at the west edge of the rubber. First and Second Platoons joined us there.

It was past 0845 when we began our sweep by forming on line on the road then moving slowly north. At noon Jackson had a series of messages from Squadron and turned us back toward the road. "Something is happening with the convoy. We're being called back to Hampton."

We traveled back through the area we had just checked at much higher speed. We went back to the road and on to Checkpoint 18. When we got there Jackson said there was a change of plan. "Foxy, First Platoon's going down to Checkpoint 12, the rest of us are going to Hampton." I radioed in First Platoon's route as well as our current location.

We pulled into Hampton at 1400. We sat there doing nothing. Whatever had brought us in changed or got finished, because after 45 minutes we were sent back to spend the night in the hard site again. First Platoon left Checkpoint 12 for FSB Wood about the same time we left Hampton. From Hampton to the hard site was over thirty klicks. With civilian traffic on the roads and in the villages, it took us over an hour to get there.

March 28

Jackson had already briefed the Platoon Leaders on a conventional road clearing drill when he got new instructions at 0645. Division had intelligence that the convoy was going to be ambushed in the Cau Khoi or Ben Cui Rubber. We were instructed to clear Road 239 to Checkpoint 36 then Highways 26 and 19 all the way south to Trang Bang. An hour later we were approaching Ap Suoi Cao when Squadron passed on a report that the road team clearing Route 22 north of Go Dau Ha had found a fifteen foot crater in the road six feet deep. The hole wasn't anywhere near the Cau Khoi Rubber or the Ben Cui Rubber, but if it wasn't filled in would force the Tay Ninh part of the convoy to go up Highways 19 and 26 past the Cau Khoi Rubber.

When we got to Checkpoint 18, Jackson sent First Platoon to clear the road to Go Dau Ha, then outpost the bridge. The rest of us continued on down Highway 19 to Trang Bang. Then we turned around and Second and Third Platoons outposted the road between Trang Bang and Ap Suoi Cao. "Foxy, Squadron says Division has ordered two Cobra teams to fly cover over the convoy from Checkpoint B all the way into Dau Tieng and Tay Ninh. Somebody's getting serious."

The platoons dropped off tracks in groups of two or three for outposts without anyone telling me where. Six Track and the Medic Track

8—Cau Khoi Rubber

joined the most northerly outpost. An hour after our outposts were set, the first serial of the convoy moved north past Six Track, led by a Commando armored car. Vehicles in the convoy were supposed to maintain a fixed interval between vehicles with a much greater distance between the serials of vehicles. Most of the vehicles were two and a half or five ton trucks, with jeeps and other specialized trucks mixed in. At least one Duster self-propelled antiaircraft gun went past. The gooks didn't have any aircraft, but the twin barreled 40mm antiaircraft gun mounted on a light tank chassis was capable of very effective direct fire. The rounds were more like big grenades than artillery rounds, but they could be fired accurately as far as you could see and the gun had been designed for rapid fire. If you could see where a group of people were shooting from, one Duster could make them stop.

After a few serials had passed, just after 1000, Jackson got very busy on his radios. It was quiet and I could hear what he said, so I had some idea of what was happening before he told me. "Foxy, Alpha's popped an ambush in the Cau Khoi Rubber and we're going to join them as soon as we're relieved by a company of the First of the Fifth." The 1st Battalion, 5th Infantry was a mechanized infantry battalion.

I nodded and checked to make sure that I had the right map ready. The Cau Khoi Rubber was on the northeast side of Highway 26 beginning a klick toward Tay Ninh from Checkpoint 36. It stretched along the side of the road for about five klicks and extended away from the road for two or three klicks.

Once Alpha Troop uncovered the enemy troops waiting to ambush the convoy, the convoy had stopped and no more trucks passed Six Track. We could see some trucks parked along the road in Ap Suoi Cao, but no trucks were in sight on the road toward Trang Bang. I assumed that the reason we were waiting to be replaced was that we were the protection for all of the convoy that was now stopped and exposed to attack along the road. There were RF and PF forces scattered in the villages along the road, but if the gooks had a complex plan, the ambush that Alpha Troop found could have been planned just to stop the convoy and draw in its escorts so that other units could attack unprotected trucks stopped along the road.

It was just before 1100 that our relieving unit radioed Jackson that they were about to move into our stretch of road. I never saw any of the mechanized infantry that replaced us. I could hear Jackson on the radio and he was pulling in our outposts just in front of where the replacement company reported its lead element was.

While all of this was going on, radio traffic on the Artillery net told me a little about what was going on. Alpha's forward observer reported where the unit was infrequently. They hadn't moved very far from the road. He hadn't reported any casualties, friendly or enemy, or called in any artillery fire. I had seen enough gunship teams headed in their general direction that it made sense that no artillery had been called.

Two of Third Platoon's APCs from the first relieved outpost went past us on the road toward the ambush without stopping, then two more APCs and a Sheridan. I got worried about keeping track of where they were. "Captain Jackson, where are they going? I need to call them in." "Don't worry. They're just going down the road to the head of the convoy. It's stopped near Xom Bao Don. We're assembling there. First Platoon's meeting us there as soon as they're relieved from the bridge. Alpha's reported three killed and eleven wounded. One air strike has gone in and there are two more waiting on station."

As we talked, another group of tracks, including the Third Platoon Leader's, went past. After brief delay came two groups of Second Platoon vehicles and finally Six Track, the Medic Track and the two Second Platoon APCs with us followed on. We were the furthest north and the last group to move north. As soon as we reached the edge of Ap Suoi Cao we started passing trucks parked on the right side of the road. They were parked bunched up between the two PF outposts on either end of the village. The drivers didn't seem too concerned. Some were sleeping in their cabs. A few were trying to talk to young women and others were just standing in small groups next to their trucks. Only one or two were carrying rifles.

As we headed north up Highway I listened to the Artillery radio net. The Alpha FO still wasn't calling in any fire and reported little. I was strangely exhilarated. We knew where the enemy was. We were going into a fight prepared, not ambushed in the brush. It was daylight and a rubber plantation didn't offer great cover to the enemy. We would be able to see on the ground. All the ambushes and fighting in dense brush would be made up for. We were going to get a clean shot at them in the daylight.

We found Third Platoon and the rest of Second Platoon stopped on Highway 26 just beyond the edge of Xom Bao Don. About the time we closed on the assembly point, Jackson got word that the Mech Infantry Platoon that was to relieve First Platoon had reached Checkpoint 18 and was headed toward Go Dau Ha. Jackson radioed Carlson to move out, stop and brief the Infantry Platoon Leader when he passed him on the road and get to us as fast as possible. We waited another fifteen minutes or so for First Platoon to get close and started up Highway 26.

It took us about fifteen minutes to cover the ten klicks to the intersection at Checkpoint 36. First Platoon was traveling flat out and caught up with us before we got to Checkpoint 36. I called in Checkpoint 36, as I had other checkpoints, as much to let the Alpha FO know where we were as anything else.

8—Cau Khoi Rubber

Checkpoint 36 was about three klicks from where I thought the fight was going on and, in addition to the unusual number of helicopters in the air over the road ahead of us there was also a wide column of dust and smoke rising as we approached. I released the magazine from my M16 and operated the bolt several times to make sure it was working smoothly. Chico had taken the belt of ammunition out of the .50 caliber and was similarly checking the machine gun's action. Charlie and Johnson checked their rifles. Between radio messages, Jackson checked his pistol, looked at me and smiled.

When we reached the rubber we stopped. The trees in the plantation had been cut down for fifty meters from the edge of the road, but the cut trunks of the trees had not been cleared away. Staring into the smoke and dust that obscured vision into the trees beyond the edge of the cut area, the joy of going into a battle that wasn't a surprise drained away. There was a Duster parked in an open area off the road on the other side, a bit further away from the fight than we had stopped. I could hear the sound of sporadic firing in the rubber trees, but couldn't tell exactly where or how far away. I noticed that the whole Troop was stopped nose to tail on the road. Maintaining a proper interval in a tactical formation had been forgotten. If a gook had fired an RPG at us then, there was barely enough space between the vehicles for a miss to go through.

As soon as we stopped a motorbike pulled up right behind the column. The Vietnamese guy driving was wearing olive drab fatigues without insignia, a red baseball cap and sunglasses. You could almost see him thinking as he turned his head toward the smoke, dust and noise north of the road. After minimal reflection he turned and sped back the way he'd come. The girl in the micro skirt behind him just held on.

Jackson ordered a turn to the right to get in a line formation to enter the trees. The line tracks started off the road to line up while Six Track and the Medic Track stayed where we were on the road. While they were maneuvering into formation, I looked at the Duster on the other side of the road again. It had only a jeep with an M60 machine gun with it. The two of them were to our right rear as we faced the Rubber.

Six Track had turned toward the Rubber, but was almost behind the right end of our line because we had been well back in the column arriving. I was looking off to our right when two NVA soldiers in green uniforms and sun helmets stood up fifty meters to our right about five meters from the edge of the road and started running toward the rubber, bounding over fallen tree trunks. I started shooting and yelling at the same time. "Gooks on the right! Gooks on the right!"

I fired a full magazine in two bursts and grabbed for a new one. When I looked back for my targets, I saw no sign of them. I had heard the Duster fire seven rounds and could see the smoke of recent explosions near the ground at the edge of the standing trees. The runners could have been inside the tree line before the Duster fired. I don't think that anyone else shot at them. Jackson kept the Troop headed straight into the rubber. Neither of the gooks appeared to be carrying a weapon as they ran, but I still felt a chill when I realized we had passed within five meters of them at slow speed without a clue they were there.

It was a rough ride over the cut tree trunks, but when we got to the standing rubber trees it was riding down straight lanes between the rows of trees. We went in without firing for some time. Visibility was not as bad as it had seemed from the road. We could see about fifty meters ahead as we advanced. Moving into a fight without shooting wasn't much fun, but we couldn't take the chance of firing into the back of Alpha. For a long time while we were moving without firing, we didn't take any enemy fire. About 1320 we took scattered rifle fire.

Apparently we had come abreast of Alpha on our left, or at least close enough to fire forward, because Jackson ordered suppressive fire to our front. The result was intermittent machine gun fire and an occasional flechette round down one of the bowling alleys between the rubber trees. Shortly after we started firing, we stopped moving. For almost twenty minutes we maintained a slow steady fire into the rubber trees. About 1430 Jackson ordered a slow back up by all vehicles with firing maintained at the same rate to the front. After a hundred meters of backing, we turned and headed out at higher speed. The last napalm of the day went in behind us, about where we had stopped before backing out.

The convoy to Tay Ninh had passed behind us after we moved into the Rubber. They took the alternate route down Route 22 to Go Dau Ha on the way back. The crater in Route 22 had been filled by then. As soon as we got out of the rubber, we were ordered back to Xom Bao Don to escort the returning Dau Tieng part of the convoy toward Trang Bang.

We didn't have much of a wait. Six Track went with Third Platoon to lead the first serial. Second Platoon followed the first serial of the convoy and First Platoon followed the end of the convoy. We pulled off Highway at Checkpoint B and watched the trucks go by. Second Platoon pulled in behind us shortly. As soon as First Platoon reached Checkpoint 18, they just headed to Hampton. When the tail of the convoy passed Checkpoint B, we went back to Checkpoint 18 and did the same. At Go Dau Ha, Second Platoon went directly to the bridge. We went with Third Platoon to Hampton to join First for a hot dinner and sit down toilets.

Jackson held an informal after action debriefing with Carlson, Evans and me after dinner. When Alpha cleared the stretch of Highway 26 next to the Cau Khoi Rubber, they had also put tracks on line through the area of the cut down trees traveling parallel to the road. When they approached a rubber processing building further on than we had gone, enemy troops in the building fired at them. The first vehicle hit was a Sheridan hit by a recoilless rifle and an RPG. Three of its crew were Alpha's killed.

Much more had gone on with Bravo Troop than I realized. We had dismounts down while advancing in the Rubber and they recovered ten enemy bodies, four AK47s, an RPG launcher and a German World War II submachine gun. Alpha had recovered 38 bodies, fourteen AK47s, a light machine gun and an RPG launcher.

When we stopped before withdrawing, the line tracks were halted at the edge of a road across our front that was used as a control line to mark the edge of the area where the gunships were firing and air strikes going in. The Platoon Leaders had forcefully ordered their Track Commanders not to go on the road. After we were back and in Hampton, one of the Third Platoon's Track Commanders said he was sad to leave a machine gun behind. He had not told Evans that there was an abandoned enemy machine gun in plain sight just in front of his track sitting on the edge of the road. It was still there when we left.

Carlson joked about the Mechanized Infantry Platoon Leader who had relieved First Platoon. As instructed, he had stopped for a brief conference when they passed on the road between Go Dau Ha and Ap Suoi Cao. Gary had passed on the little there was to say about guarding the bridge and was about to leave when the Infantry Lieutenant made some comment about Carlson being lucky to command a company as a First Lieutenant. "I just looked at him and said, This is just a platoon, and drove off."

Several times Gary had explained to me with pride that an Armored Cavalry Platoon was the smallest combined arms team in the Army. On paper, his platoon had an armor section, a scout section, an infantry squad and a mortar section. In our current reality it was just vehicles, crews and dismounts plus a mortar track that rarely fired its mortar. Gary clearly liked the idea of leading a platoon that looked big enough to be a company. By then I shared his attitude. Anybody who led a platoon with only four APCs was a poor benighted fellow deserving pity.

9

The Citadel

March 29

    First and Third Platoons left Hampton for road sweeps at 0635. Second Platoon came in from the bridge just after that. After the road sweeps, we went with First and Third Platoons and then outposted Highway 19 between Checkpoint B and Ap Suoi Cao. Second Platoon stayed in Hampton.
    After the convoy passed, Jackson assembled First and Third Platoons a little south of Ap Suoi Cao and we spent the rest of the day sweeping and searching light brush on the east side of Highway 19 south of the village. We were close enough to the road to hear the returning convoy going past, but kept on with the search for a couple of hours after that. After we were done, we joined Second Platoon at Hampton at 1730. Third Platoon left after dinner for Go Dau Ha bridge.

March 30

    First and Second Platoons repeated yesterday's road sweeps. Third Platoon came in for breakfast then held the fort. Once the road was cleared, we outposted the same stretch of Highway 19 as yesterday. After the convoy passed in the morning, the outposts assembled on Highway 19 just north of Checkpoint B, moved on line three hundred meters east of the highway then swept south two klicks. That brought us back to Highway 19 that we crossed and continued south for another two klicks to Route 1 a few klicks northwest of Trang Bang. We turned right and were in Hampton at 1645.
    I was asleep when seven mortar rounds hit. The tracks on the east side of Hampton reported that five rounds had landed outside the berm and two behind them where the Artillery battery had been. No one was hit and it was too dark to check the craters. I asked Jackson to tell them to call me if they found a crater in the morning and not to disturb it.

March 31

I found an impact crater in an open area between some of the unoccupied Artillery bunkers. At Ft. Sill we were taught how to tell which way a mortar round came from based on the spray pattern of the crater. The crater was quite small, but the pattern was distinct. Almost all of the dirt was thrown in a fan to the west side of the crater, centered due west. That meant the mortar round had come from due east. I told Jackson which way the round had come from, took a shower and had breakfast.

Third Platoon was away before 0700 to clear to Ap Suoi Cao then south to Checkpoint B. On reaching Route 1 just outside Hampton they saw signs of digging that they confirmed to be a mine. They blew it and continued. Second Platoon followed into Go Dau Ha clearing Route 22 north to Checkpoint 22. First Platoon left last, south to Trang Bang. All the road clearing was done by 0830 and the whole Troop outposted along Highway 19 between Trang Bang and Ap Suoi Cao.

After the morning convoy had passed, we assembled just south of Checkpoint 12, formed on line on the highway and moved into scattered brush on the west side of Highway 19. A few hundred meters away from the road the area was uncultivated fields separated by light hedgerows, with a lot of houses. The houses were more substantial than the hooches in the fields south of the Boi Loi Woods, but still abandoned. After we were two klicks in, we turned and headed generally south for the rest of our day. Our dismounts found nothing in the hedgerows and homesteads. When we crossed our last hedgerow for the day, we were less than a klick across open fields from Route 1. We were about three klicks from Hampton when we reached the road and were back inside at 1655.

April 1

Road sweeps were the same as yesterday and done by 0830. The Troop assembled at Checkpoint 18. We spent the day sweeping inside the triangle formed by Checkpoints 06, 18 and 12. We found nothing. The Troop was back inside Hampton just after 1700. The Cav troopers were called for pay as soon as we parked. I radioed to ask about my teams' pay and was told to send them to Cu Chi.

April 2

Our road sweeps were repeats again and done by 0830. When Six Track left Hampton to join the reassembling Troop, Charlie stayed behind to go in for his pay.

The Troop outposted Highway 19 between Trang Bang and Ap Suoi Cao until the tail end of the convoy passed about 1100. Then we spent a few hours in the light brush near the western edge of the Boi Loi Woods. The area was open enough that it was almost doing nothing. By 1630 we were back in Hampton. Charlie was waiting when we arrived. The firing battery was back too. Apparently whatever had sent them to FSB Wood was over. As soon as we were settled, Carlson came by. Schultz was going home and Carlson was going to Cu Chi as the new XO. Gary assured me that the rear area would look better the next time I was back.

After dinner Jackson brought by First Lieutenant Eric Webster, the new First Platoon Leader. Webster was big and Black. He'd been an offensive lineman for the Morgan State football team.

April 3

After breakfast I spoke to Johnson, "Take the Cav supply tracks in to get your pay today. When you get your pay, come back on the supply tracks from Cu Chi to Hampton then back to us. When you get to the Bravo area in Cu Chi be sure that you find out when the Cav supply tracks will leave to come back. Do you understand?" He answered quietly, "Yes sir."

The road sweeps were the same as the last three days and we outposted between Trang Bang and Ap Suoi Cao until the convoy passed in the morning. The convoy cleared about 1030 and we moved to the fields south of the Boi Loi Woods. We went in a way then moved south on line into some of the areas of light brush with dismounts down. We found nothing and stopped for lunch about 1245.

We started again at 1330 moving southwest into brush that we'd never been through before. The brush wasn't anywhere near as dense as the Woods, but some of the bushes were over the tops of the tracks. Jackson was studying his map with intensity. Then he threw it down and looked at me. "I give up. Where are we?"

I showed him where I thought we were, headed toward an area the map showed as cleared. He called that location in to Squadron. Happily, a few minutes later we broke out of the brush into the northern end of a huge cleared area, about where I had said we would. The 1:25,000 map showed it as a clearing. My 1:100,000 map showed it as a rubber plantation. The

9—The Citadel

rubber trees were gone. The ground was clear and almost flat in an area almost three miles long, north to south, and a mile wide, east to west.

We set up our laager 1500 meters from the northern end and 400 meters from the western edge of the cleared area. Chico parked Six Track pointed due north. The Medic Track was twenty meters behind us pointed south. There weren't any supply tracks that night, but the evening chopper delivered a water trailer and some sodas and ice. Two troopers coming back to the Troop were on board, but not Johnson. I asked Jackson to check if he was in the Bravo area. An hour later I got a message relayed from the Bravo Troop First Sergeant that Johnson wasn't there.

April 4

I was asleep on my cot between Six Track and the Medic Track when the first mortar round landed. I rolled off the cot and sprinted to Six Track. As I ran, I heard the distinctive sound of a mortar firing before another round landed. When a small mortar fires, it sounds more like a champagne cork popping than an explosion. The back ramp of the track was down and I went through the back and was climbing up through the cargo hatch to get to my radio when I heard the next muzzle pop. I couldn't see anything, but I knew the direction the sound was coming from and that it wasn't too far away. I was reaching for my radio when the third round landed. There were no seats on top of the track. I had run to the Medic Track. Six Track with my radio was twenty meters away. As this sank in and I shrank back into the track, two more mortar rounds landed, each one louder than the last. The last round was so loud that I knew the next one would come through the open cargo hatch directly above me. I couldn't move. The time for the next round's impact passed without anything happening and the spell broke. I ran to Six Track and climbed up in my seat. Jackson was in his seat, working his radios. I got on mine. "Crusher Three Six, this is Crusher Four Five, fire mission, over."

The mortar was probably a 60mm. I hadn't lost the direction to the muzzle pop. I figured it was firing from the eastern tree line. They would have set it up where they could see us, estimated the initial range and walked the rounds into us as they saw them hit. They would certainly also leave as quickly as possible.

"Crusher Four Five, this is Crusher Three Six, fire mission, out." The reply: "Three Six, this is Four Five, from target alpha tango four five zero two, direction two four hundred, right three hundred, add six hundred, mortar firing, battery three in effect, adjust fire, splash, over."

My eastern defensive target was my standard thousand meters out.

I moved the first adjusting rounds roughly south. I knew the direction to the muzzle pops and could see from the flash of the rounds going off if they were behind or in front of the tree line. The FDC repeated my fire request.

I didn't usually ask for splash, but I needed to be sure I saw where the rounds were in relation to the tree line. Asking for splash meant that the FDC would time the rounds and give a three second warning on the radio before the rounds landed. The warning was just the word "splash." We got "on the way" as a report that the rounds had been fired, without asking for it, but that was an indefinite longer time before impact. While I was waiting three RPGs streaked in from the north, followed immediately by a Sheridan main gun firing back. After a second a shower of machine gun fire tracers flowed out from the northern arc of our laager, punctuated by rapid Sheridan main gunfire.

I radioed "end of mission" to cancel my first fire mission and started over. "Three Six, Four Five, from target alpha tango four five zero one, direction five six hundred, left six hundred, add three hundred, ground assault, battery three in effect, adjust fire, over." They repeated my new fire request.

The mortar hadn't fired again since I got to Six Track and the RPGs seemed a greater threat. The outgoing fire from the north side of our laager had slowed a little, but was still steady and heavy. While I was changing the fire mission several hand flares had been fired to the north. I couldn't see anything on the ground outside our perimeter, but I thought I could see the tree line to the northwest.

I got "on the way" on the radio and twenty or thirty seconds later I heard two barely separate explosions to the northwest. I could not see any distinct flash behind the tree line, so they were a fair distance away. "Crusher Three Six, this is Four Five, drop one hundred, fire for effect, over." "Four Five, Three Six, drop one hundred, fire for effect, out." Jackson looked over, didn't say anything and went back to his radio.

After "on the way" and the same delay, six closely spaced explosions flashed behind the tree line followed by a short continuous group of explosions that was the following twelve rounds. I could see the flashes this time behind the tree line, but it was still well away. "Crusher Three Six, this is Four Five, drop one hundred, repeat, over." "Four Five, Three Six, drop one hundred, repeat, out."

The delay and the timing was the same, but this time the bright flashes of the explosions were clear just behind the trees and one blossomed on our side of the trees. Jackson had seen it too. "Outstanding Foxy."

"Where you want it? We got any targets?" "We've got a few gooks to ground, but no identified firing positions. Put some in north of there then get illumination." I radioed in an adjustment 200 meters north and called

9—The Citadel

for "repeat." When the eighteen rounds had landed I asked Jackson if that was enough. "Enough for now. Get some light."

I called in end of mission and started an illumination mission. The first flare popped overhead just after 0230. For a while I kept two lit overhead continuously. By the time five had burned out the firing from our perimeter was sporadic and there was no sign of incoming fire at all. After four more, Jackson said to shut it off. Initially, I just stopped asking for another. After several minutes Jackson said that the Sheridan infrared searchlights were adequate and I radioed in end of mission on the illumination.

Jackson said they had two gooks down in holes fifty meters or so out and were plinking at them with the .50 calibers every time they put their heads up. We had one man with a minor fragment wound. I sat and did nothing for a while. Finally I asked the CO if I could go back to bed. Trying to sleep with a background of erratic machine gun fire isn't great, but I managed to get some sleep.

Stand to was at 0545. Almost everyone was up so it made little difference. Third Platoon was still sniping at the holes they thought they had men trapped in. Most of us ate breakfast while they were still plinking away. About 0630 two Third Platoon APCs and about ten dismounts moved out toward the holes. They pulled two men out of two holes without incident. Almost as soon as Jackson radioed they had been recovered, a helicopter came to pick them up.

Third Platoon made a careful search of the area where the enemy had been. They found seven enemy bodies, two RPG launchers, three AK47s, a 9mm pistol and twelve RPG rounds. At 0900 Second Platoon checked the tree line immediately to our west. There was no sign of enemy there. As soon as they came back, the whole Troop moved out to the north. Captain kept Six Track and the Medic Track a few hundred meters in the open and sent the platoons in to check the tree line on the western edge.

About where my first salvo had landed in the tree line, they found two foxholes and a mortar base plate. The mortar I had heard firing had been over five klicks away on the other side, so the base plate couldn't have been from the mortar that had fired. Perhaps they were setting up a second one when the hard rain came. A little further north there were some abandoned hooches just west of the tree line with bunkers dug among the hooches. The hooches were torched and the bunkers collapsed.

The searches leapfrogged north along the tree line and found more scattered foxholes and bunkers in the tree line. At about the northern end of the open space Third Platoon found what they thought were two graves less than a day old.

From there we formed on line and swept slowly north into the open space behind Ap Suoi Cao. We were settling into a laager two klicks behind the village by 1520. Our trains came in from Highway along the open space south of the village within the hour. Johnson was on one of the headquarters tracks. "Where have you been?" "The choppers were full last night and this morning."

"Johnson, I told you to be on the trains out of Cu Chi, why weren't you?" "They left before I was back from getting paid sir."

"Where were you last night?" He looked at his boots, "In the Troop rear area."

"Who did you report to?" "I didn't check in sir." "Get your radio watch assignment from Chico." I had no idea what to do with him.

Jackson called a briefing right after dinner. He said we'd be sweeping north of the "Citadel" tomorrow. One of the Platoon Leaders asked before I did; "Citadel" was the new name for the big clearing we'd just fought in. I don't know who named it.

After the briefing I visited Lieutenant Evans to ask about the two guys in the holes. He said that Third Platoon had spotted a squad of men coming out of the tree line with the Sheridan's infrared gear as soon as they had stepped out of the trees. Evans had called in the sighting to Jackson immediately. Apparently Jackson expressed less than full confidence in the report and told him to keep the matter under observation. "So I thought, OK, we'll just watch 'em real good. I had the whole platoon up and ready without making much noise at all."

When I had been convinced I was about to die from mortar fire, all of Third Platoon was silently tracking the squad trying to sneak up on us. Evans said he thought all seven of the enemy killed went down from the first flechette round. Evans didn't mention the three RPGs the enemy got off before he fired, but he did predict that his next report would be taken more seriously.

About 2100, just after I had fallen asleep, I was tapped and called to Six Track. Movement had been reported to our northeast just over a hundred meters out. At 2115 Jackson authorized firing a flechette round. It was followed by several hand flares. Nothing was spotted and after the last flare floated down to burn a few seconds on the ground, I went back to bed to sleep undisturbed, except for my radio watch.

April 5

At 0830 the trains left for Highway 19 and Jackson called the platoon leaders over to Six Track to learn our planned sweep for the day, some brush at the top of the Citadel. We moved out at 0900. It was only a short

9—The Citadel

distance to where we spread out on line and swept west generally down the center of the brush. It was a slow advance at the speed of the dismounts with frequent stops to check out anything of interest. Within an hour we had found a cluster of six fighting positions, two of which were joined by a five foot long tunnel. They pulled a tripod for a .50 caliber out of the tunnel. It was clean, oiled and had some bright wear spots on it. Instant analysis was that it had been used to mount a machine gun recently.

From then until lunch, we found nothing. After lunch, the next two hours our search found two 155mm duds, 5 RPG rounds, five 60mm mortar rounds, two AK47 magazines, a duffel bag, some first aid supplies, a homemade Bangalore torpedo and a Chicom anti-tank grenade.

By 1430 we were sweeping down the tree line that was the west side of the Citadel and the scattered brush immediately to the west. Further south than our laager where we were attacked we found a small mound about a hundred meters long with seven small bunkers dug into it. Our dismounts found one pair of blue pants, an NVA sun helmet with a hole in it and six RPG rounds. After the mound, we moved into the open space of the Citadel and laagered in the center of the open space about 200 meters south of the north end. It looked a lot like we were bait. That night we got no trains. The hash and trash chopper came in at 1700 with some ice and sodas, but dinner was cold rations.

Jackson got a report on the two prisoners from our last fight. One of them had become cooperative. He said they were in the advance element for an attack by about 140 men who had come down from the Boi Loi Woods. When the lead element was hit, the rest of the force made no attempt to complete the attack.

April 6

After I completed my ablutions, Colonel McGowan landed with Captain Thomas for a visit. I called Captain Thomas aside about Johnson. "Captain, he ignored a direct order and lied about it. I want him disciplined or replaced." "Bill, I agree it's a serious matter. I'll talk to the Headquarters Battery CO."

I couldn't formally discipline Johnson. I was his superior and his supervisor, but I wasn't his commanding officer. The CO of my Battalion's Headquarters Battery, whom I never met, was the commanding officer of all of the Cav's FO teams, including Johnson and me.

The day was about the same as yesterday except on the other side of the Citadel. We moved out north into the light brush for a while then looped to the east and headed south ending up sweeping down the tree line and brush behind it on the east side of the Citadel. Squadron radioed at 1400 that Senator Tower was going to fly over the Citadel about 1800 tomorrow on his way back to Cu Chi. We were able to restrain our enthusiasm.

We found nothing significant the entire day and laagered at 1550, about dead center of the Citadel. As soon as we had stopped, Chico announced there were enough clouds each day that it was time to use the tarp and asked Charlie and Johnson to help. The tarp was a canvas shipping cover that had been carefully salvaged and preserved for rainy season duty by prior residents of Six Track. First it was tied to some bits and pieces that stuck up near the edge of the right side of the top of the track, then stretched out. It wasn't designed for the task, but when it was erected we got five cots under it, out of the rain that was expected soon. You couldn't stand up straight anywhere under the tarp, but with one end of all of the cots under the lowest part you could sit on your cot at the other end.

April 7

I was on radio watch in Six Track at 0115 when Lieutenant Webster called in that the First Platoon listening post had spotted three individuals 200 meters east of our position walking south. He said they were firing at them with .50 calibers as soon as they were far enough south to put the LP out of the line of fire. I went to get Jackson. The machine gun fire started and stopped before he got to the radio.

Wake up was at 0540. After a standard morning drill, we were on our way checking the tree line and brush beyond on the east side of the Citadel, starting east of our laager and working south. By 1035 we were about two klicks south and found ten 50-pound bags of rice in abandoned hooches that we loaded on the tracks, as well as two bicycles that we crushed by driving a track over them.

We were done at 1515 without any more finds. Our laager was 300 meters south of where we had been the night before. At 1600 three APCs from Second Platoon were sent to meet our trains coming in from Highway 19. They didn't cross the west tree line coming back until 1800. I didn't see it, but I heard it. The first track coming through the tree line hit a mine right at the edge of the trees. The right tread and two road wheels were blown off and the drive sprocket was damaged. There weren't any casualties, but it took half an hour to get the track towed into our laager. Once it was in place on the perimeter, they started working on repairing enough of the suspension to mount the right tread and tow it out in the morning.

9—The Citadel

April 8

At 0715 the whole Troop went west to Highway 19 with the trains and the damaged APC. Third Platoon cleared the road north to Checkpoint 18 followed by the trains, while the rest of the Troop went south to Trang Bang to load some RFs. When the RFs were on board we went back to meet Third Platoon at the turn south of Ap Suoi Cao and then spent the day poking around at the south edge of the open area nearest the village. The RFs were our dismounts and our troopers mostly just rode and napped. The RFs found twenty foxholes and bunkers, a sawed off carbine, some soap, a uniform, a hammock, some food and one stick of C4.

We started back out to Highway 19 before 1400. We took the RFs back then met our trains south of Checkpoint 12, moved east through the brush into the Citadel and laagered near the north end by 1515. I had my defensive targets for the night radioed in before Chico and the crew started putting up the tarp. The FDC advised me that Charlie Troop was near the southern end of the Citadel, about three klicks south of us and I couldn't fire further south than my southern target.

It was beginning to change from dusk to dark when an order came in at 1915 to move out immediately to recover an LRP team at a location just east of the eastern end of the Lower Boi Loi Woods. At least that's where we ended up. When we moved out no one told me where we were going.

We left fast. We just untied the tarp from the side of Six Track and drove away. The tarp flopped down on our cots and whatever else had been put out. Jackson commented as we left that LRPs, the exalted Long Range Patrol units, were just overloaded infantrymen who were quick to yell for help and a pain in the ass to extract. When we left the laager, forming a single file column on the move, part of the Troop was left behind to secure the laager area, but I didn't know how much. I know that we left the mortar track from each platoon and our trains, maybe more. Jackson said Charlie Troop was sending a platoon north to join our stay-behinds.

The move was frightening. A single file column clearly was the best for keeping the unit together and headed in the same direction in the dark, but the formation gave none of the sense of security that a line formation did. As it got darker the ride got rougher and rougher because Baker couldn't see the rice dikes well enough to drive over them carefully. We were not moving as fast as we could because losing contact with each other in the dark would have been a disaster, but we were moving too fast to avoid the jolts each time the track first hit then came down off the top of each of those little dirt walls.

I was sure we made enough noise moving to be heard all the way to the Woods. I was afraid that as it got darker a company or so of NVA would come down from the Woods to ambush us from behind one of the rice dikes that paralleled our route. In the dark, ten men with RPGs behind rice dikes could have stopped us.

While imagining this battle that never happened, I was trying to keep track of where we were, and failing. We had spent enough time in the area that I could read the map easily, but as it got fully dark, I was quickly lost. I couldn't estimate our speed well enough to use dead reckoning. I couldn't see anything as a reference point.

If we had been hit, I could still have adjusted fire. I would have started by firing at someplace where I knew we weren't, say the southern edge of the Woods, and adjusted from that. By the time I had absolutely no idea of where we were, other than south of the Boi Loi Woods, we crossed Provincial Road 6A, and I had a decent idea of where we were again.

After we crossed the road the line tracks formed up in a tight line on the east side of the road facing north. The platoon leaders, Six Track and the Medic Track were close behind. We started moving north through low brush that was next to the road. There was no sound of any contact or firing in the area. We moved north slowly until I assume the LRPs reported that they could hear us quite close. We stopped at about 2030 and word was passed that the LRPs were going to be walking in to us from the north and not to shoot at them. Not shooting was not a reassuring idea in the dark when you have no idea where your enemy is. I didn't see the rest of his team, but shortly after we stopped, a Second Lieutenant in LRP gear climbed up on Track Six. We never saw any sign of the people who had spooked them.

The way back was the same as the way out, but now it was pitch black out. The chance of being ambushed seemed all the worse because we had already passed this way before. Once we were well away, Captain Thomas called in a fire mission into the area where LRPs had been. There may have been no gooks there, but the sound of the rounds landing behind us was reassuring.

We went on in the dark for a while, then the CO spoke, "Hey Foxy, get us some illumination." Artillery illumination was faster than calling in a helicopter to drop flares. I guessed where we were and called in a fire mission for a single illumination round overhead. When it popped, I hadn't done too badly. It was within a thousand meters. The light from a single flare is not great, but it is a lot better than utter darkness. Then a second flare popped overhead. I had only called for one. Jackson told me to cancel my mission, one of the Troop's 4.2 inch mortars had fired illumination by dead reckoning and it was good enough for the trip home. I canceled my request for illumination and the mortar fired illumination irregularly to bring us home.

9—The Citadel

We got back to the laager about 2130 and sorted ourselves back into the right parking places with a general sense of relief. The LRPs assembled, inventoried their equipment and sharpened their knives. A few of our troopers wondered aloud where the enemy we had saved the LRPs from had gone. The Charlie Troop platoon pulled out as we returned. Their return to their laager must have also been a little unpleasant, but it was a lot shorter and their route had almost no cover for an ambush.

On return I found that the illumination was courtesy of Super Lou's First Platoon mortar. Apparently Super Lou heard Jackson had asked for illumination and decided to supply it. Our mortars rarely fired high explosive, but carried lots of illumination rounds for self illumination if we were hit at night. I have no idea what Super Lou's real name was. I don't think he was the Track Commander of First Platoon's mortar track, but he seemed to be its leader.

10

Country Store

April 9

    A new LRP team to arrive by chopper at 0900 on a slick that took out the old team. We went out of the northern end of the Citadel then northeast into the light brush. When we came close to an area of denser brush, we changed into a line formation and did a stay-behind insertion. As soon as we cleared the heavy brush on the other side, we loaded our dismounts and headed east.
    We continued through the untended fields, passing just south of the Country Store. It was 1100 when we approached some clusters of brush north of our fight on March 2. The platoons searched separately. Six Track and the Medic Track waited in an open area. After two or three searches by each platoon we moved to catch up, stopping in another open area near the center of where the platoons were then.
    At 1230 Third Platoon found a new trench and Jackson called the entire Troop over to search that area. The Troop ate while the search was going on. The trench turned out to be about 70 feet long with five attached bunkers. In the bunkers were an anti-tank mine, an antipersonnel mine and a case of AK47 ammunition.
    About 1400 we finished our last search of the day and headed west toward the Country Store. We were just starting to veer to the south to pass around when Jackson called the troop to a halt and put the Troop on line headed west toward the northern half of the brush donut. "What's up?" "Chopper pilot reported some movement in the north end of the Country Store."
    As the line tracks approached the edge of the brush, Jackson ordered a halt and a reconnaissance by fire. The result was .50 caliber fire from all the tracks. It wasn't the explosion of noise of an initial response to enemy fire, but it was still quite a din.
    Johnson was sitting on the open cargo hatch immediately to my left and a little behind me. His knees were almost next to me, shaking wildly.

10—Country Store

I put my hand on his knee, "It's OK." He didn't say anything but his knees kept shaking.

Dismounts got down from the line vehicles and we started forward very slowly. The machine gun fire continued at the same steady rate and was punctuated by grenade explosions and occasional M16 fire filling a gap in the machine gun noise.

The brush we were moving through was like small trees with a fairly wide crown of green eight or nine feet off the ground, but narrowing down to a small cluster of stems near the ground. In front of us I could see dismounts putting grenades in holes near the base of two or three clusters of brush. They were just a little in front of the tracks that were steadily firing beyond them into the brush ahead. One of the dismounts would approach a hole firing his M16 at the opening until he was close enough to drop a grenade in the hole. As soon as the grenade went in the hole, the troop who threw it would run to the nearest track. The grenades were loud enough to cut through the machine gun background noise and were visible from the cloud of smoke and dust blown out the hole's opening.

I had radioed in our location and that we were in contact. I didn't call in any artillery because I had no good idea where to put it. Jackson didn't ask for artillery fire or gunships. We had started firing and moving into the brush at 1430 and I heard Jackson acknowledging reports of recovered enemy bodies by 1440. By 1515 we had passed through the ring of brush into the clearing in the middle of the Country Store. Jackson shut off the shooting and we turned and swept back the way we had come, this time without firing. Jackson reported to Squadron that we had pulled thirteen bodies out of the grenaded holes and picked up two RPG launchers, an AK47 and four RPG rounds. Two other RPG launchers had been destroyed by explosions. We had one lightly wounded trooper dusted off at 1545.

When our dismounts were done re-checking the contact area, we continued on toward Ap Suoi Cao. We pulled into a laager near the edge of the village fields at 1730. Our trains and a couple of repaired tracks arrived to join us within minutes.

After dinner, Jackson called the platoon leaders over to Six Track and announced that we were going into the Michelin Rubber Plantation tomorrow. The Michelin Plantation was on the other side of the Saigon River, beyond Dau Tieng. It was substantially larger than the rubbers in our area. I checked my maps and found that the only map I had that covered the Michelin was the 1:100,000. Jackson said we'd get 1:25,000 maps tomorrow before we got there.

April 10

By 630 we headed north on Highway 19 toward Dau Tieng. Squadron told us that we were following the 11th Cavalry Regiment's Operation "Atlas Wedge" in the Michelin. Whatever we were doing apparently didn't merit a name. A little past Xom Bao Don we stopped just long enough for a chopper to land with new 1:25,000 maps covering Dau Tieng and all of the Michelin. When the maps were distributed, we continued up Highway 19. At Checkpoint K, where we had always stopped before, we crossed the Saigon River bridge into Dau Tieng. Our route through Dau Tieng was dominated by Third Brigade's base camp along the north side of the road. It looked like Cu Chi, but smaller.

The evenly spaced rubber trees of the Michelin Rubber Plantation began immediately east of the town. The plantation had an irregular outline, covered about 25 square miles and had a grid of east-west and north-south roads one klick apart inside the outline. When we were into the plantation, Jackson ordered the column off the road and onto a cleared strip on the right side of the road. About twenty meters were cleared on each side of the road. The rubber trees beyond the twenty meters had almost no brush between them and that meant that we could see a fair distance. No brush also meant that the plantation was still operating, even while being used as a staging area by the NVA and VC.

About seven klicks into the plantation, a French car passed us on the road going the other way. It was a black car with a long hood, big curved front fenders and bug-eyed headlights. He was driving on the road. I wondered how he knew the road wasn't mined.

Just before we reached the main road that went north through the middle of the plantation, we passed the largest enemy emplacement I had ever seen. It was an X shaped trench. Each of the four arms of the X extended about forty meters from the center. It would hold a typical enemy infantry company. Almost any way an attack came from, half of the unit could fire on the attackers. The X shape emphasized firepower, while the standard American circle of fighting positions emphasized protection. Usually we stopped to blast or crush even small bunkers or foxholes, but paid no attention to this trench.

When we reached the northernmost east-west road we turned west to parallel it through the rubber trees to near the plantation's edge. The CO ordered the Troop on line and we began a slow sweep of the area. Almost immediately we found nine half-finished bunkers with logs for overhead cover plus one NVA uniform. At one of the plantation road intersections a mine on top of the road attracted attention and we found two more buried in the road nearby.

About 1530 we set up for the night in a clearing next to the edge of the plantation. The other side of the clearing was the beginning of the heavy brush at the base of a short line of hills called the Razorbacks. The peak directly across from us was only about 300 meters high, but even 1500 meters away that seemed huge when everywhere nearby was flat.

The evening chopper brought a water trailer slung under it, but we got no trains and dinner was C-rations. After dinner, I went over to see Evans. When I walked up to his track, I didn't see him. "Where's Lieutenant Evans?" "Click-Click's inside."

"Who?" "Click-Click, Lieutenant Evans." Before the night was over, the name was explained. Evans carried a personal .32 caliber revolver. In the Country Store the day before Evans had spotted a gook in a hole next to his track, drawn his weapon, pointed and pulled the trigger twice. The result was merely "click-click." He had forgotten to load it. The gook died shortly thereafter from a dismount's grenade. Evans' crew thought it was hilarious and the nickname stuck.

April 11

Our second day in the Michelin was about the same as the first. At wake up there was no sign of the night's brief rain. We found nothing before lunch or after. At 1530 we stopped and laagered in a different clearing between the edge of the plantation and the brush at the foot of the Razorbacks.

April 12

Our drill was the same as yesterday. After two hours of sweeping back and forth and finding six foxholes and one 155mm dud, we headed toward Dau Tieng. Just outside Dau Tieng we stopped for refueling. A fuel truck with one APC as a guard was parked next to the road. The Troop's vehicles formed two lines passing on both sides of the fuel truck to top off their tanks.

By 1530 we were through Dau Tieng and on the west side of the Saigon River. From there we retraced our path down Highway 19. About a klick north of Ap Suoi Cao we pulled off the road and waited for no apparent reason. After all the Troop was off the road, Jackson said we were waiting for part of the 11th Armored Cavalry Regiment to pass going the other way, back into the Michelin. In a few minutes vehicles like ours started passing going the other way. All displayed the rearing black horse symbol of the

11th Cav. As they passed I thought they looked a little odd, but wasn't sure why. Then I realized it was because they didn't know that this was a "safe" stretch of road and what looked odd was that almost all their troopers were holding their weapons and keeping careful watch. On the same road in the afternoon our troops would have looked relaxed and unconcerned. I didn't count the vehicles, but it seemed that about a full Cav Squadron passed, then a self propelled Artillery Battery followed by a Cav Platoon. When all of that had passed, we got back on the road, made the turn at Checkpoint 18 and were inside Hampton by 1730.

After we got in, I was told to report to the Battery command post. There was a message for me to call my Artillery Battalion's S3 on the Battery's telephone. He asked why I had canceled the illumination mission on our LRP extraction on April 8 after only one round. I explained we got substitute illumination from the Troop's 4.2 inch mortar and wondered, without asking, why they cared. He then asked if I had any reason to believe that the gun had not fired accurately. I said I wasn't sure enough of where I was at the time to question or confirm the accuracy of the shot. It seemed hard to get my message through. Finally he asked me to sign a written statement that I had not canceled the mission because of the inaccuracy of the first round. I wrote the statement and left it at the Battery Headquarters for delivery to Cu Chi.

April 13

We left at 0730. Just past the PF outpost on the eastern edge of Go Dau Ha, two Sheridans broke down almost simultaneously. Jackson called for an M88 to tow them in and the rest of the Troop moved on arriving at Checkpoint 18 at 0800.

South of Ap Suoi Cao we went east and then north past the eastern end of the cultivated fields. We spent the day sweeping light brush in the area just south of the disused part of Highway 26. Our score for the day was twenty empty bunkers. Jackson called off searching about 1530. We were back in Hampton at 1645.

Captain Thomas found me after dinner. He said that Battalion had decided to spread the experience in our FO teams more evenly and I would be getting an experienced Recon Sergeant who was currently with the Alpha Troop FO team and Johnson would be going to Charlie Troop's FO team. If all the transportation could be worked out, the switch would be tomorrow afternoon. He said not mention it until the transportation was confirmed. Neither of us said it, but it was clear that Johnson would not be disciplined.

April 14

Two platoons were on highway sweeps by 0730. Second Platoon north to Checkpoint 22 and Third south to Trang Bang. Almost immediately after leaving Hampton Second Platoon reported about a hundred dirt mounds on top of the asphalt over a 350 meter stretch between Hampton and Go Dau Ha. None of the mounds had wires leading to them or registered anything on a mine detector. Each appeared to be just a pail of dirt dumped on the road. Within twenty minutes they had checked out all of the mounds and passed on into Go Dau Ha. On a beach it would have been the remnants of child's play; on a road just outside a town it was a political statement.

As soon as Second Platoon cleared town, Jackson moved us to Go Dau Ha with First Platoon to pick up some RFs. By the time we were loaded, Third Platoon had returned from Trang Bang and we all followed Second Platoon up Route 22. Second Platoon reached Checkpoint 22 then came back to wait for us on the side of the road just south of Ap Bao Dung, the town we stopped in before our fight on February 2. We moved off the road to the northeast and by 0930 were sweeping a hook shaped area of rubber trees that extended out of the south side of the Little Rubber. After we finished that part of the rubber, we turned south and swept through the general area of our February fight. There were very few civilians in the area, but about 1100 our RFs detained two 35-year-old men without any identification papers. They were choppered out within the half hour.

Our lunch stop was uneventful, as was the remainder of the day. We returned the RFs to Go Dau Ha about 1440 and were joined by our trains. We went to Ap Suoi Cao, circled their fields and laagered northeast of the village, a klick southwest of where we had searched the day before. Shortly after we stopped, Captain Thomas radioed, asking for me personally. He said that my new Recon Sergeant was on the evening chopper and I should put Johnson on the same chopper to go to Charlie Troop. I got off the radio and called Johnson over. "Johnson, we're shifting some of the FO teams around. You're going to Charlie Troop. Get your gear together and be ready to get on the evening chopper in a few minutes."

We didn't know everything that happened to the other Troops, but Charlie Troop seemed to have the worst luck and take the most casualties. Johnson didn't look happy. While Johnson was collecting his gear, I told Charlie that a new man who outranked him was arriving and he was back to RTO. Charlie showed no concern. Johnson got on the chopper without comment when it arrived. The new man who got off was Specialist Fifth Class Pickens. He apparently actually had some training in calling in artillery fire. He was much older than most of the troops, maybe older than me. He was white and thin with jet black hair and a slight Southern accent. I didn't ask any personal questions, but he looked like he'd grown up in redneck country.

April 15

We were ready to move by 0615, but didn't. I asked Jackson, "Why are we waiting?" "They're holding our morning chopper at Cu Chi for some LRPs coming to us, but they haven't shown up yet." Eventually we were advised they had showed up. Twenty minutes later they arrived. Jackson put them with Third Platoon.

We left at 0810 and moved north toward the scattered brush we had swept two days before. We stayed in fairly open areas and were near the north end of our prior search area when we switched to line formation and headed into a fairly large clump of dense brush within sight of Highway 26. Our dismounts and all of the LRPs were down as we approached. We moved into the clump and stopped for a standard stay behind insertion.

We started the rest of our day's work in scattered brush two klicks east of the center of the Citadel. Over the next six hours, including a lunch stop, we carved an irregular path about seven klicks long and checked all that we passed carefully. Nothing significant resulted. When we were done, we moved to a laager about 300 meters from where we had spent the night before.

April 16

At 0745 we started with the trains toward the southwest corner of the fields behind Ap Suoi Cao. From there the trains headed to Highway 19 with two APCs that needed repairs. We headed east toward the Country Store. We moved into the southwest edge of the brush donut at 0950. Once we were in the Country Store, it seemed we hardly moved at all. Jackson had the dismounts checking everything very carefully. It must have been good intelligence that sent us there. At 1030 Second Platoon found a hastily buried rice cache of three holes with twelve 100-pound bags of rice in each hole. Each hole had been covered by some plastic sheeting with leaves and debris scattered on top of the plastic.

We spent the rest of the time before lunch going over the immediate area carefully. Actually it wasn't "we." I radioed in our location and the find, then sat on top of Six Track and watched. The first step was to pull the bags out of the holes and pile them on the ground. Jackson had Six Track parked in sight of where the rice was being piled. After I got tired of watching rice bags being piled, I had a tepid Coke, smoked and read. While Second Platoon was recovering the rice, the other platoons were searching the immediate vicinity. By the time Jackson told the platoon leaders to break for lunch, the only other find was two unopened cans of Folgers coffee.

While we were eating, Jackson got word from Squadron that we should pack out the rice for helicopter pickup at our laager in the morning. They also advised us a television news crew was on its way to document our find. Six Track and the Medic Track were close enough to the edge of the brush to cover a chopper landing in the open next to the Country Store. When it was close, Jackson popped the smoke and walked out to meet them. The chopper deposited a newsman, a cameraman and an escort officer. They started by filming an interview of Jackson with troopers picking up rice behind him. It was close enough to Six Track that I could hear most of it. They asked him where we were, why it was called the Country Store, how much rice we'd found and how much we'd found here before. Mike answered all the questions and volunteered that the enemy rice would be donated to local Allied forces and orphanages. They took some close-up shots of the troopers moving rice and filmed a few bunkers being blown up.

The filming seemed over when Colonel McGowan landed. As soon as the newsman saw McGowan, they shot another interview with him. Then the news crew's chopper and McGowan's LOH came back and they all left.

Loading the rice took some time and had continued throughout the filming. After each APC in Second Platoon had taken three bags, APCs from the other platoons took the rest. Most of the APCs put two bags inside the track and carried the third on top of the open cargo hatch at the back of the track. Some of the troopers in the APCs rode away sitting on that thick rice cushion.

We were all loaded and left the Country Store at 1440 to laager a klick to the southwest. As soon as the circle was established, each track that had carried rice piled its bags a few meters behind the track, then went on with the normal evening drill.

We got two Hueys that night. The first brought a water trailer slung underneath. When the water trailer was unhooked, the chopper moved outside the laager to unload some returning troopers, mail, other junk and two heavy duty cargo nets. The second Huey arrived a few minutes later with cooks, supplies and some hot food.

April 17

The rice was piled on the cargo nets outside the laager. The morning chopper picked up the cooks, their gear and the drained water trailer just after 0730. A few minutes later the first inbound Chinook radioed for smoke. As the Chinook came in, Lieutenant Webster gave the hand and arm signals for the pickup. The first pilot made an easy hookup, the second not so much.

When the rice was gone, we and headed north passing a klick east of the Country Store toward the Boi Loi Woods. We formed on line when we got close to the edge of the Woods. Once we were in line formation, Jackson had an extended radio conversation with the Platoon Leaders. The entire line opened up into the Woods in front of us with machine gun fire. I snapped my head toward Jackson. "No sweat. Just a recon by fire."

When the brief firing stopped, we rolled forward into the brush. I hated going back into the Woods. It was always the same; hot, dead, humid air and brush high and thick enough that you couldn't see much. Any fight in the Woods would start with an enemy you hadn't seen firing at close range. As soon as we were well stuck in, Jackson had the Troop pivot left and we moved slowly west close to the southern edge of the Woods. We came to an area of less dense brush and some clearings straddling a footpath that was old enough to be on the map. Jackson ordered a halt and put down dismounts to search carefully. If I had read my map right, the footpath led south out of the Woods to the north end of the Country Store.

Within a few minutes it was clear that we had stopped at the right place; First Platoon reported a rice cache. They were closest to the Country Store. Jackson moved Six Track down to the First Platoon area to see what was going on. They had several holes with 100 pound rice bags inside. The whole Troop made a very careful check. Third Platoon, on the right end of the line, found nothing and Jackson shifted them to the other side of First Platoon to search on the south side of the discovery.

We found nothing more, but the rice cache was forty more 100 pound bags. Orders from Squadron were to pack it out. The loading drill was the same, but took a lot longer because it was harder to maneuver the tracks. As soon as all the rice was loaded, we moved a hundred meters past the footpath and turned left to leave the Woods. We didn't usually move through the Woods in column, but we were close enough to the edge that running into an enemy unit seemed unlikely. We came out, and took a long route swinging around the Country Store to laager on its southeast. That night we only got one chopper with cooks and the cargo nets.

After dinner Jackson passed on news about Johnson. Yesterday Johnson had gotten on the evening chopper leaving Charlie Troop's laager.

They located him today in the Artillery Battalion's area in Cu Chi. He just decided to leave and left.

April 18

The rice was flown out by Chinook. As soon as it was away, we headed to the southern end of the Country Store and swept counter-clockwise around the donut. It was slow movement with dismounts down. We broke for lunch just after 1145 then continued on around the donut. About 1500 Jackson looked over at me. "That's enough, let's go home." "OK by me." We hadn't gone all the way around the donut, but were close. We moved out of the brush and headed toward Ap Suoi Cao. We were in Hampton at 1650.

After dinner I checked in at the Battery headquarters and got an update on the inquiry about the canceled illumination mission from the Battery XO. One round from the Battery had fallen in a friendly village, while the other five fired at the same time had properly hit their intended target. Because the error was one of direction not distance, it wasn't a defect in the projectile or in the loading of the powder charge. Either the gun's aiming stakes had been improperly laid or there had been an error in aiming. The gun that dumped the boo-boo in the village had fired our single round of illumination on April 8. They thought the gun had been laid properly, but my cancellation of illumination cast doubt on that.

They had found the error. The gun had been properly laid and there was no human error in aiming. The scale inside the sight had slipped. A slipped scale was unheard of. If they had done a visual check of the guns before firing, they would have noticed that one was not parallel to the others, but that safety check was for stateside training, not combat.

I was awakened at 2300 by two explosions followed by rifle fire. Jackson and I got to Six Track about the same time. The firing stopped before he got on the radio. The explosions were two RPG rounds that had been fired into Hampton. Lieutenant Webster was on First Platoon radio watch when it happened and authorized the men on watch on three of his tracks to fire back with M16s. Go Dau Ha was too close to the direction the rounds had come from to fire anything heavier than rifles. When it was clear that was it, I went back to bed.

April 19

First and Second Platoons cleared the roads to Checkpoint 18 and Trang Bang. Six Track and Third Platoon waited until they were done and headed back before leading north up Route 22. First Platoon fell in behind followed by Second Platoon. We stayed on the road until we were just south of the part of the Little Rubber adjacent to the road. We turned off the road to the northeast and went a little over a klick to the hook extending out of the Little Rubber. We swept on line through the rubber trees for a klick then pivoted south into an area of scattered brush, homesteads and hedgerows. Jackson directed the platoons to search separate areas. When we stopped for lunch, we were over two klicks south of the rubber.

After lunch we headed back north reversing the pattern. We reached Route 22 at 1505 and were back in Hampton at 1540.

April 20

Third Platoon left at 0730 to Checkpoint 18 then north to Checkpoint 25. Second Platoon followed to Checkpoint 18 then south to Checkpoint B. We stayed with First Platoon in Hampton.

When Second Platoon reached Checkpoint B, they found the culvert blown. They reported a twelve foot long hole across the road, five feet deep. The convoy to Dau Tieng had to go up Route 1 to Go Dau Ha then cross over to Ap Suoi Cao rather than coming up Highway 19 from Trang Bang. Second Platoon stayed at Checkpoint B to cover the engineer repair crew. Third Platoon laagered between Ap Suoi Cao and Xom Bao Don. Jackson moved First Platoon out of Hampton to laager near the RF outpost at Checkpoint 06.

That was pretty much where the Troop stayed for the day. Six Track and the Medic Track stayed with First Platoon until the convoy passed on its way north then went to stay with Third Platoon until the convoy came back. Sometime during the day Engineers with several dump trucks of gravel arrived and replaced the culvert at Checkpoint B.

When the returning convoy passed, Six Track, the Medic Track and Third Platoon followed the tail of the convoy to Checkpoint 18. The convoy turned toward Go Dau Ha and we continued south on Highway 19 to join Second Platoon. Jackson radioed First Platoon to join us there as soon as the convoy passed them. The Troop probed the brush near Checkpoint B for about an hour finding nothing. Then our trains arrived and we moved into the middle of the Citadel to laager at 1700.

April 21

Second Platoon escorted our trains and two tracks in need of repairs back to Highway 19 and was back in half an hour. We moved to the southern end of the Citadel and continued south into the brush beyond. Once we swept slowly through a few hundred meters of light scattered brush, we came to another relatively open area running generally north to south with a border of tree lines and hedgerows. For about two hours Six Track and the Medic Track stayed in the middle of that area while the platoons searched its borders. There were a few abandoned homesteads in the tree lines that got particular attention. While we sat in the middle, Charlie and Pickens spent most of the time napping on the ground in the thin band of shade next to the track.

At 1130 the platoons came to join us in the middle and break for lunch. Lieutenant Webster's track was parked near Six Track, on my side. A little after we were all assembled I looked his way and he said, "What the fuck, over." I answered, with proper radio procedure, "What the fuck, out." Eating done, we moved south on line toward the scattered brush and homesteads that marked the southern end of the open area.

When we got near the end of the open space we stopped and Jackson dispatched the platoons separately again. From where we were parked with the Medic Track, I could see the dismounts moving into whatever area they were searching. They looked at each stretch of tree line a long time before they stepped into it and at each hooch door before stepping through.

At 1420 Second Platoon was stopped next to a fairly large brush grove that appeared to have two or three hooches in it. They radioed in that they had found warning signs in English and spotted several booby traps in the brush around the hooches. I heard Jackson say, "Just mount up and come back here, we'll have Foxy blow the booby traps away."

He called back the other two platoons and moved further north. We stopped about 800 meters away from the booby trapped homestead with a clear view of it. Six Track was in the center of a line of vehicles stretching from east to west, all pointed south. Everybody was mounted and waiting. Jackson just pointed back at the grove and said, "Clean it out."

"Crusher Three Six, this is Crusher Four Five, fire mission, over." The response and confirmation was prompt as always. I called for adjusting rounds on what I thought was the homestead's grid location. The FDC confirmed with "wait." The wait for clearance seemed long. After fifteen minutes, Jackson was interested, "What's the delay Foxy?" "Don't know. Maybe Squadron can move something." He went back to his radios. Clearance was announced by "on the way" in a few more minutes. The first rounds were close.

If someone had been shooting at us, I would have called for fire for effect, but this time there wasn't any rush so I asked for two more adjusting rounds a hundred meters closer to us. Before they landed, Captain Thomas radioed that he was overhead and would take over the mission. Apparently Jackson got the same message from Squadron. He looked at me and said, "Sorry." My rounds were almost in the hooches, but Captain Thomas called in an adjustment that moved them further away. His next adjustment was no closer.

Jackson wasn't happy with the delay so he asked Colonel McGowan on the Cav net to take his chopper away so that Captain Thomas would have to give the mission back to me. Promptly, Captain Thomas radioed me to take over because they were leaving station. I had watched the rounds, so one adjustment was enough to confirm on target and call for fire for effect. Normally, an aerial observer had an advantage over a ground observer, but not in this case. I had a good view of the target. He had to keep track of it while flying in a circle some distance away.

Six rounds blossomed inside the booby trapped homestead, then six more. "Is that enough boss?" "Yeah, let's check it again."

We waited a few minutes to ensure that my "end of the mission" was understood then moved on line toward the target area. When the line tracks reached the edge of the brush and stopped, Six Track was twenty meters behind. We had all seen the shells go in, but there wasn't any obvious destruction. The dismounts still approached quite slowly, but this time they went into the brush and continued on into the hooches.

When the dismounts came back to the vehicles, they reported that the booby traps they had seen before were gone and they found no more. Apparently the exploding shells had been enough to set off all the booby traps one way or another.

We loaded up and headed back north the way we had come, to the northern end of the cleared area, through the brush and into the Citadel. We continued north and laagered two hundred meters south of where we had spent the night before at 1545. Our trains and a couple of repaired tracks came in from the west side tree line half an hour later. At the evening briefing Jackson announced that after work on the 23rd we were going to Cu Chi for a four night, three day stand down.

April 22

We were up at 0500 and moving out at 0630. We reached Checkpoint 18 in twenty minutes then cleared the road to Go Dau Ha and were in the center of town in another twenty minutes. We turned north up Route 22 and our trains headed for Hampton. We reached the Little Rubber at 0745. "Foxy, Second Platoon is staying behind here and sweeping and outposting the Little Rubber."

I had already radioed in or our position at Checkpoint 22 and now reported again to add that Second Platoon would be staying there. Another five klicks on Route 22 brought us to the Big Rubber. It stretched off to the northeast, with fifty meters cleared next to the road. The Big Rubber was about three times the size of the Little Rubber.

There was a road through the center of the Big Rubber that was a right angle right turn off Route 22. We straddled the road on line with First Platoon on the left side of the road and Third Platoon on the right. Six Track stayed just to the left of the road, with the Medic Track right behind. We went about three klicks that way, then pivoted to go almost due north for another three klicks. We reached a stream that separated the Big Rubber from the southern part of the Cau Khoi Rubber and stopped for lunch. We had moved carefully and slowly, spending over three hours going in, finding nothing. After lunch, we moved over enough to avoid sweeping the same ground and swept back to Route 22 by 1540.

We picked up Second Platoon next to the Little Rubber at 1600 and met our trains in Go Dau Ha at 1620. We laagered in the middle of the Citadel. Being a little insecure of where we were north south, I fired in my east defensive target. Just after I had finished a trooper walked up. He held up a jagged piece of steel about four inches long and an inch wide, "Sir, this just went through my cot. At first it was too hot to pick up." "Sorry."

He walked away. I had only called in three rounds, all at least 800 meters away. Still, one fragment of the shell had made the trip and arrived capable of wounding, maybe even killing.

April 23

We left about 0730 and moved through the northern end of the Citadel to near the southwestern end of the Upper Boi Loi Woods.

We poked around on the edges of the Woods for about two hours, but never got very far in. About 1030 we pulled away from the edge of the Woods and moved north toward the disused part of Highway 26 that ran into the Loi Woods. We stopped unexpectedly. All of the Troop was out of the Woods in a mostly clear area with just scattered low brush. Still, there seemed to be no reason to stop.

With the Troop stopped, Six Track and moved forward to the leading platoon. When we got there, there were two 40-year-old Vietnamese men squatting on the ground next to the Platoon Leader's track. Their hands were tied behind their backs and two of the troops gathered around were carrying their M16s.

Nam got down from the Medic Track and started asking them

questions. He didn't wait for the CO to tell him what to ask. The initial questions were pretty obvious. We weren't deep in Indian Country, but there was no explanation for civilians being there. Nowak came over and explained that they had spotted the two men watching from the edge of some brush as they went past and just charged and caught them. Nam's interrogation didn't last long. Nam said the men had identified themselves as "military civilians" and admitted that they had been watching our movements. Nam said that military civilians was what the VC called supporters who were not armed, but watched our troop movements and guided VC troops.

Jackson had radioed in the capture as soon as he was told that the prisoners were connected with the VC. When Nam said they wouldn't tell him any more, Jackson said not to worry about it, that a chopper was coming to take the prisoners back to an intelligence unit for formal interrogation.

After the military civilians were picked up, we paralleled the trace of Highway 26 to Xom Bao Don. At Highway 19 we stopped and waited for the tail end of the returning convoy. It passed about 1530. We fell in behind and followed the convoy into Trang Bang and south on Route 1. At the town of Cu Chi we turned off Route 1 and got to Cu Chi base camp about 1700. Dinner was grilled steak. Dessert was cold beer at the Squadron Officers' Club.

April 24

Charlie borrowed a jeep and drove me to the Artillery Battalion area to draw my pay that wasn't sent home. I had two months coming. Half way to the S1's office I met the S3 walking the other way and saluted. "Good morning sir."

He returned the salute. "What's that Cavalry brass. Take it off. Why are you wearing a mustache? Professionals don't need a mustache." I took the Cav brass off my collar. Underneath was the standard camouflage Field Artillery insignia. My mustache was specifically allowed by regulations. While I was fumbling, the Major switched tone. "Can you stay for lunch?"

I put the brass in my pocket. "No sir, I'm giving my team a class in fire mission procedures as soon as I draw my back pay." My excuse was conveniently true. "Excellent idea. Come to our mess some other time." He walked on as I said, "Thank you, sir."

The S1 was quite efficient counting out pay in his office. On the ride back to our Troop area, I put the Cav brass back on. Within a few minutes of getting back to the Troop area, Pickens and Charlie met me at Six Track as planned. No one was working on the track at the time and we used it as our school.

"Before we review the fire mission formats, I want to go over more important things. The most important thing is knowing where you are. Our primary job is knowing where we are. We can't all hold the map, but you both need to be staying aware of where we are. We spend a lot of time in the same places. You need to know where they are on the map. Check the map from time to time and if you have any questions, ask me. If you don't know and I'm not there to answer when it matters, ask the CO or a Platoon Leader. If you don't know where you are and you can't find out, the next best thing is to know where you aren't. If you know we're not in the Woods, or not in the Citadel, or not on the other side of the road, you can put your first rounds where you know we aren't and adjust from the impact."

"You know that I put out almost the same night targets every night. Target bravo tango two three zero one, one klick north; zero two, one klick east; zero three, one klick south; and zero four, one klick west. Six Track is parked pointed north almost every night. That means that one is straight ahead, two is to the right, three is behind and four is to the left. Check with me every night about where the targets are. If there is a night attack emergency and you don't know where the targets are for sure, don't panic, just call a target. If a target is plotted at FDC, it's not where we are. If, when you fire it, it isn't in the right general direction, knowing where it is may orient you so you can ask for the right one. Use correct radio procedure whenever you can, it's faster. If you don't know the correct procedure, tell them what you do know and ask for help."

"You should always start a mission a klick away. Don't bring things in closer than 100 meters at a time unless you are damn sure the last rounds were way too far away. We shoot primarily to freeze the gooks. No reinforcements, no maneuver, no withdrawal. Rounds landing 400 meters away put enough hot steel inside our position to risk friendly casualties. Don't fire closer than that unless the CO or a Platoon Leader asks you to. Before you do, make sure he understands that you think it may cause friendly casualties. If you are alone and you are sure that not firing closer means the unit will be overrun, come closer. Be sure it's the last chance because you will be betting your own life and the rest of the Troop."

I wasn't sure Battalion would fire really close even if we asked. Pickens and Charlie sat very quiet. We finished with several dummy radio fire mission requests for each of the three standard fire mission request formats: from the observer, beginning with a direction and distance; from a pre-plotted target, beginning by naming the target; and from a map location, beginning with a map grid location.

April 25

Carlson, now Troop XO, had made the showers available only certain hours of the day. When they were open all the time, they were almost always in use. Gary also said that if they put more water in the showers, the Vietnamese hooch maids would use it to wash clothes. This morning I got to the showers just at the end of the morning period and found the hooch maids pounding wet clothes on the shower's concrete floor. I said to myself screw it and used a shower at the other end. I have no idea if they cared, but I didn't care enough to give up the shower.

The Squadron XO saw me outside after breakfast and stopped me to tell me what happened to Johnson. The Cav could not formally discipline the FO teams, but the Artillery Battalion CO had kept them informed. Johnson had accepted Article 15 punishment, been busted to E1 and reassigned to the Battalion ammo handling team. It was the lowest pay grade there was, the same rank and pay a draftee gets on the day he's inducted, and the ammo handling team was the hardest physical work that the Battalion had, but Johnson wasn't likely to get shot at any more. Johnson had left his post "in the face of the enemy," but there was no court martial.

It wasn't really all that hard to figure out, the Headquarters Battery CO and the Artillery Battalion CO knew their personal performance evaluations would be hurt if their court martial rates got too high. The problems that might build up from not court martialing malingerers probably wouldn't show up until after the CO who decided not to make a fuss had rotated home. Johnson got less pay and harder work, but while he was doing that, somebody else was getting shot at in his place. In exchange, his COs avoided being dinged for high court martial rates. The Squadron XO reported the results to me without expressing an opinion and I thanked him for the information without expressing an opinion.

We had an award ceremony before dinner. I got another Bronze Star for the fight on February 28. The citation referred to my helping to evacuate our seriously wounded driver while I was stunned from being knocked off the track by enemy fire. Then, alone and exposed to enemy fire, I remounted the track and called in artillery fire until the enemy position was completely saturated. Like last time, I recognized the outline, but some of the details were new.

After dinner at the Officers' Club I sat with Carlson. He had a big push on, making sure that everybody in the base area worked hard. Even before we came in, a lot of people with some minor medical disability had voluntarily come back to the field early because they'd rather be in the field than working fourteen hours a day painting hooches or working on other chores Lieutenant Carlson kept finding. After his tales of fix up projects and the responses and evasions of various troopers, Gary alluded to his wife's advanced pregnancy. Apparently he thought I already knew. "When's she due?" "May." "Number one. Have a beer." He was planning a July R&R in Hawaii with wife and child.

April 26

I skipped breakfast and didn't get up to shower until the platoon leaders were long gone. Today the hooch maids hadn't set up their laundry shop yet. When I was done I had nothing to do. I ate lunch with Click-Click and Webster. The CO had been there when they started. They passed on his request that we all meet at 1400 to go to the Delta Troop area for a recon flight over our tour for tomorrow, the Hobo Woods.

When 1400 arrived the platoon leaders and I were all waiting outside the Troop Headquarters hooch. Jackson came out, showed us the area on the map that was called the Hobo Woods and told us the other two Troops had been in there for three days now. They'd had a few casualties from booby traps, but hadn't found the enemy. He led us across the road to the Delta Troop area next to the landing strip. There was a LOH waiting when we arrived. As we walked up, the pilot didn't get out or say anything, he just revved the turbine and engaged the rotor. As the engine picked up speed you could see the landing skids flex as part of the weight was lifted by the rotor. The LOH had an empty copilot seat in front and a bench seat in back. As Jackson headed around the nose of the chopper for the copilot seat he yelled over the engine noise. "Nowak, Foxy, you two wait for the second trip."

Webster and Click-Click got in back on the bench. Jackson was putting on a radio helmet as the chopper took off. Nowak and I made small talk and smoked until the chopper came back in about twenty minutes. As soon as it landed, Webster and Click-Click got out and Nowak and I got in.

A LOH looks a lot like an egg on its side with a tail boom. The front was almost all curved clear plastic. As built, a LOH had two back doors with big plastic windows on each side, but every one I saw in Vietnam had both back doors taken off and the bench in the back was open to the outside at both ends.

As soon as we hit the bench, the pilot lifted off. Jackson took off his radio helmet and yelled back at us. It was noisy enough that I'm not sure exactly what he said, but the gist was clear. We were going to fly over the Hobo Woods to get a look to compare to our maps. I had the right map with me and was able to locate map features on the ground as soon as we stopped climbing. There was a village near these woods named "Hobo."

I had no idea what "Hobo" sounds like in Vietnamese. We just used the English pronunciation.

By the time we got over the Hobo Woods, it was easy to see on the ground. There were no surprises from a thousand feet up, the roads, streams and villages looked just like the map. The map showed the Hobo Woods as areas of rubber trees mixed with areas of heavy brush and woods. That part didn't match, the ground had no trees or major vegetation, just scattered brown debris.

11

Helmet Fight

April 27

We cleared the Cu Chi main gate about 0730. Even seeing it for the second time, the long line of Vietnamese civilians at the gate lined up to be checked in by the MPs was an impressive sight. They were coming in to their jobs, and we were going out to ours.

To get to the Hobo Woods we turned right off Route 1 onto Provincial Road 7A about eight klicks short of Trang Bang. We traveled up 7A six klicks to Trung Lap, a village with a large RF outpost. The RF outpost looked more like a movie version of a French Foreign Legion fort than anything else I'd seen in Vietnam. Most of the RF outposts were small squares or triangles made out of earth berms with bunkers and firing positions built into the wall with a barbed wire belt around it. The RF outpost at Trung Lap was a lot bigger than usual, with very high walls. Strangely, it didn't have much wire around it.

The RF fort was on one side of the road and the village's huts were lined up well back from the road on the other side. There was no sign of RFs in the fort. As soon as we were past the fort, we got off the road and moved parallel to it in the adjacent field. At 1030 we reached a stream with a small concrete bridge, 1500 meters beyond the fort. At the near end was a large sandbag bunker with a low dirt wall around it and three rows of barbed wire concertina outside the wall. There were four RFs visible outside the bunker. The Troop pulled back on the road just long enough to cross the bridge. Three klicks beyond the stream we turned left away from the road and headed toward the Hobo Woods five klicks away.

Arriving at the edge of the Woods on the ground confirmed our aerial reconnaissance. There were no standing trees. The area had been bulldozed. A jumbled carpet of felled trees still covered parts of what had been the woods, but nothing was green. There had been some decay, but the large pieces were not yet rotten. Apparently the local civilians were making some use of the wood, because some areas had been cleaned of large pieces of wood. Maybe the VC were using the logs to make their bunkers and tunnels. The area must have been sprayed with defoliants because there were few plants growing, just the remains of dead trees.

It wasn't very pretty, but a traditional VC hiding place and staging area had been eliminated, or almost eliminated. It was still Indian Country and we were there because someone thought some gooks were still there, but the Hobo Woods no longer provided cover for a walking man and was little barrier to our tracks. The vegetation to hide an enemy battalion from aerial observation was gone.

Sweeping, we found some small bunkers, some miscellaneous supplies and a couple of RPG rounds. Then one of the tracks hit a mine in the middle of nowhere, no road, no trail, just in the middle of what had been a forest. The shock of the blast knocked the driver's head against the front edge of his hatch opening and the hatch hit his head from behind. His helmet prevented serious damage, but it was still quite a blow. The damage to the APC was a broken left track, near the front.

The driver jumped out of the driver's compartment and stamped away in the same direction the vehicle had been headed, yelling at no one in particular. "That's the fifth fucking mine I've hit! The fifth fucking mine! I ain't never driving that fucking track again! I ain't driving that fucking track ever!"

His tirade was embellished with more elaborate curses as he strode away from the track. By the time he was through yelling, he was over thirty meters from his vehicle. He stopped and looked back. None of the small group that had gathered to inspect the damage paid any attention to him. The driver stood muttering with his hands on his hips glaring back at the track.

The Track Commander got into the driver's seat and backed the APC up very slowly about six feet. Only the right track was working, but he got it to move back almost straight far enough to get the end of the broken left track out where it could be worked on. One of the other men on the track had found two spare track links. The Track Commander shut off the engine and joined him in removing the damaged track link on each of the loose ends of the broken track. Nowak arrived, said a few words and got out of the way. The driver walked about halfway back to the track and stood with his hands in his pants pockets watching and muttering.

About the same time that the damaged track links had been removed and replaced, the Platoon Sergeant arrived with two track jacks. A track jack is a tool to pull the ends of a separated track together, not to lift anything, It can be extended or contracted by turning a long hexagonal nut shaped center piece that two threaded rods screw into. Each of the threaded rods had a sort of hook at its end. A couple of the watching troops held the two ends of the track close enough together to attach two extended hooks behind the last link at each end.

The driver walked over and joined the group watching the work from up close. He said nothing and no one spoke to him. The two men actually working were tightening the two track jacks with wrenches. They tightened at the same speed and the separated ends of the track were drawn slowly together. When the track ends were pulled close enough together, there was an interlude of cursing by the workers, with verbal assistance by the observers, as they struggled to line up the two end track links to insert the pin that would connect them and complete reassembly of the track. When the pin was finally driven in and the track jacks were loosened enough to remove them, the crowd broke up in anticipation of the order to move out. The driver climbed back into his seat without comment and drove off when the order to move out came.

Another APC and a Sheridan also hit mines that day. Neither had any casualties and the Sheridan wasn't even damaged. One of the men working on the APC set off a second mine by stepping on it. He was severely injured and evacuated by chopper immediately. Our laager was 1500 meters south of where we had found the last mines.

All of our overnight supplies were brought in by Chinook. The chopper arrived with a water trailer suspended under it. It set the water trailer down inside the circle and hovered. As soon as the sling was unhooked someone signaled the pilot and the chopper slipped to the side to set down. Then a mine exploded under the helicopter. The chopper hesitated then rose and hovered. Apparently there was no damage to the chopper. No one on the ground was hurt. After a bit, the pilot set down and our cooks got off gingerly and unloaded our dinner and miscellaneous packages. The incident was forgotten quickly. It was the only helicopter mine I ever saw. The simplest helicopter mine was supposed to have some kind of a propeller on a shaft above ground. The downdraft from a landing helicopter spins the propeller and that sets off the mine. There were also reported to be more sophisticated fuses that were set off by the higher air pressure under a landing helicopter. The chopper left as soon as unloaded. There was no natural cover for an enemy nearby, it was still light and we were not moving. It was almost a relaxing situation.

April 28

A Chinook arrived right after full light and collected our cooks and the water trailer. By 0830, we were moving slowly north through the forest's debris. Fifty meters or so at a time for the tracks, by platoons with the platoons close together, then waiting for the dismounts to make a thorough search of the land in the vicinity vehicles.

We hit no more mines, but found a few bunkers with six rifles in them. The rifles were a big hit. They were bolt action rifles and could be taken home by the men who pulled them out of the holes. Five were a Russian model that was used by the Czar's army in World War I and by the Red Army in World War II. The sixth was the standard rifle of the French Army at the beginning of World War II.

We laagered where we stopped sweeping. It was a substantially clear area big enough for the Troop about in the middle of what had been the Woods. Cokes, cooks, dinner, water trailer, a few returnees and other bits and pieces arrived by Chinook without incident.

April 29

Breakfast cooked on a portable grill wasn't much, but it was better than C-rations. As soon as breakfast was done, the cooks and their gear were choppered out. At 0900 we headed to the northwest. At our first stop to inspect, less than ten minutes later, two of our dismounts were wounded by a booby trap, one badly enough that they put him on the dust off on a stretcher. Individual men and vehicles moved further, but the center of the Troop moved less than three klicks in the next six hours. We lost one more casualty to a mine.

Shortly after 1500 we laagered at the northern edge of what had been woods. Several helicopter flame baths dropped into a nearby area we had not gone into and each drop produced at least one secondary explosion. I don't know who designed the flame bath, but the Aviation Battalion made them at Cu Chi. A flame bath was three barrels of aviation fuel slung beneath a Huey on a long tether. Somewhere inside the cluster of barrels was a detonator with an explosive charge. The chopper moved over the target slowly and dropped the load. The detonator blew when it hit the ground and converted the three barrels of aviation fuel into a fire ball. It was a poor man's napalm. The Division commander thought they were a great idea.

While the flame baths were going in, our evening chopper came and went. Again, our laager area was a little more cleared than the rest of the "woods." We could see a long way and that always seemed like safety.

I asked to fire two of my defensive targets to confirm their location and ours, but was denied without any explanation. I wandered around Six Track in the center of the laager a little. I watched the troops and talked to those I knew as they passed. There wasn't anything more for me to do, so I climbed up into my jeep seat to read until dinner.

One of the troops walked toward Six Track from the left front. About ten feet from the vehicle he stepped on a mine. I never want to know how it sounded to him, but to me, twenty feet away, quiet just disappeared into noise. His right foot was blown off cleanly at the ankle. One of the medics appeared with a syringe and a dressing before the smoke cleared. Between the massive shock from the explosion and an immediate injection, the kid probably didn't feel any pain until later when they started easing him off morphine.

A small crowd gathered, but most of the troops stayed near their vehicles. I just stared at the hole. The crater was only a foot deep. The smell of the explosion lingered a long while after the smoke was gone. I had wandered past the mine several times before he set it off. How far away had I been? Four feet, a foot, two inches?

The sanctity of our laager had been violated. The wandering around stopped. There could be other mines in the same area and it was instinctive to return to your track, to your crew. The dust off helicopter arrived quickly, as always, and the broken man was carried away to excellent treatment. No one stayed to treat the rest of us, but our symptoms were gone surprisingly quickly. Within half an hour, dinner had pulled almost everyone away from their track for at least a while and the laager returned to almost normal.

April 30

We started out just after the Chinook picked up the cooks and the water trailer. We swept up to the northern edge of the bulldozed woods then west and south along the edge of wet ground and low brush that marked the course of the stream that was that part of the boundary of the Hobo Woods. We moved slowly, searched carefully, found nothing and took no casualties.

Jackson stopped our sweep at 1430 and moved us a klick to the southeast to laager. Again, we were in an area with little large debris inside our laager. A Chinook load of cooks, food, soda, ice, mail and stuff arrived before the RPG screens were all up.

May 1

We left at 0740 and crossed the little bit of Hobo Woods to the south on line without incident. We continued on across the fallow fields beyond, moving slowly and stopping occasionally, but found nothing.

About 1100 we approached the back side of the RF fort at Trung Lap. Jackson ordered the Troop into column when we were three hundred meters away and we started a long loop around the fort to get to Road 7A. As we came around the fort we could see several Cav trucks moving on the road.

When one of the trucks blew up, Jackson ordered the Troop on line as we moved toward the trucks at relatively high speed. There had been no sound of a weapon firing before the explosion, so it was a mine. There was no firing after, so it wasn't an ambush. By the time we reached the trucks, the four drivers from the other trucks, all armed, had already pulled the driver out of the blown truck. The rescued driver was bleeding from both legs. Two of his rescuers stayed with him while the other two walked away from the mine crater toward the village on the other side of the road. One of the drivers found the two-stranded telephone wire they were looking for about ten meters from the crater. The wire meant the mine had been command detonated. Someone at the other end of the wire had decided when to blow it. All the while we had been in the Hobo Woods and the other troops before us, there had been frequent Cav traffic on the road. Even if the mine had been put in the night before, there had been several vehicles over it before it was blown.

Squadron ordered us not to go into the village to hunt for at the other end of the wire. Two tracks from Squadron Headquarters arrived from somewhere to secure the site for dust off and we went down the road toward Route 1 without waiting for the chopper to arrive. I never heard if they found out where the wire ended. Probably the RFs were supposed to check it out. The same RFs who hadn't noticed a mine being planted in the road next to their fort.

Six klicks down the road we were back to Route 1. A right turn and eight klicks on Route 1 brought us to Trang Bang. We turned north of Highway 19 and stopped, about midway between Checkpoint B and Checkpoint 12. All the vehicles turned right on the road and we began sweeping east on line. Six Track, the Medic Track and the Platoon Leaders fell back to their appointed positions as the line moved.

Our sweep through the western tree line of the Citadel brought us to the center of the Citadel at 1500. We moved a little north to quit for the day. Within an hour after we laagered, our trains arrived from the north with two repaired line tracks.

May 2

At 0710 Second Platoon escorted the two cargo carriers and headquarters track through the western tree line of the Citadel to Highway 19.

11—Helmet Fight

As soon as somebody's road clearing party passed, Second Platoon came back to us and we were on our way.

We went through the eastern tree line of the Citadel and spent the day working slowly north by sweeping back and forth through a two klick wide zone of scattered brush clusters on the eastern side of the Citadel. We found nothing and suffered nothing. By 1530 we had laagered near the eastern end of the Ap Suoi Cao fields. Our trains arrived from Highway 19 half an hour later.

I was awakened near midnight by the sound of a steady rain on the tarp over my head. I was dry and went back to sleep easily.

May 3

After our trains departed toward the west, we moved east. An almost straight line through open areas took us past the southern end of the Country Store then a little beyond. Our day was spent searching scattered homesteads and clusters of brush southeast of the Country Store. The Platoons were pretty much on their own with only general assignments from Jackson. He called the Troop together for lunch, then more of the same. There were only a few minor finds. At 1500 Jackson called it off.

We headed to just east of the Country Store and started curving counter-clockwise fifty meters out from its edge. The northern end of the Country Store, at its closest point, was only two hundred meters from the Boi Loi Woods. From that narrowest point we continued on around our circle for a bit then turned west. Shortly after that turn we headed north on line straddling a small trail. As we started north, I questioned Jackson. "Why the change?" "A helicopter spotted some movement north of here, in a clearing."

I radioed in our position and new direction. The troops I could see were tensed up. Jackson may have passed word of the sighting down through the platoon leaders. An abrupt change of direction into brushy country near the end of the day was unusual enough by itself to make them nervous.

It was only a short distance into the brush until we reached a clearing. It was thirty meters north to south and almost two hundred meters east to west. The line tracks were facing north. We advanced across the clearing slowly and stopped with the line vehicles on to the north edge of the clearing. When we stopped at the edge, the center platoon put down its dismounts, That wasn't really any particular formation. Each of the line APCs kept a driver, track commander and a third man on board. The dismounts were the eight or ten men in the platoon left after that.

The dismounts went slowly up the trail into the brush until they were all out of sight. Shortly after they disappeared, there were three or four bursts of machine gun fire. Some troops claimed to be able to tell enemy weapons from ours by sound. I couldn't, but this time I was pretty sure it was an enemy machine gun because the next sight was of our men running back into the clearing. By the time our men were back to the vehicles, the firing had stopped. There was silence for a minute. I heard the CO calmly speaking into his radio, "Are they all out?," "Are you sure?" Then he ordered the Troop to open fire. As always, it was a godawful noise, twenty-five or so .50 caliber machine guns plus an equal number of M16s and M60 machine guns. Once the firing started, the track in front of us exploded. Then it really exploded.

The second explosion snapped my head back. I had no real sensation of impact, but something had hit my head. I touched the front of my helmet with my right hand and felt a hole in the camouflage cover above my right eye. Immediately I knew that there was a hole in my helmet and in my head; that shock was protecting me from pain; that the shock would ebb; then a terrible pain would come and I would die. I snatched the helmet off and turned it to look at the hole. The cloth was ripped and the helmet was dented, but unholed. As soon as it registered that I was not dying, I realized how stupid I was taking off my helmet in the middle of a fire fight just to look at it. The dent showed the benefits of wearing a helmet.

Once back from confirming that I was still alive, I radioed in a fire mission with the initial rounds a klick north in the Woods. As I radioed, there was nothing in our wall of sound to let me know if the gooks were firing anything. I could hear the punctuation of the steady firing of Sheridan main guns.

Waiting for the report that my mission had been cleared, I saw two litters on the ground next to my side of Six Track. I hadn't noticed them arrive. Each held a body in a U.S. uniform with the head and chest covered with a poncho. There wasn't any sign of a fire, but the legs of their pants were charred and thin wisps of smoke rose from both.

My FDC radioed, "Crusher Four Five this is Crusher Three Six. What is your unit's status? Do you have casualties? Over." "Crusher Three Six this is Crusher Four Five. I'm staring at two smoking corpses. Get me rounds! Fucking status reports later. Out."

The clearance came and the first rounds landed about due north. I pulled them in to about six hundred meters north of us and fired three 12-round volleys just in case anyone was moving toward us or away. The APC was burning almost directly in front of me, but it wasn't much of a fire. By the time I finished my third fire for effect, the Troop's fire had about petered out. Erratic .50 caliber fire continued but the Sheridan main guns had stopped.

A few minutes after the firing slowed down, Six Track, the Medic Track and a mortar track headed south out of the clearing. We went back to about where we had turned north to start the show and were met almost immediately by a dust off helicopter coming in. Three walking wounded who had been riding in the Medic Track boarded the helicopter. The medics and two men from the mortar track loaded the two corpses and the chopper left.

As soon as the helicopter took off, we were on our way back to the rest of the Troop. Jackson was on the radio with Squadron and apparently they decided not to move into the brush we had probably cleared of enemy with our fire. Dusk was coming and nothing required that we stay. The line tracks all backed up about twenty meters, stopped, turned left and headed west again. The cupolas and turrets stayed pointed to the north. The brush at the west end of the clearing didn't amount to much and we were in fairly open space almost immediately.

We stayed in the open to Highway 19 then across to Go Dau Ha. The sun was setting as we pulled into Hampton. Dinner and a pay call for the Cav troopers were waiting when we arrived. Before I went to dinner Captain Thomas came over with a skinny white PFC. "Watson, this is Private Lewis. He's your new RTO. Pickens is going in to Cu Chi on the evening chopper." "Welcome aboard Lewis. Does Pickens know?" "I caught him a few minutes ago."

Charlie hadn't left for dinner yet either. "Charlie come here. Meet Lewis, our new RTO. You're back to Recon Sergeant. Show him where to stow his stuff and where all of our team gear is. Introduce him to Chico and Baker. Lewis, you had dinner?" "Yessir."

"Charlie, you're going in for pay tomorrow on the Cav supply convoy. Lewis, make sure you know our frequencies and where our batteries are."

May 4

As always, shave and shower at Hampton were more enjoyable than the field drill and the remains of the breakfast offering that I picked at looked almost good. The platoons swept to Checkpoints 18 and 22 and to Trang bang. When Six Track left, Charlie stayed behind.

The Troop assembled at Ap Suoi Cao then went east near the southern edge of the village and its fields. On the way over I pointed out the checkpoints on the map to Lewis as I called them in. I also told him what I knew about places and things that we passed. We stayed in the open spaces to about a klick south of our fight yesterday. Once we were south of the fight, each track turned left onto on line and we swept north. We reached the clearing and the burned out APC without incident. Our dismounts confirmed there was no one in the brush immediately north of the clearing.

While the dismounts moved a little further into the brush, the hulk was carefully checked. It didn't look like the gooks had scavenged it, but there wasn't much left that was of any value. We really didn't do much. Poking around the burned out track went very slowly and turned up nothing.

Lewis asked, "Was that ours, sir?" "Yup. Yesterday." I let him stare at it in silence a while then explained where I had fired and why.

Jackson decided the hulk could be towed out. We towed it out of the brush then to Highway 19. We left it alongside the road, just south of the PF outpost at the southern end of Ap Suoi Cao. I don't know who picked it up or when, but the next time we passed by, it was gone. Charlie was at Hampton when we arrived.

12

War Correspondents

May 5

Our road drill were the same as yesterday. When it was done we assembled at Checkpoint 06, then moved north off the road. We passed by every time we went to Ap Suoi Cao or back, but had never gone into the area immediately north of the road before. It was a lot like the area south of the Boi Loi Woods.

About two klicks in, we passed through a hedgerow into large fairly flat open area outlined by hedgerows. There was no indication of cultivation, but there wasn't any brush. It was about 500 meters across and two klicks wide. We had come close to the field's north side before, but never into it.

Jackson stopped near the center of the field and sent the platoons off to search assigned sectors of hedgerow. Once I had radioed in our position, I had nothing to do for the four hours that the platoons searched the borders of the field. After lunch I got a *Life* magazine that someone had just finished. One of the articles in the issue was about the first coeds at Princeton. I knew women had been admitted, but the article's photographs were my first view of my new schoolmates. The story was mostly that the new coeds were all very bright and clever, but what I noticed was how pretty they were. One was especially fetching standing next to her orange and black tiger striped bicycle. Looking at the pictures and remembering where I was, I wondered if I had made a serious timing error.

When the searches were over, we went out the way we came in and arrived at Hampton earlier than usual.

May 6

Our morning road drill was the same again. There wasn't much town after we turned right on the road to Ap Suoi Cao, but I noticed a woman sweeping her front yard with a broom that was just a bundle of long twigs. Her front yard was about ten square meters of packed dirt. To begin her day she cleaned her dirt. Every day, just like us sweeping the road, she had to do it over again.

From Ap Suoi Cao we went to search by platoons the homesteads and brush clusters immediately east of the Citadel. Six Track went with the center platoon and I kept the Artillery informed of the slow southward movement of our center of gravity. When we stopped for lunch, the platoons were all in sight of Six Track. After lunch, we spent another three hours slowly moving south. All day we found nothing. At 1600 we laagered a klick southwest of the Country Store.

Half an hour later a Headquarters track plus a Sheridan and an APC returning to the Troop escorting a cargo carrier towing a water tank with our cooks, dinner and the supplies for tomorrow's breakfast on board arrived from the west.

May 7

Colonel McGowan arrived by LOH as the cooks were cleaning up. Jackson called me to join him on a recon flight. Jackson got in the right front seat next to the pilot. I got on the bench in back. Once we were up, there wasn't really much to our trip. We flew just over the southern edge of the Lower Boi Loi Woods. The few trails and clearings shown on the map were visible on the ground. At the end of our pass over the Woods, we headed back toward the laager. As soon as we were well away from the Woods, the pilot went into a short dive and pulled the nose up sharply. The chopper reached about forty-five degrees, paused and slid off to the left.

As the chopper started up, I grabbed the front of the bench on both sides of my knees. When the LOH side slipped out of its climb, I spent a few seconds staring down at the ground through the missing door below me with my hands clamped on the seat to keep from sliding out. When the chopper leveled out, I relaxed my grip and shook a little. When we landed, Jackson was smiling and gave the pilot a big thumbs up as he walked away from the chopper. Colonel McGowan yelled a greeting that was drowned out in the chopper's noise as he boarded and left. When we left the laager, Jackson was still joking about trying to loop the LOH. He said he and that pilot were determined to be the first to do it.

We went across the open area that separated us from the Lower Boi Loi Woods, formed on line fifty meters from the edge, then moved slowly in. Our days were hot as soon as we got up in the morning, but it got still hotter as soon as we passed into the Woods. Swimming though the brush in the Woods put a dryness in my throat that water didn't cure. Cigarettes helped.

My dread was real, but nothing came. We swept an arc to the right in the Woods north of the Country Store and found nothing other than old enemy positions and a couple of duds. We broke out of the Woods by 1530, continued south around the Country Store then headed west. At 1600 the CO got a radio message, passed it on to the platoon leaders and then told me: Charlie Troop was sweeping a brushy area south of Ap Suoi Cao that we'd been in the day before and had flushed a small group of gooks who were on the run between us and Charlie Troop. I put my M16 across my lap.

We hadn't heard any firing before and didn't hear any as we moved on 1500 meters to the west. When we approached a large cluster of brush near the western edge of the open space there was a flurry of fire from several automatic weapons. The column stopped immediately. I turned to my right and fired an M16 burst into a clump of brush just to the right of the vehicle behind us. There was no sign of anyone there, but the bush was too damn close. No one else in the Troop fired. What I had thought was an ambush was Charlie Troop firing. I found out later the CO had ordered the platoons not to fire without his order because we were so close to Charlie Troop. Me, he had neglected to tell.

Shortly after my firing, a man in black pajamas ran out of some thick brush thirty meters in front of us headed diagonally across our front toward some other thick brush thirty meters off to our right. At first no one fired at him. He ran almost twenty meters before the firing began, one .50 caliber machine gun, and couple of rifles and an M79 grenade launcher. You couldn't see where the bullets were going, but two of the M79 grenades seemed to explode next to his back foot as he ran. Almost immediately after I had annihilated a menacing clump of brush, I didn't shoot at him. It seemed almost impossible, but he disappeared into the brush without any sign of being hit. The shooting continued for a few seconds after he slipped into the brush. He was only the third live enemy I had seen who wasn't captured or surrendering.

We never saw Charlie Troop. After the runner disappeared, we sat for a while, then moved to laager at the eastern end of the Ap Suoi Cao fields. Apparently Charlie Troop left while we were sitting.

May 8

After breakfast our trains and an APC in need of repairs took off for Highway 19. As they left, the Troop moved out toward the Woods. We formed on line at the point of the western end of the Lower Boi Loi Woods and rolled on in. The impact of crossing the edge of the Woods was the same. Although there was no apparent change in the Woods or our speed, we got much further than we had the day before in about the same time. When we paused for lunch, we were in the middle of the Woods north of the Country Store. After lunch we pivoted to the southeast and, after a brief rain in transit, broke out of the southern edge of the Woods. The result of our sweep was the same nothing as yesterday.

Out of the Woods we laagered a klick southeast of the Country Store. No trains came out. The evening chopper bought a half filled water trailer slung underneath and our cooks and food inside. After dinner the CO called me and the Platoon Leaders in for a briefing. He had just been radioed that tomorrow morning we would be the escort for one of the Division's Assistant Commanding Generals while he did a ground inspection of a recent B52 bombing run.

May 9

The Troop's morning activities were standard. There was a last call to fill jerry cans, then the water trailer was drained on the ground. The cooks and trailer were picked up by Huey at 0720 then we left. We took the clearest path to Highway 19, then continued north to Xom Bao Don.

We passed the RF compound and turned left on Highway 26 toward Tay Ninh. Xom Ba Don stretched almost a klick along the edges of Highway 26 and we had to slow down for traffic in the village. Five klicks beyond the village we stopped. Jackson radioed the Platoon Leaders that our guest was in the air out of Cu Chi and would be joining us shortly. He had all the vehicles ahead of Six Track in the column pull ahead thirty meters and stop. When the General's pilot radioed he was two klicks from us, Jackson threw a smoke grenade on the road and the chopper landed on the road. The General wore the distinctive polished black leather pistol belt and holster. His aide, a Second Lieutenant, had the "Colt Commando" version of the M16. The rifle was pretty, but nobody I ever saw with one carried any extra magazines.

The General was greeted by Jackson and offered my seat. I sat next to him on the cargo hatch so I could use my radio. The General's aide sat next to me. Charlie and Lewis moved to the Medic Track. Once the General was settled aboard Six Track, we turned right and headed toward the brush a klick on the other side of the fields next to the road. We moved into the brush on line. Initially the brush was fairly light, but it increased in density and height. It wasn't as dense as the Boi Loi Woods, but there

12—War Correspondents

were similar scattered small clusters of trees and brush that looked similar. It was in those clusters that we came to the edge of the craters. They were neither regularly spaced, nor close together, but they were big, four or five meters wide and maybe three meters deep. All had standing water at the bottom. The tracks had to drive around them, they were too big to cross.

We crawled slowly among the craters without clear formation and the General looked at them. He didn't say much. Nothing indicated why this area had been bombed. About 1100 the General announced he'd seen enough and asked Jackson to take him back. We were well out of the brush at 1130 and the General's chopper was overhead almost as soon as we stopped. The General's aide popped smoke as the General shook hands with Jackson then left.

I moved back into my seat and Charlie and Lewis came back. We ate lunch where we had stopped. After lunch we spent the rest of the day finding nothing in light brush near Highway 26. When we were done for the day, we went back to Ap Suoi Cao. In the afternoon there was enough civilian traffic on the highway to slow us down. Our trains were waiting for us at Checkpoint 18 and joined the end of our column for the trip to laager near the east end of the Ap Suoi Cao fields.

Lieutenant Webster stopped by Six Track say goodbye before leaving on the evening chopper. He was about to be promoted to Captain and off to a job as liaison to some ARVNs. At the evening briefing First Platoon was represented by its acting Platoon Leader, an E6.

May 10

We waited at our laager in the morning for a helicopter with some correspondents and the Division Information Officer. Secretary of State William Rodgers had come to Vietnam with a large complement of diplomatic correspondents. He was off to tour somewhere in the Delta and all of the correspondents they had room for went with him. For the left overs, second prize was a field trip with a combat unit.

When they arrived there were three correspondents with the IO. The correspondents were wearing flak jackets over their civilian clothes, but no helmets. The IO looked like the rest of us, except all his gear was clean. He carried a .45 caliber pistol. One of the correspondents was put on Six Track, sitting on the cargo hatch just to my left. The other two and the IO rode on the Medic Track. The Track Commander of the Medic Track, our head medic, was now a tall blond Spec5 who had replaced our prior head medic a couple of days ago. As was common, he immediately became "Doc" and his real name was forgotten before it was learned.

All morning we moved slowly east through the open area south of the Boi Loi Woods spot checking this and that. Between radioing in our slow progress, I spent most of my time talking to the correspondent. He was a German who had become a U.S. citizen after World War II. At the very end of the war he had been part of a group of teenagers drafted into an antiaircraft unit in Berlin. When the Russians were closing in on the city, their Sergeant told them to go home. He said he just took off his uniform and took a trolley back to his parents' house.

About noon I apologized to him that we weren't doing anything interesting. Within minutes I heard the Charlie Troop FO radio to the FDC that Charlie was in contact. The CO didn't tell me what was coming in on the Squadron net, but his radio traffic increased at the same time. A few minutes later on our Artillery net the Alpha Troop FO advised the FDC that they were being called in to join Charlie. Fifteen minutes later, we were headed back west, toward Charlie and Alpha. We had been invited too.

We were moving fast enough that crossing the rice dikes was noticeably more unpleasant. The driver slowed some to climb the dike, but there was still a jolt when the front of the treads made contact. The bump coming off on the other side was worse. Our driver probably knew what was happening, but he just went as fast as he was told to. "Guess I spoke too soon. Sorry about the ride." The correspondent didn't say anything; he was concentrating on not getting bounced off.

We continued west at high speed until we reached the scattered brush at the western end of the open area. We went into the brush in column, then each track turned left and we started sweeping south. By the time we turned south we could hear small arms firing further south. We moved south at a fast walking speed, but didn't have any dismounts down. As we moved south the firing in front of us got louder, but none of it was very close. The other troops weren't in heavy contact, but apparently they had found someone to shoot at.

As we got closer to its sound, the firing was to our right front. I would guess we were still 700 meters from the firing when we stopped. Jackson spoke, primarily to the correspondent, "We're holding here for an air strike." A few minutes later he gave the warning, "Here they come."

I heard the plane before I saw it. The sound was straight ahead. The jet came in fast and low, headed straight toward us. Normally our supporting air strikes went in across our front, from left to right or right to left. Bombing errors were more likely over or short than from side to side. Today, we were the over. The plane was an F100. I could identify it by the distinctive hole that was the beginning of its fuselage. There were two big pointed tanks hanging under each wing. Sitting there, the main thing I noticed was that the plane seemed a hell of a lot bigger headed toward you. The plane seemed on top of us when one tank on each wing started tumbling down. The plane passed directly over us before the tanks hit the ground. The tanks landed close enough that we felt a heat flash when the napalm lit up, but on the ground it was 200 meters or more away. A second F100 followed and did the same again.

As the smell of the napalm in the distance dissipated, a sniper fired two or three rounds at us from our left rear, somewhere off in the brush. While Jackson talked on the radio, the left platoon responded with a few minutes of machine gun fire in the direction of the shots. The correspondent got down inside the track and sat on the right side bench motionless with his hands clasped in his lap.

The line vehicles did tight right turns to reverse their direction and passed us sweeping back the way we had come. The Platoon Leaders fell in behind the line as it passed and we fell in behind the Platoon Leaders. When we passed the Medic Track, it turned to follow. The Information Officer and the other two correspondents were still sitting on the back. After we passed the Medic Track and it began its turn to follow, a couple of single shots were fired right behind us. When I looked back I saw the IO fire three or four more shots from his .45 at something behind them. Doc radioed to the CO that the IO had seen a gook running to the south in the brush. We kept going the other way.

Apparently the right side of the line saw something from time to time because they fired in a couple of bursts as we moved on. Captain Thomas was overhead with Colonel McGowan and fired some artillery in front of us. He put it in a hell of a lot closer than made any sense when we weren't heavily engaged and two of our troopers were hit by small fragments. He stopped after that. After the artillery was cut off, the fight was over. We never got really close to the other troops, but there were no more sounds of fighting from what was now behind us and none of our tracks saw anything more to shoot at.

As soon as we reached a big enough open area, a chopper arrived for our correspondents. They said goodbye quietly as they left. The IO glowed with exhilaration as he marched to the chopper. After they were gone we continued north a little further then turned west. Our trains were waiting at Checkpoint 18 and, as soon as we reached Highway 19 south of the village, they joined us. We went south on the highway, turned back to the east and went into the Citadel. Our laager near the center of the Citadel was about four klicks southwest of where the napalm had been dropped.

13

Sergeant Major Turner

May 11

Third Platoon escorted the trains and two malfunctioning tracks north out of the Citadel then came back to us. On their return, we crossed the eastern tree line. We went to about where the sounds of Alpha and Charlie Troop's firing had come from yesterday. Jackson said we were supposed to check out the area where the enemy troops appeared to have been dug in. Six Track and the Medic Track stopped and the platoons started poking around on their own. After radioing in our position and plan, I read for a while.

"Foxy, Third Platoon has found six fresh bodies and is opening another grave. We're going down to look." The Third Platoon vehicles were in sight, but far enough away that we couldn't see clearly what they were doing. When we arrived, there were six dirty corpses next to the holes they had been pulled out of and one man was digging into the side of a rice dike. He was wearing a gas mask and even at a fair distance there was a stench in the air. It was Lieutenant Evans. Everyone else was standing fifteen or twenty meters from him as he dug furiously alone. We were supposed to dig up graves to check the corpses and to make sure it wasn't a weapons cache instead of a grave. When the troops first doing the job had broken through to the smell they had recoiled. Click-Click put on a gas mask and continued the digging rather than ordering anyone else to do it.

There appeared to be four more bodies in the new hole, all substantially decayed. There was nothing to check for intelligence information. When all of the bodies were reburied our investigation of the site was over. We spent the rest of the day moving slowly east, searching by platoons. When the afternoon's searches were over, we went back into the Citadel. Fifteen minutes after we arrived, Jackson sent First Platoon through the western tree line to pick up our trains.

After we were settled, Jackson said Evans was going in. Evans was being promoted to Captain and, even without a replacement in sight, he was through being a Platoon Leader. "Don't have a real Platoon Sergeant. Sergeant Major Turner's good, but he's got no real experience. First Platoon's the same, led by an inexperienced E6."

Sergeant Major Turner was a twenty-year-old Black trooper whose first name was Major. He was a Staff Sergeant, E6, not a Sergeant Major, E9, the highest enlisted rank in the Army. I never heard anyone call him anything but Sergeant Major Turner. There weren't many puns in the Army and nobody wasted this one.

I went to congratulate Click-Click on his promotion. He was stuffing a duffel bag when I arrived. He was pissed that he was leaving the Cav. "Fuckin' ring knockers. I've done good work and this fuckin' West Point club is still dumping me to a Mech Infantry unit." "Look at the good side, you'll still be in Vietnam!" He laughed. "Anyway, good luck with your new unit."

Half way back to Six Track, a steady rain started and I ran for cover under our tarp. When I reached shelter, the rain stopped. Click-Click came over to Six Track as soon as we got warning that the evening hash and trash was inbound. He had his bag on one shoulder and his revolver on his pistol belt. He shook hands with the CO and me before the chopper landed. Two troopers and a small load of junk and mail got off. Click-Click got on.

May 12

When we left the laager, I noticed that one of Third Platoon's Sheridan had crossed thigh bones and a skull wired to the front of the vehicle, Jackson saw it too.

Second Platoon lead our column out of the north end of the Citadel then west to Highway 19. Six Track and the Medic Track went north on the highway with Second and Third Platoons. First Platoon went south to Trang Bang. The trains stopped to wait at Checkpoint 18. At Xom Bao Dom we turned left on Highway 26 and continued to Checkpoint 36. Someone must have decided that something had changed because we cleared at high speed the same stretch of Highway 26 that we had cleared with mine sweepers on foot two months before.

When all the road had been cleared, the Troop outposted Highway 26 between Xom Bao Don and Checkpoint 36. Six Track and the Medic Track stayed with Second Platoon near the middle of the stretch. It was a day of sitting. The Tay Ninh part of the convoy passed at 1030. Colonel McGowan dropped in by helicopter an hour after the convoy passed. He passed on a recent observation. Flying in, Colonel McGowan had noticed what looked like a trooper in the grass some distance from one of our vehicles and had his pilot turn to investigate. He could see that the kid was screwing a prostitute. Colonel McGowan demanded nothing specific, but reminded Jackson of the health and security problems of the men going off with prostitutes.

On the main roads from time to time we would see a Vietnamese man, usually in vaguely military clothes, on a motorbike with a woman in a short tight dress on the back of the bike. The couples varied, but the drill was the same. If there was a group of GIs near the road, the bike would stop and the man would offer the girl's services. Often the GIs just insulted the pimp and told the pair to get lost with varying mixes of humor and vindictiveness. However, somebody said yes often enough to keep the teams in business.

The returning convoy passed us at 1430. We stayed in place until we got word at 1520 that the Dau Tieng part of the convoy had passed through Xom Bao Don then went to Hampton for the night.

May 13

The Troop left Hampton just after dawn down Route 1 to Trang Bang. Leaving, Six Track passed the Sheridan whose pirate decorations had been removed. At Trang Bang we turned north on Highway 19 for about a klick where we took a right fork, Provincial Road 6A. Once past the RF fort, we moved off the road, formed up on line and headed north cross country. We had so few tracks in the field that Jackson ordered the Platoon Leaders' tracks on line. The area we moved through had scattered two and three hooch homesteads partially surrounded by light hedgerows. The Troop moved generally north in fits and starts, stopping to check each homestead we came to.

By the time we stopped for lunch we were about six klicks north of the RF fort in an area with scattered bushes two to three feet tall. There weren't any more homesteads to check, just clumps of brush. As we moved north after lunch, the brush got thicker. It was still clusters of low bushes that didn't interfere with seeing into the distance, but the clusters got closer together as we went north.

A little further on there was an explosion in front of Six Track. The track directly in front of us, Sergeant Major Turner's track, had been hit. I didn't see where the track was hit, but I did see a small cloud of grey smoke at the base of a clump of brush to the right of his track. The Troop initially kept moving forward but then stopped and all of the line tracks opened up to our front with machine guns.

13—Sergeant Major Turner

The delay between the initial explosion and the Troop's response was just long enough for Jackson to get some idea of what happened and order our halt and firing. By the time Six Track stopped, the clump of brush where I'd seen the smoke was directly to my right. The smoke was almost gone and I could see a small hole with partial overhead cover near the base of the brush. Of more immediate concern were the forearms sticking out of the hole holding an RPG launcher. There was no projectile in the launcher. I fired a long burst at the hole. As I fired the forearms disappeared into the hole. The Troop's initial flurry of fire ended about the same time.

In the silence that followed, I stared at the hole and paid little attention to two sharp cracks that broke the silence. They were answered by another machine gun hosing from the Troop. I yelled at no one in particular, "Give me a grenade!"

I got no answer. Apparently my personal battle had gone unnoticed and Charlie and Lewis had gone off to help with casualties. I wasn't sure we had any grenades on Six Track and wasn't going to take my eyes off the hole to hunt for one. While I was wishing for a grenade, Jackson yelled at me. "Foxy, Sergeant Major Turner's hit. There aren't any other qualified NCOs in the platoon. Can you take over Third Platoon and get them moving?"

Doctrine is that an FO isn't in the chain of command for the unit he's supporting, he just works for whoever is in command. There was nothing to fire artillery at yet, but I wasn't supposed to take on a job that would keep me from firing later if it was needed. I don't know what I would have done with just doctrine to worry about, but I damn sure wasn't going to leave my hole unguarded. I yelled without looking back at him. "Captain, I can't do that. I've got a gook in a hole over here. Do we have any grenades?"

He didn't answer, I could hear him calling up an NCO from Second Platoon. There was no mention of my gook. I yelled, "Have him bring a grenade."

There was no sign of activity in the hole. I fired the rest of the magazine in my M16 at the opening of the hole and inserted a full magazine. A track had pulled up behind us and a Staff Sergeant came running up on my side. He didn't have a rifle, but he was carrying one grenade. I pointed at the hole with my rifle, "Put it in there."

He slowed, pulled the pin and dropped the grenade in the hole. He kept going, running toward Sergeant Major Turner's track. It seemed a longer delay than a grenade should have, then there was a sharp explosion inside the hole that shook the cover on top and sent a plume of dirt and smoke out the opening. I had just enough time to flinch when a second explosion came. It was about as loud as the first, but sounded like it came from deeper in the hole. A secondary explosion meant there wasn't too much risk that anyone was going to come out of the hole to fight.

By then, Charlie and Lewis were back from carrying Sergeant Major Turner to the Medic Track and Jackson started the Troop forward. For a while the Troop fired sporadically as we advanced, but there was no return fire or any other sign of the enemy. We moved on a klick north into an open area and called in the dust off. The chopper arrived almost immediately. When Sergeant Major Turner was loaded, he was on a stretcher with a field dressing wrapped around his chest and an IV in one arm.

After the dust off we continued sweeping north without incident until we came to the southern edge of the open area south of the Woods. We switched to column and took the clearest route to Highway 19 and on to Hampton for the night. Jackson never said anything to me about my not taking the platoon or about the gook in the hole.

The stuff waiting for us at Hampton included new Signal Operating Instructions. At midnight our Artillery call sign changed to "Grapeshot." I became One Niner; the FDC, Two Seven; and Captain Thomas, Five Three.

May 14

After road clearing between Checkpoint 22 and Trang Bang and over to Ap Suoi Cao, the Troop assembled and went east along the southern edge of the village's fields. There wasn't much in the Ap Suoi Cao fields, but the ones closest to the village were being cultivated with something and we never rode over the crops. At about the end of the cultivated area there were three kids with two water buffalo standing at the edge and watching us. The kids were staring at us like we were the most fascinating thing that they had ever seen. The buffalos were not.

We spent the day in the area south of the Woods checking clusters of hooches to the south. About 1000 a large, dark cloud passed slowly over us leaving behind fifteen minutes of torrential rain. The searching stopped and the troops put on whatever rain gear they had and kept watch. When the cloud passed, the full sun returned and the water burned off about as fast as it fell. We found nothing of interest before lunch. Lunch was uneventful as were the first two hours of searching after lunch.

Two hours after lunch we had worked to within a klick of the band of brush and hedgerows that separated the eastern end of the area from Road 6A. Second Platoon was working furthest to the east. Jackson got a burst of radio traffic and Six Track took off to the east at high speed. Jackson yelled that Second Platoon was chasing a man who had run out of a hooch as they approached it. We were close enough to see the tracks moving to the east, but couldn't see the runner. We had crossed about four rice dikes when two .50 calibers fired three bursts each, then nothing.

We kept on. I could only hear fragments of what Captain Jackson was saying on his radio. "Are you sure he's dead?" "Don't touch anything till I get there."

The two APCs that had actually been chasing were stopped just beyond the next homestead. Lieutenant Nowak had come over and the rest of the Platoon's vehicles had stopped nearby. The man was lying face down and a good portion of the back of his head was missing. There was a huge bloodstain that covered most of the back of his shirt. Lieutenant Nowak was standing near the body. The rest of the troops were still on their vehicles. One of the Track Commanders still had his .50 caliber pointed at the corpse. Jackson got down and went over.

They rolled the body over to look for pockets. There weren't any pockets in the black shirt or shorts. Underneath the black clothes were an olive green blouse and matching rolled-up long pants. The dead man looked twenty. He must have known that his disguise wasn't good enough if he stayed at the hooch. A twenty-year-old man in civilian clothes was unusual enough in the area to be stopped and searched. Running in an open area wasn't much of a plan either.

"The gook was wearing a uniform under the black pajamas," Jackson said as he climbed back on Six Track. "Sure am glad we didn't kill some old farmer just because he was scared of us. Where'd he think he was going to run to?" Shooting the runner was effectively the end of our day. The Troop went back to Hampton for the night.

May 15

Road clearing was the same as yesterday. The platoons reassembled at Ap Suoi Cao.

We went to the Country Store. We spent the whole day going around the brush circle on line. Or at least where the brush used to be. There were still some clumps, but most of the brush that was there in February was gone. Some of it had been shot or blown away, but mostly it had been worn away by being run over. With a lunch break, it took the whole day to complete the circle. Other than fresh sandal prints on some trails, we found nothing.

At 1630 we laagered a klick south of the west end of the Woods. Our trains arrived with a repaired Sheridan a few minutes later. Before dinner the hash and trash chopper brought a new First Lieutenant, Sonny Wright. I think Jackson gave him Third Platoon because it was almost out of sergeants. He checked in to say hello to me shortly after he arrived.

May 16

Jackson called the Platoon Leaders to Six Track to show them we were going to the Thumb. The eastern end of the Lower Boi Loi Woods was close to a tiny stream that flowed north into the Saigon River. On the other side of the stream was a low ridge. The contour lines that showed its slight elevation on the map were shaped like a thumb pointing at the river, hence the name. The base of the thumb was a little north of where we picked up the LRPs in middle of the night in April.

We moved east past the end of the Woods, passing through a gap in the band of hedgerows and homesteads next to Provincial Road 6A. We continued to the northeast through scattered brush on the other side of 6A until we were at the base of the Thumb. The centerline of the Thumb was higher than the ground around it, but less than twenty meters higher. The 6A road curved to the east and marked the base of the Thumb. We formed on line headed north, crossed the road again then swept up the center of the ridge with dismounts down. It was the usual go, stop, search drill in dense, low brush. We found nothing.

When we got near the tip of the Thumb, we stopped for lunch. The trip in had been tense. The end of the Thumb was close to the river and we didn't know how often the enemy visited. The brush was low, but dense enough to provide cover for someone determined to hide. Once we stopped anxiety began to fade. The bushes in the immediate area became familiar. Soon the troops were walking from one track to another without flak jackets or helmets.

The Thumb ended with a slight rise and I could see over the vegetation for quite a distance. To the west was the Lower Boi Loi Woods with the edge of the Upper Boi Loi Woods peeking out to its north. To the southeast was the edge of the Hobo Woods, rudely cleared scrub land stretching off in the distance. To the north and northeast was a line of thick vegetation that marked the banks of the Saigon River, unseen just beyond. On the other side of the river, a rounded ridge paralleled the river's bank.

As I ate I stared at the ridge. The other side of the Saigon River belonged to the 1st Infantry Division. Throughout the day there had been scattered interruptions on my radio with strange call signs, probably 1st Division units. The ridge looked like the hills of the artillery target range at Ft. Sill. I got out the binoculars my predecessor left behind for the only time I used them. I scanned the ridge, just like we had at Ft. Sill. Instead

13—Sergeant Major Turner

of following the instructor's directions to identify a practice target, I was looking for a real target.

If I could find a target on that ridge, they'd be too far away to shoot back. Just one lousy target, even five gooks marching down one of the trails on the side of the ridge. We were far enough away that they might think that we couldn't see them. I could work it through the binoculars the way we'd been taught. Carefully I scanned the side of the ridge. Nothing. Please just one target, one real target I could see. I'd call in the mission and ask for "splash." Then I'd tell the troops, "Watch the hill, Foxy's goin' to make it rain." No sweat, just a little show. Eighteen high explosive rounds would plow the gooks into the ground and the troops would cheer.

A full fire mission ends with a report of the damage inflicted. What do you report when you've decided to stop firing artillery because nobody's shooting at you anymore? With a real target across the river, I could give a report, "End of mission, platoon dispersed, estimate ten killed." Just one fucking target.

Jackson must have guessed what I was thinking, "Foxy, you see anything over there?" "No sir, not a thing." "Too bad, time to move out." We went back the way we came and laagered a klick south of the Woods west of the Country Store. Three repaired tracks and our trains arrived from the west half an hour after we did. They were accompanied by two guest tracks; an APC with a Vulcan 20mm Gatling gun mounted in a small open turret and an APC ammo carrier, The gun was designed for antiaircraft fire, but was being evaluated for ground fire. Jackson had our guests park near Six Track and the Medic Track.

Before dinner I fired in my north defensive target at the edge of the Woods and the easterly one to nearest edge of what was left of the Country Store. I wanted them to be where someone observing, sniping or waiting to join an attack was likely to be. Jackson spent a lot of time talking to the Lieutenant who came with the Vulcan. When I looked, it seemed to me that most of the insides of the Vulcan track were snakes of flat rectangular plumbing to feed the 20mm rounds to the six barreled gun at 3,000 rounds per minute.

Rain began midway through my radio watch and was over before I woke Chico for the next watch at midnight. My cot was still dry when I went back to it.

May 17

We left our laager moving north. Fifty meters from the edge of the Woods, we spread into line formation and rolled into the Woods. Ten meters into the motionless hot damp air my throat was parched. We had no dismounts down, but the tracks still stumbled through the tangled vegetation much slower than walking speed. Our antiaircraft team just followed Six Track. We didn't know if the rough going was having an impact on their complex machinery, but nothing fell off.

We slowly wheeled right and headed somewhere in the main body of the Woods. Within half an hour of our turn, I had little idea of where we were. All I was sure of was that we were in the Woods and east of where we laagered the night before. When we stopped for lunch, surrounded by brush in the middle of nowhere, I asked Jackson where we were. He had no better idea than I did. He had far less reason to be concerned. If he called for air support, a gunship or FAC would confirm seeing us before doing anything.

After lunch we kept crawling generally east. An hour after lunch, Colonel McGowan's chopper passed over. "Grapeshot Five Three, this is Grapeshot One Niner, are you over us, over." Captain Thomas answered, "One Niner, this is Five Three, affirmative, over."

"Five Three, this is One Niner, where am I, over." "One Niner, this is Five Three, from Foxtrot Six, up four point two, right three point five, over."

"Roger, from Foxtrot Six, up four point two, right three point five, out." "One Niner, this is Five Three, don't get lost now, out." As soon as I knew where we were, we wheeled steadily to the right until we were headed southwest. Half an hour later we broke through the edge of the Woods into the open well east of the Country Store.

Once in the open, our column headed around the southern end of what was left of the Country Store to laager within 200 meters of last night.

Our trains brought out the usual stuff and an ARVN First Lieutenant. I hadn't noticed before, but Nam was gone. Jackson said that Nam had leave to visit his family and the Lieutenant was his replacement as our interpreter. Nam's English was limited enough that calling him an interpreter was a bit of a stretch. The Lieutenant spoke better English, but his uniform was too well tailored to inspire confidence. Jackson introduced him to the Platoon Leaders, told him to travel on the Medic Track and privately reminded Doc to be polite to him. The only gear the ARVN carried was a .45 caliber pistol.

Just before it got truly dark, there were two quick rifle shots from somewhere to our south. Jackson got a radio report from Second Platoon that they had spotted muzzle flashes in the window of a hooch 500 meters south of us. The Vulcan crew had mounted at the sound of the firing. Jackson sent them to the southern edge of our perimeter, between two Second Platoon tracks. They moved out and he trotted in the same direction.

Jackson joined them almost as soon as they settled in place. I saw him point toward the hooch and the Lieutenant riding on the back of the Vulcan track nodded. Within ten seconds the gun let out a weird sound, more like a loud moaning than the sound of a gun being fired. Without the orange hosing coming out of the barrels I wouldn't have been sure that it was firing. The first spurt was only a few seconds, but all of it was into the hooch. Then a brief delay followed by a second loud moan and orange spurt.

The second firing was the end of it. The hooch was burning brightly. Our troopers on the south side whistled and yelled. Every second or third round had been a tracer and the two bursts were like fire bombing the building. When the hooch was fully engulfed in flames, the Vulcan track moved back to the center of the laager. There was no more sniping.

As soon as they were back, they started reloading from the ammo carrier. They opened several cans of 20mm ammo to replenish the two or three hundred rounds they had fired in the two short bursts. It was a lot of ammo just to burn down a hooch, but I dearly loved the show. I also liked the empty 20mm ammo can that they gave me. It was twice the size of a .50 caliber ammo box with a clamp down top with a waterproof seal. I strapped it to the top of the track in front of my seat and filled it with loaded M16 magazines.

May 18

By the time we were ready to move out in the morning, our new interpreter was wearing a flak jacket. Our Vulcan friends left with our trains. I was sorry to see them go after their demonstration.

We started the day moving south until we approached the southern edge of the open space. From there Jackson assigned areas to the three platoons and they went off on separate searches. Six Track and the Medic Track sat and waited in wide open space where we could see all three platoons most of the time. It took all morning to search the initially assigned areas and find nothing. For lunch the platoons were called back and parked in a rough circle around us. Our ARVN Lieutenant was offered lunch from a previously unopened case of C-rations.

After lunch the Troop moved two klicks east and the platoons were again given separate searches. After radioing in our new location, I settled back into reading, sweating and smoking.

An hour after beginning our second search, Second Platoon reported finding an occupied hooch. All the others had been vacant. Jackson radioed the Medic Track to take our interpreter to the hooch. We sat for a few minutes, then Jackson decided to follow. When we approached the hooch, most of the platoon was gone. One line track was parked near the hooch with everybody on board watching. The Medic Track was parked off to the side a bit. As we drove up, I could see a woman in the doorway with a small kid holding onto her leg. Our ARVN was twenty feet in front of the house, next to a low wall around a well, holding a ten-year-old boy. As we got closer, I could see he had his pistol out and was slapping the kid and yelling. As we stopped next to the Medic Track the ARVN lifted the kid and held him head down by his ankles over the well. Jackson jumped down, motioned for the troopers on the line track to come over and strode briskly to the well. Jackson and two troopers arrived about the same time. When Jackson arrived, the ARVN put the kid back on his feet and let him go. The kid ran to his mother. Jackson came back with the ARVN following, a little behind. "What'd he say?" "Said he was just trying to scare the kid into talking." "What did you tell him?" "We don't beat kids and won't let him."

We spent two more hours searching before quitting for the day with nothing found. Our laager was within 200 meters of last night. No trains came out, but the evening chopper brought cooks and hot food. Our interpreter ate alone and stayed away from Six Track.

May 19

The morning chopper took out the cooks and their gear and brought two blocks of ice, a pleasant surprise in the morning. Like magic, a sergeant from each platoon materialized and quickly divided the ice into three roughly equal shares, using field knives as ice picks. It wasn't exact, but there never were serious disputes. Big chunks lasted longer and every split wasted some pieces too small to save at all, so precise adjustments weren't done. Every minute spent dividing the ice meant some more melted before it got inside a cooler. It worked because they tried to share fairly and everyone knew it was only ice. The same thing happened again within each platoon, a rough distribution to individual vehicle coolers. If there wasn't enough ice to cool a soda for everyone on the track, somebody went without and an appropriate entry was made in an unwritten account. When a lot of ice came in, somebody would bring a chunk for Six Track. When there was only a little, like today, none came. Noblesse oblige.

Colonel McGowan's LOH arrived as the last of the ice disappeared. Jackson invited me for a recon flight while McGowan circulated among the troops. The flight wasn't much. We climbed to about five hundred feet as we flew south to the edge of the open area, turned east and flew the three klicks to Road 6A. On the return leg we flew much lower and the pilot zigzagged over the brush and scattered hooches at the southern edge of the open area. When we approached the laager, I put my map under me and got the best grip I could. The chopper pulled up sharply, hesitated and fell off to the side as the loop attempt failed. Being ready made it a little better, but I still spent too long a time staring down out the missing back door and wondering if I was going to slide down the bench and out the door.

Before Colonel McGowan left, I heard him tell Jackson that he'd delivered written instructions for our interpreter to match the Troop's orders. As McGowan boarded his chopper, I asked Jackson what orders. "We're going to tell all the civilians along the south edge to leave. They've all been told before, but we're going to tell them again."

When we left our laager we went to about where we stopped yesterday, then a little further east. Almost all of the apparently inhabited huts were between there and Road 6A. When we got to the first cluster of huts, Six Track stopped near the north edge of the cluster. The rest of the Troop just stopped spread out around us. Our interpreter got down from the Medic Track and yelled out something in Vietnamese. A small group of children, women and old men slowly collected and listened passively to a short speech in Vietnamese. Jackson said he was supposed to be telling them to clear out. Everyone in the whole area had been told to move to a government relocation center long ago, but obviously not everyone had.

We worked our way east and visited all of the hut clusters to the edge of Road 6A. The drill at each was the same at each cluster. I couldn't tell if our interpreter was changing his announcements, but they seemed to get louder. It was an easy day for the Troop, just sitting and listening to the town meetings. We finished the last cluster at 1520 then waited out a short rain squall before we left to laager just east of the village fields. We saw no sign of anyone getting ready to leave as we departed.

First Platoon's new Platoon Leader, First Lieutenant David Hughes, was on the evening chopper. As soon as he had unpacked his gear, Jackson called the evening briefing and introduced him.

14

Hoi Chan Fight

May 20

    Jackson announced we were waiting for a Hoi Chan, a VC who had "rallied" to the government a day or two before. He had reported the location of an NVA hospital at the eastern end of the Lower Boi Loi Woods. We couldn't just go where he said it was because he couldn't locate in on a map. Even if he could have, I'm not sure that they would have accepted his story without sending him along. Taking him with us discouraged leading us into a horrible trap. When he arrived by chopper, he wasn't a very impressive sight. Just a thin, scared looking fellow in lightweight green shorts and short sleeved shirt. He was barefoot. When he arrived, Jackson and our ARVN interpreter talked to his escort for a while then the escort got back on the helicopter and left.
    Jackson brought the Hoi Chan back to Six Track and sent the interpreter to the Medic Track. Jackson pointed to the top of the track and the Hoi Chan climbed up. Jackson got into his seat and pointed at the space on the cargo hatch next to me. When our Hoi Chan sat down, he made a little grin at me. "That ARVN ain't worth shit. I'm not sure what he was saying to our friend here, but it sounded like he was being mister tough guy and our Hoi Chan was just getting more and more frightened. I think I'd rather have him friendly and not know what he's saying than the other way around. They say he can't read a map, so I'm not sure what good he can do us anyway."
    I offered him a cigarette and he took it. He got a lighter out of his pants pocket. It was a crude old thing, like a lipstick tube with a wick on top and a striking wheel and flint mounted to the side. He flicked the wheel with his thumb, lit the wick and lit my cigarette then his. He put the lighter out by pushing over a little cap that pivoted to snuff the wick.
    We headed east. Six Track was in its normal place just behind the lead platoon leader's track with the Medic Track immediately behind us. We made good speed because we stayed in the open and avoided all the brush

14—Hoi Chan Fight

we could. The Hoi Chan just sat there. He couldn't have known too much about what was going on. Every time I looked at him he smiled. Twenty minutes on I offered him another cigarette. Again his lighter came out for my cigarette then his.

A klick past the Country Store, we turned generally northeast, headed toward a 400 meter gap between Woods and the north end of the band of brush on the west side of Road 6A. Through the gap we stopped close to the stream that flowed to the north past the eastern end of the Boi Loi Woods into the Saigon River. I couldn't really see the stream, but there was a strip of lush, low vegetation between us and the road. Jackson looked over at the Hoi Chan and pointed to the northeast up the dark green vegetation strip. The Hoi Chan nodded his head and pointed the same way.

Jackson radioed Doc for the interpreter and he came up from the Medic Track. "Ask him if this is the way to the NVA" was followed by a brief exchange in Vietnamese. "He say go that way." "How far?" was followed by more Vietnamese. "He not sure. Maybe five hundred meter. Maybe eight hundred meter. Not sure."

"Are the NVA in the woods?" More Vietnamese. "He say in woods. He say near edge, he know where to turn. He tell you when if you go that way." "How many NVA?" More Vietnamese. "Only a hospital and guards when he leave."

We moved out generally parallel to the vegetation along the stream. We could stay a hundred meters from the edge of the Woods without getting into the really wet ground. About 800 meters on the Hoi Chan pulled on my sleeve and pointed at the Woods just a little in front of us. "Captain, I think he's found it." Jackson looked at where he was pointing and nodded. We kept going until Six Track was a little beyond where the Hoi Chan had pointed and stopped. Jackson pointed at a spot where there was a gap in the brush at the edge of the Woods and the Hoi Chan nodded his head.

Jackson radioed the Platoon Leaders to turn left on line and point the center platoon at the spot the Hoi Chan had identified. The tracks turned and started forward slowly. By the time the line had moved twenty meters toward the edge of the Woods, Six Track and the Medic Track were close behind the middle platoon leader. Our Hoi Chan was getting a little fidgety, so I gave him another cigarette.

Ten meters from the edge, an RPG hit a Sheridan in the center platoon. I heard some enemy automatic weapons fire before the Troop opened up. Then came our wall of noise. The Sheridan that had been hit didn't fire, but the other six with us fired four flechette rounds each as fast as they could load. All of the Track Commanders, including the Sheridans', were firing their .50 calibers. The Medic Track raced past toward the silenced Sheridan with a shocked looking ARVN Lieutenant hanging on in the back.

Colonel McGowan must have been watching over us because Captain Thomas started a fire mission before I did. I could tell from his transmissions that he was inside a helicopter. He called for first rounds about 800 meters inside the Woods. I yelled at Jackson over the firing, "The Liaison Officer has started a fire mission! I'll be in the Woods!" "Roger, gunships are on the way!"

The Troop's fire had slowed some, but was still fairly steady. Chico had our .50 half cocked, but wasn't firing. The crew of the hit Sheridan had bailed out, but it hadn't caught fire. One seriously wounded man from the Sheridan's crew and a less seriously wounded crewmate were being treated at the Medic Track.

Six Track moved up to the right rear of the hit Sheridan and Chico started spraying the Woods in front of the Sheridan with his 50. The Platoon Leader's track had pulled up to the other side and was doing the same. I joined in with my M16, just firing into the Woods in front of me. Four or five bursts from each magazine, then insert a new magazine and do it again. When I released an empty magazine, I just let them drop through the cargo hatch into the track. While we were shooting, one of the Sheridan crew crawled back into the driver's compartment and tried to back it out. The engine wouldn't start. Through it all the Hoi Chan sat quietly beside me.

The Platoon Leader's track traded places with the APC on line to the left of the Sheridan. The line track turned as it backed up until it was behind the Sheridan pointed the other way. The man who had tried to start the Sheridan had come back with its cable and the APC was cross cabled to the Sheridan. The first gunship runs were going in about a hundred meters in front of us into the Woods when the APC slowly pulled the Sheridan straight back. Our fire was not suspended for the helicopter runs and they fired from much higher altitude than they normally did. They were also firing further from us than they normally did.

Whatever damage the Sheridan had suffered, its treads weren't jammed and the APC pulled it back. When the APC and Sheridan had about a fifty meter head start, Jackson ordered the whole Troop to back out. The line backed up at very slow speed maintaining a steady fire into the Woods. When we stopped a hundred meters back, the damaged Sheridan was about as far behind the line as Six Track. The APC that had towed the Sheridan returned to a place on line. The two men left from the Sheridan's crew were on it. Apparently there was still enough battery power to move the turret. They traversed the turret to the rear and stood guard over our backside. The Troop had stopped firing and the gunships were firing rockets into the edge of the Woods directly in front of us.

When the gunships finished, Captain Thomas resumed his fire

mission and had rounds coming in not too far from the edge of the Woods. We got several live shards zinging past and I asked him to move them away. He only got off another battery about two hundred meters further away from us before a helicopter flame bath team arrived. Jackson radioed that he wanted the drop just inside the edge of the Woods directly in front of the center of the Troop. Smoke was popped to mark our center. The first drop looked just right. All the flame was in the Woods, but we could see lots of it, so it had to be close to the edge. The second drop was just a little to the side of the first. While the flame baths were going in, a dust off chopper landed close in behind us and took off the two wounded from the Sheridan and two other walking wounded.

When the flame bath choppers were clear, Captain Thomas moved the artillery fire another two hundred meters away from us and we started forward. The damaged Sheridan stayed where it was with a mortar track left behind with it. Fifty meters from the edge of the Woods the line tracks opened up, not maximum, just steady. We reached the edge of the Woods without any sign of opposition. The line tracks had crashed through about five meters of thick brush when an RPG hit one of the APCs on my side of the line. The sound of the explosion was all the command the Troop needed. The rate of firing went from steady to frantic and the Sheridan main guns joined in as fast as they could load and fire. Every M60 that could be was fired and everyone on a track not driving or firing a machine gun was firing an M16 or M79.

One man was killed by the RPG, but the APC could still drive. As soon as Jackson was sure of the situation, he ordered the Troop to back out again. The process was the same as last time, except the rate of fire was much higher until we were fifty meters away from the Woods. We backed up to where we had stopped before, but stopped firing at fifty meters from the Woods. Almost as soon as we stopped firing, the first Cobra began strafing the edge of the Woods in front of us. The first pass was rockets, then the second of the team with rockets too, then the first again with minigun, then the second with minigun, then two more rocket passes and finally two more minigun runs. When the second team of gunships began the same sequence, I offered the Hoi Chan another cigarette. When he got out his lighter, I got mine out and gestured to trade. He smiled, handed me his lighter, took my Zippo and lit our cigarettes.

While the second team was making its runs, Jackson said that we confirmed four enemy bodies in the five meters we had gotten into the Woods last time. When the second team of gunships left, Captain Thomas was back on the Artillery net to put some rounds into the Woods. Captain Thomas was moving the rounds uncomfortably close when he got shut off for more flame baths. The flame bath choppers hadn't watched us pull back, so we popped smoke for them. This time it was in the middle of the right platoon, instead of the center of the Troop. The result was the same, two large fire balls near the edge of the Woods, directly in front of the smoke.

As the second flame bath Huey pulled away, the line tracks started forward. I asked Jackson before Six Track started, "Once more into the breach?" "Yeah, show time. Keep that artillery far enough out."

At about fifty meters from the Woods the line tracks began steady machine gun fire as we rolled very slowly forward. Captain Thomas was firing again, about six hundred meters inside the Woods, I think. We crossed the fifty meters again without incident and the line tracks had crunched into the brush again before the first RPG hit. This time it was an APC to the left of center. The Troop's full frenzy was the response. I think I heard the sound of two rockets missing off to the left before our noise closed off the world, but I could hear nothing of the enemy after that.

As soon as the firing started again, the Hoi Chan dropped down inside the track. I immediately reversed my rifle so that the barrel was toward him instead of the outside of the track. I didn't think there were any weapons inside, but there were smoke grenades and flares. He picked up the magazines I had dropped and a bandolier of cartridges then sat down on the bench right under me and started reloading the empty magazines. I don't think he saw me move my rifle. Charlie had noticed. "I'll watch him sir."

Our advance had halted immediately with the first hit and Jackson was initially concerned with damage reports. The hit APC had two seriously wounded, but could still drive. Apparently the gooks were also firing other weapons, because there were other wounded. Once the situation was confirmed, the order was to reverse out again. For fifty meters we backed out while maintaining a heavy fire. While we were backing out, the Hoi Chan climbed back up to his seat and offered me five reloaded magazines. I'm not sure I would have trusted him with a rifle, but I don't think he wanted the fight to end with him explaining to his comrades why he was with us. "He put eighteen rounds in each magazine sir." "They must get the same training we do." I took the magazines and nodded. The Hoi Chan smiled.

As we backed over the fifty meter line and stopped firing, the gunships began again. We continued backing up to the Sheridan. When we stopped some of the crews started shifting ammo between tracks. We turned over six cans of .50 caliber to three runners from one of the platoons. This time when the first gunship team was done there was a gap, an almost eerie silence. The spell was broken by an Air Force spotter plane making a low pass and firing two white phosphorus rockets into the Woods directly in front of us. A F100 roared past from right to left across our front, depositing two wing tanks of napalm where the rockets had gone. Once he was well away, his wingman came in for the same. I heard Jackson radio, "right on target," and each jet made a second napalm run after a brief delay.

Before a team of helicopter flame baths went in near where the napalm had gone, I noticed that two APCs were being cabled together and to the damaged Sheridan. Crossed cables connected the two APCs nose to tail and the rear APC was cross cabled to the front of the Sherman. It was well past 1600 and we were far from any friendly place.

While the flame baths went in, Jackson said we were going out the way we came in. After the flame baths, Captain Thomas resumed his mission, but kept the rounds well away. Jackson radioed the platoon leaders to confirm that all personnel were accounted for and that our remaining ammunition had been redistributed. When he was sure, we were off, the way we had come in. Most of the vehicles had their turret or cupola traversed toward the Woods, a few to the other side. We were behind all of the leading platoon and the two APCs towing the Sheridan were immediately behind the Medic Track. Captain Thomas fired a few volleys after we started back, then ended his mission. The only sound now was the noise of the moving vehicles. As loud as that was, it was a frightening silence compared to the rest of the day. Any enemy left in the area showed no further interest in us.

An M88 armored recovery vehicle and a scratch detachment of four headquarters APCs was waiting for us in the middle of the gap we'd passed through in the morning. The M88 took over towing the damaged Sheridan. With an M88 to tow, we traveled at normal speed and retraced our path to Highway 19 and on toward Hampton. We stopped near Checkpoint 06 where a chopper landed to pick up the Hoi Chan. Jackson pointed at the chopper when it landed and the Hoi Chan walked over to meet his escort. I waved at him, he flashed a grin and climbed on the chopper.

The sun was almost down when we arrived at Hampton. Before anybody went to dinner two trucks circled the perimeter dropping off ammo to the tracks. Refueling waited until after dinner. Our ARVN Lieutenant took the evening chopper back to Cu Chi.

After dinner I visited Doc to ask about a wounded man I had seen loaded on a chopper with a needle taped to his arm and nothing connected. "The biggest threat from most serious wounds is blood loss. My job is to slow the bleeding and get an IV going. It's just salt water to replace lost blood volume. Men who arrived at the hospital alive have died because the hospital team couldn't get an IV needle into their collapsed veins before they died of shock. If the dust off arrives before I have an IV hung, I have to decide whether to ship him or not. If it's a real dust off chopper with a medic on board, he should be able to start the IV on the way in. If it's just a Cav slick, it's a tougher choice. The guy you saw had a capped IV needle in his arm. I had time to stick him and tape it to his arm. I thought he could get to the hospital without a risk of shock. If I was wrong, at least they wouldn't have had to hunt for a vein."

May 21

Our platoons cleared Route 1 north to Checkpoint 22 and south to Trang Bang, the road over to Checkpoint 18 and Highway 19 between Trang Bang and Xom Bao Don. The Troop reassembled at Xom Bao Don to load fifty RFs with a U.S. Sergeant advisor, then headed to the south side of the open area south of the Woods. One or two of the hooches we visited on the 19th had been vacated, the rest had not. We stopped at the clusters of hooches and the people were again told to move to the government relocation center. The RFs found a few chickens and a pig to requisition. We saw one family packing and finally moving off in a buffalo cart piled with all of their household goods. The cart had two huge wooden wheels, a small body and two poles in front with a lumbering water buffalo between them.

Two of the houses had unusually large rice supplies. More than a year's supply for the family in the house, a family that had not planted a crop the prior season. Most of that rice was confiscated. It was either VC supply or certain to become so. The rice was donated by us and the RFs to the RFs.

When we were done for the day, we mounted up all the RFs and took an open path back to Highway 19. When we got to the compound at Xom Bao Don, the RFs were all in good spirits as they carried the confiscated rice in. Almost as soon as we stopped, an RF came running out with big glass of beer with ice in it for the advisor Sergeant. There were beads of humidity condensing on the outside of the glass. The Sergeant was kind enough to walk away from us before he started drinking it. We went back to Hampton.

May 22

After the same road work as yesterday, we reassembled at Checkpoint 18 and then went south to spend the morning investigating brush east of the Citadel. In the morning, we found nothing. After lunch, we resumed the same program. At 1320 we had a ten minute rain break. About 1400 we took an incoming round and Jackson pulled the platoons together on line pointed at where the shot seemed to have come from.

We were facing west. The platoon leaders' tracks were right up against the line and we were closer in than usual too. When we started forward, there was sporadic rifle fire from what appeared to be scattered individuals hiding in the brush. Whenever one of the enemy fired, there was a spirited burst of return fire, but there was not a continuous blast of fire from our line tracks. There had been no RPGs fired and the enemy fire was more like sniping than a fire fight. The CO didn't request any artillery and I didn't have any idea where to fire, there wasn't any direction that serious fire was coming from.

I couldn't fire my M16 at anything, because we were behind our own tracks and they were too close together to fire between them. All I could do was sit and wait. I dozed off. "Foxy, wake up. We're getting shot at. Nobody should be sleeping!" When I looked at the CO, he laughed. The fight, such as it was, was about over. It just petered out. We stopped getting shot at, pushed on for a while then turned around.

On our trip to Hampton there was a short rain between Ap Suoi Cao and Go Dau Ha. By the time we got back to Hampton, it seemed everyone in the Troop knew that I had fallen asleep while we were getting shot at. Some of the troopers kidded me as if they thought it was a sign of bravery. I think it was being afraid and not being able to do anything.

May 23

We cleared the same roads again then went to the RF compound at Xom Bao Don to pick up some of the same RFs as two days before. This time there seemed to be more of them and there were more officers. I think they liked our success at finding rice. After the RFs were all loaded, we went back to Ap Suoi Cao and stopped near the south edge of the space below the Woods. The RFs searched the first hooch we came to, then set it on fire. Colonel McGowan arrived by helicopter and told Jackson that U.S. troops should not burn a hooch. The RFs repeated search and burn for several empty hooches. Colonel McGowan called his helicopter back and left.

Finally we came to a hooch where a family remained. The RFs pulled out an old man, a woman and a boy. After a great deal of yelling the RFs set the place on fire. I don't know if they offered one more last chance to clear the hut, but nothing came out. When the smoke from five or six huts on the west end of the fields was curling toward the sky, we could see the remaining residents in the area rapidly packing, some already on the move in buffalo carts.

Jackson announced that one of the Assistant Division Commanders was about to land and visit us. Colonel McGowan was in the air over one of the other Troops nearby and landed before the General arrived. When the General's helicopter approached, Colonel McGowan popped the welcoming smoke. The General got out, spoke to Colonel McGowan near the helicopter and left quickly. From a distance we could tell that all was not well. The General's posture was entirely formal and as he talked, he stood much closer to Colonel McGowan than normal. When Colonel McGowan came back to Six Track, he was not happy. He told the CO to stop the RFs from burning any more huts.

The General had reminded Colonel McGowan of a standing Division order that U.S. troops were not to be present when any homes were burned. Having seen the smoke from the burning hooches, the General probably had landed to give the message personally because he didn't want to use the radio. Corps Headquarters sometimes monitored the radio transmissions of lower commands and the General didn't want to discuss hooch burning over the radio and take the chance of being overheard. Part of the problem was that smoke from a burning hooch was visible from far away. Any newsmen in the area would try to get to the smoke if they could cajole a helicopter pilot to get them there. Stateside, before I came over, I had seen the press coverage of a Marine setting fire to an empty grass hut and I'm sure that the General didn't want publicity like that screwing up his career.

As soon as the General left, we stopped for lunch. Jackson, the senior RF and his advisor discussed the General's visit and the senior RF agreed not to burn any more hooches. It may have had something to do with all of the rice we had been donating to the RFs. The afternoon was spent searching hooches without burning them. Maybe the point had been made anyway. We saw several buffalo carts leaving and all the hooches we searched in the afternoon had been left before we got there. Of course they were still there for anyone who needed a roof for the night.

Burning a few hooches had emptied the others in the area very quickly, but we burned no more that day, or ever again. As we finished up the searches for the day, several hooches were damaged by passing tracks that may have deliberately misjudged the clearance, but no more were burned down. Most of the hooches stayed vacant, or least vacant when we were in the area, but a few families started filtering back within weeks.

We often took the time to crush the crudest bunker that we found, some just a foxhole with half a roof, but we were prohibited from burning down huts that were grand hotels by comparison. Faced with the possibility that denying shelter to the enemy might generate bad press, our leaders opted to leave them shelter.

At the end of the day, we took the RFs back to Xom Bao Don with a small load of goods they had collected. We retraced our route to pick up our trains at Checkpoint 18 and laager east of the Ap Suoi Cao fields. After dinner Jackson got a message from the First Sergeant that Gary Carlson's wife had delivered a healthy daughter on May 21.

May 24

A Second Platoon track passed close to Six Track with a Track Commander who was bare chested and wearing an NVA sun helmet. Jackson was on the radio to the Platoon Leader immediately, forcefully explaining the multiple errors involved. Apparently Lieutenant Nowak was equally forceful when he contacted the Track Commander because he was dressed in fatigue blouse, flak jacket and radio helmet within a few hundred yards. Going out without a helmet and flak jacket was bad enough; wearing a distinctive item of enemy uniform was idiotic.

At the highway, Second Platoon turned south to Trang Bang. The rest of us headed north. The trains stopped to wait at Checkpoint 18 while we continued on to Xom Bao Don. Our pickup was about forty RFs, There was one older guy who was followed by an RF with a radio. I think he was a warrant officer.

Second Platoon rejoined us south of Ap Suoi Cao and we took our conventional route south of the village fields to just south of the Country Store. We turned south, then slowed to form on line as we approached the brush that marked the southern edge of the open area. As soon as we were on line we stopped and the RFs and a few of our troopers dismounted. Nobody hurried, but I was surprised that the RFs stayed well in front of the tracks. Our troopers stayed close to the vehicles. We stopped often and the RFs searched several areas very carefully, but they stayed in front of the tracks all morning. When it was time for lunch, we stopped and waved them back.

About halfway through lunch, twenty RFs moved rapidly into the brush to our south. "Captain Jackson, where are they going?" He looked up, "I don't know. Damn, what are they up to." He was on the radio immediately. A query on the Troop net apparently brought no information. He tried Squadron to check in any information was coming in from any RF liaison. He was still trying four or five minutes after they left where there was a sharp burst of automatic rifle fire, due south of us. I couldn't tell what the weapons were, but I could tell that they weren't shooting at us.

Jackson checked the platoons and ordered all the vehicles started and ready to move. Then he went back to the Squadron radio net, with no result. Two RFs came back into view smiling and waving some gook gear about the same time Jackson got some information from Squadron. "RF command at Xom Bao Don has reported overrunning a squad of VC at lunch. Looks like it was our batch that did it."

We loaded the RFs and moved slowly south through the brush. Two hundred meters on we found the rest in a small clearing. They had two dead gooks, a wounded prisoner, one AK47 and the remains of a small cooking fire. Some of the RFs were eating what looked like hot fresh rice off big leaves. They had put a field dressing on the prisoner's biggest wound. Doc put the prisoner on a litter, hung an IV and started covering all of his wounds.

After a bit of pantomime, it was clear that the RFs thought that the rest of the gooks had headed south. Jackson gestured for them to lead and we followed on line. As soon as we reached a clearing large enough, Six Track and the Medic Track paused to load the prisoner on a dust off.

We didn't find the rest. Eventually we reached the open area that extended across the bottom of the Citadel and Jackson called a halt. He whistled for the RFs and waved them back to load up. Our troopers were quicker than usual to offer a hand to pull an RF aboard. Most of the RFs waved goodbye when they got off at Xom Bao Don. The old man just got off and never looked back. Our tracks pivoted on the road and headed back to Ap Suoi Cao to pick up our trains. We laagered two hundred meters south of last night.

At our evening briefing Jackson passed on the prisoner's initial interrogation. He and his friends were NVA recently sent to join some VC main force battalion. They were just starting to eat when the RFs blew them away. Three or four of the lunch party were unaccounted for. It made no sense. Enemy soldiers gathered around a boy scout campfire during daylight? They hadn't heard us two hundred meters away? It had to be true, there were two corpses and a prisoner.

Jackson told us Rome Plows were going into the Upper Boi Loi and then casually mentioned that we were going in on stand down tomorrow night. Both were good news, but the stand down was more immediately good. After the Platoon Leaders left, he said that he was scheduled to rotate out of the field June 5.

May 25

At stand to, our laager was decorated by puddles. After breakfast, First and Second Platoons went with the trains to Highway 19 then swept to Xom Bao Don and Trang Bang respectively. We stayed with Third Platoon. When the roads were done and both platoons returned, we did nothing for a while, then formed on line and headed north. For a klick we moved very slowly through nothing. When we finally reached some scattered brush, each bush was carefully checked. Some stretches were moderate vegetation, but we never got near the edge of the Upper Boi Loi Woods. At noon when we stopped, we hadn't even reached the trace of Highway 26 into the Woods.

At lunch Jackson referred to our mission for the day as a "pre-stand down special." Squadron knew there was nothing where we were looking, but on the Division map, it looked like we were in the brush like any other day.

After a leisurely lunch we pushed on, slowly, to the unused part of Highway 26 then turned down the road into the back of Xom Bao Don. When we reached Highway 19 at Checkpoint 25, we stopped pointed at the intersection waiting for the returning convoy. It was an hour until we got a message that the head of the convoy was less than a mile away. We pulled on Highway 19 before they arrived and proceeded south at road speed through Ap Suoi Cao, Trang Bang and points down on Route 1 to the town of Cu Chi and my favorite left turn to Cu Chi base camp.

Dinner was hamburgers and hot dogs with real ice cream for dessert. After dinner I went straight to the Officers' Club. A new NCO bartender was there and opened the bar a little early for me. Folks dribbled in as I nursed a beer. When Carlson stopped by, his newborn daughter was sincerely toasted by Bravo's officers, joined by all present.

May 26

There was a memorial service at 1000. It was the same as the one in March, but this time there were only three pairs of boots next to the door. When we were in last month, we hadn't needed a service.

May 27

After dinner, beers in the Officers' Club were interrupted by a cry of, "Hey that's Bravo." AFVN TV was rebroadcasting the network news story about Bravo in the Country Store that had been filmed on April 16. They showed the Colonel McGowan interview, but nothing with Jackson. He got kidded a little about being left on the cutting room floor, but he didn't seem too upset. "Rank has its privileges."

May 28

At 1540 a steady rain fell on Cu Chi. I was inside the officers' hooch when it started and stayed inside for twenty or thirty minutes until it stopped. Word at the officers' table at dinner was that the 25th Aviation Battalion Officers' Club was the place to be tonight. They were having a "smoker" with several films. Carlson had to stay in the Troop area, so we took his jeep.

15

Baby Dumpling

May 29

Leaving Cu Chi was like all the other times. I don't know when he arrived, but Nam was back on the Medic Track. When we got to Trang Bang we turned north on Highway 19. We turned right at the south edge of Ap Suoi Cao. Jackson said that the Third Platoon was going on to Checkpoint 18 to complete our road sweep, then catching up with us.

We spent the day searching at the southern edge of the open area south of the Country Store. We found close to nothing and laagered east of the edge of the village fields, I called in three standard targets, but fired in the east one right on the edge of the Woods.

May 30

I had to move my morning shower to avoid a puddle where I normally would have stood. I always made some mud showering, but the puddle from the night's rain would have overwhelmed my shower clogs.

We pulled out of laager and headed south toward the Citadel. We avoided brush until we broke through the Citadel's northern end. We were halfway between the east and west sides. Second Platoon peeled off to the west as the rest of us continued south. About 800 meters on, Six Track and the Medic Track stopped and First Platoon headed west. Third Platoon continued on to the southwest. Jackson said the platoons were going to do separate searches and we'd be sitting for a while. We sat for several hours as the platoons worked south, then moved south a klick to get near their center.

After lunch, I heard Jackson radio the Platoon Leaders to pull back into the center of the Citadel and identify their troops from Texas, Utah and Tennessee. "Where you from, Foxy?" "Oklahoma." "Sorry, you don't get to play. Our visiting Senators only want to meet lads from their home states."

We formed a rough laager and waited half an hour for further word. Something came in on his radio and Jackson called for the home state detail. There were ten troopers who qualified. The CO formed them in a line just outside the laager about the same time a couple of slicks came overhead and somebody popped smoke. One landed and Colonel McGowan, two other officers and five civilians in khaki safari suits got off. Three of the civilians, who turned out to be the Senators, took off their flak jackets as soon as they got off. Jackson was introduced to the three Senators and led them to meet the selected troops. The two other civilians kept their flak jackets on and spent all of their time filming the Senators shaking hands and talking to the troops. I noticed that two Senators often politely withdrew from camera view from time to time so that the third could be photographed alone with one of the brave boys from his state. I guess that's why they held a formation in Indian country outside the laager and the Senators took off their flak jackets; better photographs.

The review took about fifteen minutes, ending with each of the Senators being filmed shaking Jackson's hand with the Troop in the background. The last Senator to get on the chopper turned and waved to the rest of us just before climbing on. I don't think they got that on film. Jackson walked directly back and climbed aboard. "Well there's another critical fact finding tour successfully completed. Our prize is that we're done for the day."

We went out the north end of the Citadel and on to a laager behind Ap Suoi Cao, fifteen hundred meters west of the Woods. Like the night before, I put my eastern defensive target in the tree line. Our trains arrived an hour later. At the evening briefing after dinner the Platoon Leaders kidded Jackson about his high level protocol and liaison skills. He told them to worry about their LPs and he'd handle Congressional relations.

May 31

The morning chopper brought Warrant Officer Walker from the 25th Military Intelligence Company with a very fancy radio and a motion sensor he was going to plant in the Country Store.

We went to the Country Store. Even with most of the brush gone, the trails through the remnants still showed heavy traffic. After searching that found nothing, Six Track ended up next to a cluster of brush near a heavily traveled north-south trail. Line tracks and dismounts were scattered all around us. Our spook got off and went into the brush alone. Ten minutes later he came back.

"Watson, where do you put that clump on the map?" I used my pen to point on the map where he'd put the sensor. He compared that to where he'd marked it on his map.

"I agree." He turned on his radio and called in a report that I assume included reporting the sensor's location. The Troop continued on to complete the search of the remainder of the Country Store. After lunch, we headed south and the platoons were cut loose for separate searches. Most of the time Walker and I shared cigarettes and chatted about nothing. The center of the Troop was moving so slowly that I rarely had any reason to call in a new location. At 1400 Jackson called in the platoons and we headed toward the eastern end of the village fields then turned north.

Walker spoke, "Watson, I've got motion." "What?" "I've got motion on the sensor. Can you shoot it? We're not set up yet."

"Are you kidding?" It wasn't even dusk yet. "Can you tell what it is?" "No joke. I can't tell what, but something's moving." I called in a battery three mission on a "motion sensor report" at the location we'd plotted "at my command." Clearance came very quickly. Walker confirmed that there was still motion and I called for "fire for effect." "On the way" came soon and a distant rumble behind us soon after that. "Could you tell when the rounds landed?" "Yeh, they shook it up real good. Can't tell exactly where they landed, but I think they were close, close enough to scare the crap out of anybody who survived."

By the time the mission was over, Six Track had stopped pointed north and the laager was forming up around us. We were a little north of the opening between the Upper and Lower Boi Loi Woods, about a klick from the edge of the heavy brush. There weren't any more motion readings after the fire mission. The evening chopper arrived a few minutes after the trains. I walked with Walker to the chopper. "Good luck, Lieutenant. Next time you're in Cu Chi come see me." "Luck to you, Walker. Blow 'em away."

At the evening briefing Jackson said we were further north than usual because Alpha was spending the night in the Upper Boi Loi with the 60th Land Clearing Company. They were starting to Rome Plow the Woods. Lieutenant Nowak suggested paving it.

June 1

We were all up at 0600, on our way by 0730 and approaching the southern edge of the Lower Boi Loi Woods northwest of the Country Store at 0800. The drill was the same as usual, form on line in the open, approach the edge and enter the hot, humid embrace.

For the next two hours I smoked and sweated continuously as we moved slowly through the tangled brush to the northeast. Most of the time no one was dismounted. At the end of the two hours, we were almost in the center of the big end of the Woods' pork chop shape. At least I think that's where we were.

We pivoted right and headed about due south. Our speed and progress were about the same, but at least we were headed out. After another hour and a half we broke through the southern edge of the Woods a klick east of the Country Store. When we turned west through the narrow space between the Woods and the Country Store I was very careful to radio our position frequently. We might be shaking the ground in the Country Store. We continued west and stopped for lunch at 1220 in a rough laager four hundred meters south of the western end of the Woods.

At 1320 we started off again. We went around the west end of the Woods and headed north to a little less than a klick south of Highway 26, near our February and April fights in the Upper Boi Loi Woods. Then we headed east on line. We went into the Woods for half an hour or so then turned and came out. Jackson never said what we were looking for or why we had done sweeps in widely separated parts of the Woods. We broke back out of the Woods at 1510 and headed south. We took a standard route back to Hampton and were inside at 1620. The Cav S1 had a table set up for pay call next to the dinner line.

It started raining just after dinner and continued for half an hour. Jackson, Charlie and I stayed in Six Track with the hatches closed and the back ramp down. I read until it stopped raining. The rest of our crew kept dry in the bunker next to the track.

June 2

We left Hampton at 0730. Charlie stayed behind to go in for his pay. The whole Troop cleared the road into Go Dau Ha and across to Checkpoint 18. We went south of the village fields, then turned north toward the Upper Boi Loi Woods. Alpha Troop was babysitting the Rome Plows that were cutting and clearing a big "X" in the Upper Boi Loi Woods. The Rome Plows were bulldozers made in Rome, Georgia, and specially equipped with heavy duty brush cutting blades on the front and a cage of steel pipe with a roof to protect the driver from falling trees and brush.

They had done a lot on the line of the X that started on the edge of the Woods a little north of where unused Highway 26 ran into the Woods and went northeast to the edge of the Woods near the Saigon River. They had cut an initial swath all the way through and were working on widening the cut. The cleared area still had the felled brush and trees in a jumble on the ground. The ride through the cleared area was rougher and slower than through open rice paddies, but faster than in the standing brush and trees plus you could see.

We started up the cut at 0840. We came up on the working parties before we were too far in. There were two separate teams of three bulldozers working to widen the strip. The three dozers of each team worked quite close together with an Alpha platoon standing by. The platoon stayed on the cleared side, not in the Woods, just out of falling tree range. The two teams and their guardians were only a couple of hundred meters apart. We didn't see them, but apparently Alpha's third platoon was in the Woods nearby.

We kept going up the cut until we came to a spot where the other line of the "X" crossed. That was the Rome Plow's and Alpha's nightly laager. A larger area had been cleared. The bulldozers had pushed up an earthen berm in a rough circle with four gaps for gates. The Alpha Six Track, Medic Track and two other APCs were still there. The other line of the "X" was much narrower, but still wide enough to speed our passage and give a few meters open space on each side of the column. We turned northwest up the crossing cut, went on a klick then moved into the Woods on the right side of the cut and began moving on line parallel to the cut. We stopped for lunch for forty-five minutes, then resumed the sweep.

We had only done two klicks when one of the APCs threw a track. Putting a track back on in the heavy brush was a horrible job. The circle of the track had to be opened then the track laid out in a straight line for the vehicle to be driven back onto the track. In the open it wasn't all that bad a job, but in the Woods, it was a nightmare that took well over half an hour to get done. The APC was back in operation at 1530 and we moved into the cut strip and went back out the way we had come in. When we got to the edge of the Woods, we paralleled Highway 26 to Highway 19 at Xom Bao Don and were back in Hampton at 1700. Charlie was standing in front of the bunker at Six Track's parking place when we pulled in.

June 3

We were out the gate at 0730. The puddles from the night's rain weren't much of a problem, except they watered the mud ring inside Hampton. Today Lewis stayed behind to go in for his pay. We cleared the road to Checkpoint 18 and went in behind Ap Suoi Cao to the gap between the Upper and Lower Boi Loi Woods. We stayed on the south side of the stream, then changed to on line as soon as the northern edge of the Lower Woods moved close to the stream. The left end of our line was in the almost open wet land next to the stream; the middle was in light brush and the right end in the Woods.

We had done less than a klick on line when a Sheridan near our left end hit a mine. There were no casualties and the damage to the vehicle was minor. The track wasn't even broken, but we stopped long enough to replace two damaged track blocks.

The map showed dirt trails on both sides of the stream and scattered huts in the gap. There was no sign of trails or huts on the ground. We didn't find anything, but we still moved carefully and slowly. It took us about three hours to sweep another five klicks to where the opening started to get wider, about at the most northerly point of the Lower Boi Loi Woods. Where it was wide enough to give a sense of comfort, we stopped for lunch. At 1350 we headed back the way we came. We were back to relatively open space at 1515 and in Hampton at 1610. Lewis was waiting where Charlie had been the night before.

June 4

Our morning road drill was the same as yesterday. When we got to Checkpoint 18, we headed north to Xom Bao Don and picked up forty RFs. From the RF compound we went parallel to Highway 26 to where the southwest arm of the X cut began at the edge of the Upper Boi Loi Woods. It appeared a little wider than two days before. We formed up just inside the cut on line facing the southeastern edge of the cut. Ten meters into the Woods we stopped and our dismounts and the RFs climbed off and poked around a little. When they'd had long enough to find anything that might be there, we backed out, side slipped toward the center of the X and repeated the cycle. Then again for several times. Our searches were close together, but we didn't search everywhere as we moved sideways toward the center of the X.

At lunch time we were near Alpha's hard site in the center of the X. That time we didn't push the vehicles into the brush, just moved to the edge of the cut and sent the dismounts in a little way on foot. As soon as they came back, we broke out the C-rations, gave some to the RFs and ate.

After eating we continued up the northeast arm. It was also noticeably wider than last time. We did several similar shallow searches into the edge of the arm. By 1515 we were almost out of the Woods toward the Saigon River. Our turn to head back through the track on a Third Platoon Sheridan. After a while with no success, Jackson radioed to Squadron we couldn't get the track remounted where we were. "We're towing it to Alpha hardsite. They've got a reasonably cleared area. The crew should be able to put it back together tonight and we'll pick them up in the morning."

I nodded. It was only a few minutes until another Sheridan was connected to the defective one. Towing in the mess was slow, but the Alpha hard site wasn't very far. When we arrived our column passed by the hard site, but the towing Sheridan went directly inside the berm and deposited the damaged Sheridan. As soon as it disconnected, the towing vehicle joined us. In the whole day's searching we had found nothing.

We went back to Xom Bao Don the way we had come in and dropped off the RFs. At 1800 we pulled off Route 1 into Hampton. At our night briefing, Jackson reminded us tomorrow was his last day as CO, "so let's do it right."

June 5

I was shaken awake and called to the Squadron Headquarters about 0100. Alpha's position in the Upper Boi Loi had been mortared just after midnight and was still under attack. Every night since they started the X they had taken a few rifle rounds, just enough to let them know that they were not welcome. Apparently the VC or the NVA had decided to hit harder. No plan was announced, but we knew we had been called in for the horrible possibility that we would have to go to Alpha's aid. From the radio traffic it sounded as if they were taking fire, but there was no sign of a ground assault, just steady fire from the fallen trees surrounding the laager. Still, Alpha had one killed, one critically wounded and fifteen other wounded.

The Squadron radio traffic included a report that the division medevac helicopter refused to land for the critically wounded man. Colonel McGowan was overhead and got the kid out on his command LOH. After an hour it seemed to be all over and we were released to go back to sleep. Our regular wake up was at 0600. We were out the gate at 0720 to pick up forty RFs at Xom Bao Don at 0800.

We went toward the beginning of the southwest arm of the X then up to the hard site. As we got close, Third Platoon's Sheridan came out to join us, apparently repaired from the day before and not damaged during the night. From the middle of the X, I could see they were working on the southeast arm. They were far enough away that I couldn't see vehicles, but I could see the top of a standing tree shaking then falling.

The southwest arm we had come in on was now almost 200 meters wide and the crossing arm almost half that. We went on a little past the hard site and started the drill of going into the Woods a short distance into the side of the northeast arm then having our dismounts, mostly RFs, search around. We repeated the cycle several times, nearing the river end of the cut then starting back along the other side. We didn't find much. We stopped for lunch at 1100, about halfway back to the hard site.

While we were eating, one of the crew of the Sheridan that had spent the night with Alpha came over. He didn't say much about the basic fight, but he was eager to talk about the dust off. We had heard about the problem on the radio. One of Alpha's men needed a critical dust off. Delta Troop Cobras were flying firing runs around the laager and taking ground fire from the attackers. The Division medevac helicopters wouldn't go into the dark small landing area under fire.

Colonel McGowan was over the area in his LOH. When the medevac pilot wouldn't go in, he decided to use his own ship. When they had briefed the ground unit and the two other pilots involved, two Delta Troop Cobras and the LOH came in three abreast with the LOH in the middle, just like a regular strafing run with the gunships firing outside the perimeter of the hard site with rockets and machine guns. The LOH made a low run in and instead of pulling up, it landed next to a strobe light near the middle of the position. The gunships finished their strafing run, pulled up and loitered until called back.

On the ground, before the helicopters came in, the wounded man had been strapped to a stretcher with an IV in his arm. When the Colonel's LOH landed, the stretcher was strapped to the rear bench and the gunships called back to strafe again on the same route. This time, the LOH joined the second half of the run, lifting off as the gunship fire was striking outside the perimeter. A few minutes later the kid was unloaded at the evacuation hospital in Cu Chi and survived.

We moved out after lunch toward the hard site. When we got to the center, we turned up the northwest arm and went about a klick before heading west into the Woods. We were traveling almost in a straight line back toward Xom Bao Don. The first klick or so through the Woods was heavy brush with scattered trees, a hot, slow, jarring ride. After the first klick, the brush got lighter as we swept toward Checkpoint 25.

We got an afternoon cloudburst in the lighter brush. I put on the civilian olive drab rain jacket I brought from home. Jackson put on a similar jacket. Half our troops put on an Army poncho, the others just got wet. All the RFs just got wet. By 1430 we were only two klicks east of the RF compound and moving easily through light brush. After unloading the RFs at their compound we pulled into Hampton at 1545.

As soon as Six Track was parked in its usual slot, our new CO came over, First Lieutenant Peter Wells. Jackson introduced him to me and Chico then to the rest of our crew. Jackson immediately pulled out his personal gear, stacked it on the open rear ramp, and shook hands all around. "Good luck, Foxy." "Good luck sir."

He picked up his bags and walked to the Squadron headquarters tent. It was a while before the evening chopper left for Cu Chi with him on it. Nowak went in with him to become our new XO. Carlson had made Captain and was the new CO of Charlie Troop. As soon as Jackson left Six Track, Lieutenant Wells called the platoon leaders to a briefing after dinner.

June 6

Beginning was the same as yesterday, out at 0725 headed for the RFs at Xom Bao Don. At 0810 we were picking up another group of forty with a new advisor. The advisor climbed on Six Track with his RF RTO. He was a lifer, a Sergeant First Class, E7. His counterpart, an RF Lieutenant with another RTO, climbed on the Medic Track.

After we were loaded we started toward the Upper Boi Loi Woods. Then we turned to the south going across the fields west of the Upper Boi Loi Woods to the western end of the Lower Boi Loi Woods. We curved around the end and formed on line then moved slowly into the Woods headed northeast. Our next hour of slow jarring progress through the heavy brush and small trees took us in two klicks to a clearing that the map showed at the junction of two foot paths. We'd been close before, but this was the first time we'd gone into this clearing. The clearing was about a hundred meters in diameter and we stopped in a circle of vehicles just inside the clearing's edge to check it out. The Sergeant muttered, "I'm too old for walking in the woods," as he got off to join our dismounts and the RFs. The search found nothing more than signs of recent foot traffic on the trails.

From the clearing we moved north for about half an hour and broke through into the gap between the Upper and Lower Boi Loi Woods. A little up the gap on the other side I could see the cleared area where the southeastern arm of the X cut ended. It was 1100 and we stopped for lunch with the mortar tracks and another track from each platoon pointed back toward the Woods we had just left. I radioed in our position, "stopped for lunch" and applied myself to some canned peaches. The Sergeant expressed a desire for a canned pecan roll because he'd "been eating too much rice and mystery meat."

We were on our way again at 1200, forming a line to go back into the Woods almost due east. Half an hour earned us 800 meters and a thrown track on an APC. Fixing it in the brush took half an hour. As soon as the track was repaired, we turned northwest to take the shortest route back to the gap between the Upper and Lower Boi Loi Woods, turned left and headed out.

At 1440 we were all the way back to near the western end of the Lower Boi Loi and Wells was coordinating a pick up of a LRP team in the brush at the end of the Woods. While the rest of the Troop stood off a little, Second Platoon pulled up to the edge of the brush on line. Eight LRPs walked out and climbed on board. Once the LRPs were on board, we went back to Highway 19 and unloaded at the RF compound then headed to Hampton. The LRPs got off at the entrance to wait for their chopper.

I met Nowak's replacement, Second Lieutenant Tim Murray, when he came to Six Track for the evening briefing. After the briefing, Wells said Murray was only a few days from being promoted to First Lieutenant.

June 7

Using Hampton's shower was a substantially greater effort now that the perimeter road was churned mud. Most of the inside of Hampton was still firm, but there was enough rain now that the part the tracks kneaded every day was horrible. It looked a lot like the canned chocolate pudding my parents sent by mail. The immediate area around Six Track was OK, but to cross the mud ring to get to the shower I wore unlaced boots. I had to be careful they didn't get sucked off. On my return I scraped off the mud so it wouldn't get spread all over Six Track.

We left Hampton at 0730 and cleared the road to Ap Suoi Cao. At Checkpoint 18 we turned south, passed our normal turn just south of the village, then turned east a little further on. By 0820 we were east of Highway 19 on line pointed south into scattered brush east of the road. For the next three hours we swept slowly keeping about the same distance from the road. We found nothing. At 1130 we turned east and swept on line through the western tree line of the Citadel. When we reached the center near the southern end, we parked for lunch.

After lunch we moved a klick past the south end of the Citadel. Six Track and the Medic Track parked in the center of an open area and the platoons started separate searches. When that area had been checked, we moved to a new area and repeated the process several times. At 1545 we had reached the northern end of a series of fields that was generally clear of brush all the way to Highway 19 due south of where we were. Wells called the Troop back into a line formation and we slowly swept south to the road.

We pulled up onto the highway at 1630 near Checkpoint Z and turned left. Minutes later we were in the center of Trang Bang surrounded by civilian bustle. From there we drove up Route 1 to Hampton at a leisurely pace through local traffic.

June 8

We were called out at 0500 and beginning road sweeps at 0630. It was a road day. The platoons cleared north on Route 22 to the Big Rubber, south on Route 1 to Trang Bang and across to Checkpoint 18. When that was done, the Troop outposted Route 22 from just north of Go Dau Ha to the Big Rubber. Other than one sniper round the day was a snooze.

The tail end of the convoy returning from Tay Ninh passed the northern end of our outposts at 1325 and the outposts followed behind it. The tail of the convoy cleared Checkpoint 05 in Go Dau Ha at 1410. Bravo was close behind and in Hampton at 1425.

June 9

The Troop left Hampton about 0730, swept Route 1 down to Trang Bang and turned north on Highway 19. We went about a klick north to a fork in the road. We took the right fork, Road 6A, and stopped at an RF compound just outside the village. The compound was smaller than Hampton, but looked more permanent. You couldn't see much inside of it. It was triangular rather than circular and the barbed wire was much more extensive. There was a path through the wire that zigzagged out to the road. The movable barriers that closed the path had already been moved out of the way.

There was no sign of anyone in the compound when we stopped, but almost as soon as we did, RFs started filing out. There were thirty of them led by a man with just a swagger stick, a Warrant Officer. Besides not carrying a weapon, he was better dressed than the others and an RF RTO followed him. Most of the RFs carried one grenade, the RTO carried a couple of smoke grenades. All of them carried some ammunition, but it didn't seem like very much. Three of them had a hundred rounds of ammo for their one M60 draped around their neck like a scarf.

Wells dismounted and conferred with the Warrant Officer and Nam. The Warrant Officer, his RTO and Nam got on the Medic Track. The rest of the RFs rode on the APCs behind the Medic Track, four or five to a track. They were all loaded about 0830. We moved northerly parallel to the west side of 6A for about fifteen hundred meters then went north through open fields for another three klicks. Then all the vehicles turned left and we were on line facing a heavy hedgerow about a klick west.

We came up slowly on the hedgerow and stopped fifty meters from it. The CO talked to the RF Warrant Officer again, then our dismounts and all the RFs got down and walked between the tracks as they advanced slowly again. The tracks stopped about ten meters from the hedgerow and the dismounts and RFs continued forward into the hedgerow. Nobody rushed in but they moved in steadily. Often it seemed that the RFs hung back whenever there was something like this to check, but today they didn't. We shifted up and down the hedgerow and checked it carefully for a couple of hours. We found nothing.

Just after noon, we went across the hedgerow on line into the open area just south of the Citadel. Almost immediately someone reported seeing gooks in the hedgerow across the field. When our dismounts and the RFs were back on board and the Troop about halfway toward the sighting, Wells cleared a reconnaissance by fire. We stopped and each platoon's APCs fired a few short bursts of .50 caliber into the hedgerow. We waited a few minutes without response then we did it again. Still no response. Wells called off the recon by fire and moved us north into the Citadel. We went a klick in and stopped for lunch at 1300.

After an hour we loaded up again and went south out of the Citadel. Just about where we had stopped before lunch one of our APCs hit a mine. There were no casualties, but a track was broken and had to be repaired. Wells put the two other platoons on line between us and the place the enemy had been sighted, while the damaged vehicle's platoon provided local security for the repairs. Our dismounts and the RFs checked the immediate area around the vehicles for signs of mines or recent activity. It took almost an hour to replace a road wheel and replace the damaged track blocks. When that was done we began a slow advance toward the hedgerow to the west. We had only moved a hundred meters when we were welcomed with sporadic rifle fire, and an RPG fired wildly up into the sky, all from the area we had fired into before lunch.

The Troop responded almost immediately with machine gun fire and continued moving slowly forward. The APC to our left front, Baby Dumpling's track, had to slow even more to cross an old trench and fell behind us. Baby Dumpling was a big, chunky, friendly dismount who rode on the track. Somebody else was the Track Commander, but it was Baby Dumpling's track. The CO halted the Troop, still a good distance from the hedgerow. As we stopped, I felt the flash of an explosion to the left behind us. An RPG had hit Baby Dumpling's track.

Almost as soon as the track was hit, Doc and our other medic were up on the back of the APC pulling a man out. The driver and the track commander were stumbling away from the front of the vehicle. Bright red flames leapt out of the open cargo hatch chasing the man that Doc and his assistant had pulled out. They brought him next to Six Track. We were the closest track, but didn't carry any special medical supplies. When they reached us, Doc checked the wounded man and stuck a capped IV needle

15—Baby Dumpling

in his left arm. The other medic had already reached the Medic Track and was running back with a stretcher over one shoulder and an IV bottle in the other hand. Within thirty seconds the fire in the burning track was being punctuated by the ammunition and grenades in the track exploding.

While Doc was working, I could see the kid's left foot was blown off at the ankle. Doc worked on getting a field dressing over the stump first. Then I saw why the IV needle had gone in his left arm. The muscle of the kid's right arm ended about in the middle of what had been his forearm and three inches of white bone stuck out past that. His face had four or five places where it looked like his flesh had been scooped out with a melon ball tool. The IV bottle was attached to the needle in his arm and suspended from a support rigged to the side of his stretcher. He made no sound.

The attention of the rest of the Troop was focused on the hedgerow to our front that was being beaten with concentrated machine gun fire and had absorbed more than twenty Sheridan flechette rounds after the RPG hit. The likelihood of any organized fire at us from the target area was nil. My fear was being shot from behind. Then I noticed the RFs. The Warrant Officer was using his swagger stick to direct eight or ten of them in firing into and grenading the trench that had slowed Baby Dumpling's track. There was no return fire. Eventually they pulled three bodies out of the trench and an RPG launcher.

By the time the RFs were recovering bodies, the dust off was coming on station. The Medic Track took the stretcher back across the field to near the hedgerow we had checked so carefully before coming across the field. A Delta Troop slick landed, three or four men jumped off, the stretcher was loaded and the chopper left. The men who got off the helicopter were Bravo troopers who had been in Cu Chi on some errand or light duty after a wound. When word that Bravo was in contact spread, they went to the Delta Troop helicopter pad to catch a chopper to join us.

The Medic Track returned and stopped beside Six Track. Doc climbed down carrying an M60 with a belt of ammo draped over his shoulder. He walked up between two line tracks and fired the machine gun from the hip, swinging it slowly from side to side. I couldn't hear his firing separate from the rest of the Troop, but I think he was screaming too. When the belt was finished he turned around, walked back to the Medic Track and climbed back on board to wait for the next wounded man.

Apparently there were no more enemy nearer than the hedgerow and the ones in there were keeping their heads down. Less than twenty minutes after it all started, a FAC was overhead with the first pair of fighter bombers waiting for his direction. Our gunships were minutes away. The RFs formed a line on foot behind the center of our line, facing the other way, and led us as we backed up to within fifty meters of the hedgerow behind us. Before we were all the way back, the bombers and gunships began ploughing the hedgerow to our front. While they were attacking, we didn't fire.

When the planes and choppers were all done, about 1600, we started back toward the hedgerow, firing to keep their heads down. About thirty meters from the hedgerow, we found out they were not done. A sharp increase in our rate of fire was my warning that the gooks were shooting back. That clue was confirmed by hearing the CO call for a dust off for another four wounded men. We again backed slowly across the field, firing as we retired past the line marked by Baby Dumpling's still burning track. We kept a steady fire up until another wave of fighters and gunships was ready. Almost as soon as the air pounding began again, Charlie Troop came through the hedgerow behind us on our right.

When the second aerial wave had broken over the enemy, Bravo and Charlie began a steady firing slow advance that drew no return fire. By 1730 we were sweeping through a defoliated hedgerow where they had been. A few minutes later the enemy's last action was an RPG fired toward Charlie from far to the north. It is hard to imagine how anyone got away under the volume of fire that was kept on the enemy position, but some of them must have. In the part of the hedgerow Bravo swept we found thirteen enemy bodies, Charlie found eleven.

By the time the search was done, the burning track had become a smoldering wreck. We left the area through the hedgerow to the east without getting close enough to Charlie's Six Track to wave hello to Carlson. We dropped the RFs at their fort about 1900 and were back in Hampton before 2000. Wells was handed his promotion orders to Captain when we parked.

June 10

We didn't leave Hampton until almost 1130. Wells said we were going back to sweep yesterday's contact site. We went down to Trang Bang then back up past the RF fort on Road 6A. The fort looked as empty as it had the day before and we didn't stop. We went about a hundred meters to the right of the road and then north, parallel to the road to the east of yesterday's fight. We stopped, turned to the west on line and swept toward yesterday's contact. We crossed 6A and approached the hedgerow a klick away. We passed through the hedgerow and moved across the open area toward the hulk of the burned out APC. About the same time we got there one of the tracks hit a mine and we all stopped. No one was injured and the tread wasn't broken. As soon as it was confirmed that the track was serviceable,

15—Baby Dumpling

the CO sent the platoons out to poke around in the brush at the edges of the open area. Six Track and the Medic Track parked near the burned out hulk.

Baby Dumpling's body had not been recovered and we were concerned that he would not be confirmed dead. It would have been cruel to his family to have him carried as missing. Wells told Doc to check the track for evidence of his death. I went to help. From the outside, the track looked almost intact. The outside wasn't even scorched. The inside was different. Fragments and lumps of metal were scattered on the floor on a thick carpet of ashes. A few of the metal pieces were identifiable. The pale green paint on the inside walls was burned to black. The back ramp of the track had been blown down by one of the secondary explosions. There was no salvageable equipment on the inside.

We tossed out pieces of metal junk as we searched the mess on the floor. Doc and I both used bayonets to stir the ashes. We didn't find any identifiable bones, but we each found a couple of teeth. After we had stirred all of the ashes and were about to quit, we checked under the rear ramp found a right elbow, forearm and hand outside the vehicle. The explosion that had blown the ramp down apparently blew that part of Baby Dumpling's arm out of the track before it was burned to ash. There was still part of a fatigue sleeve on it. I didn't feel much about this severed arm other than hoping fingerprints would be enough to confirm his death.

We put the teeth and the forearm in a body bag that was sent to the rear. Part of one arm and a few teeth was a ludicrous sight in a six foot long body bag. Later we learned that Baby Dumpling was declared officially dead based on Doc's affidavit. When Doc pulled the wounded man out of the track right after it was hit, he had seen Baby Dumpling in the track apparently dead. Doc swore to that and confirmed that the ammunition in the track blew almost immediately after that and that the track burned in his view for a considerable time thereafter without anyone getting out. I don't know if they took fingerprints from the hand we sent back. Baby Dumpling's name was on his name tag, but Baby Dumpling was the only name I ever knew him by.

The platoons investigated the brush on the edges of the field for four hours and found nothing. When they were done, we moved north into the Citadel to laager near the south end. About 2100 I was called over to Six Track. It was dark enough that our LPs were out, but I hadn't gone to bed yet. The LP to the east of the laager had spotted five people moving south down the tree line east of us. The LPs had been called back in and Wells wanted artillery fired into where the movement had been spotted. It was easy. One of my defensive targets was due east, one klick out. The two adjusting rounds landed just about due east of us. The flash of their explosions confirmed that they landed on the other side of the trees and brush on the edge of the field. I dropped 100 meters toward us and 200 meters south, the direction of movement, and called in the twelve round fire for effect. The orange flashes in the dark were almost pretty and seemed to be coming from both sides of the trees and brush. When I called in "end of mission" I had no idea if we had accomplished anything, but it wasn't worth any more rounds. As I headed for my cot, a passing trooper said, "Nice rain Foxy."

An hour later when I was shaken awake and asked for another mission. One of the LPs thought they had heard a mortar being set up about a klick to the southeast. The LPs were on the way back in to the perimeter and I started another mission. For this one the hedgerow didn't mark the target and firing where they put the target was almost guessing. I called in the mission starting with map coordinates where they thought the sound came from. The adjusting rounds landed in the right direction, but seemed too far away. I adjusted 200 meters closer by intuition and called the twelve round fire for effect. Again, I had no idea what had been accomplished when I ended the mission at 2230. There were no further reports of movement or sounds that night.

It rained through most of my radio watch. The sound of rain on the top of the track was almost pleasant.

16

CRIP

June 11

One of the platoons escorted the trains west to Highway 19 and was back at 0815. We began a day of exploring the southern edge of the open area east of Ap Suoi Cao by platoons. We finished the day with two hours in a drizzle searching the northern edge of the Country Store. About 1515 we headed west to laager 1500 meters south of the western end of the Lower Boi Loi Woods.

June 12

Second Platoon left the laager at 0800 to pick up Xom Bao Dom RFs and were back at 0915 with thirty. We then formed on line west of the Country Store. Moving into the brush remnants, one of Third Platoon's Sheridans threw a track that couldn't be fixed in the field. Wells arranged for an M88 pickup. The disabled Sheridan was towed by another Sheridan back into the open and Third Platoon stayed with it.

The rest of the Troop searched in the vicinity until Wells called it quits at 1500. We laagered about where we had the night before. First and Third Platoons made two thirds of a circle pointed back at the Woods. Second Platoon headed off toward Ap Suoi Cao to return the RFs. Second Platoon came back an hour later with the trains they had picked up at Checkpoint 18.

Wells called the platoon leaders over to Six Track after dinner. When they were all there he shut up the back of the track with just him, me and the platoon leaders inside. He said he was a bit concerned that one of our Sheridans had an all Black crew and was calling itself the "Soul Track." He asked for comments. I'd never noticed any racial tension in Bravo Troop, but we all knew there was some in the rear and in other units. Pete and the platoon leaders agreed it wasn't a big deal but still not a good idea.

Pete told the platoon leader involved to make a general reorganization of his crews so that one of the Sheridan's four crewmen was white, without making any comment on "Soul Track." The name stayed for a while, then faded. So far as I know there never was any reaction to the change.

June 13

We went to Xom Bao Don at 0720 to pick up RFs. The trip was also clearing the road from Checkpoint 18 to Checkpoint 25. Our pickup was forty men with one officer with an RTO plus a U.S. sergeant with his own RTO. Instead of going back towards the Woods, we went southwest from Checkpoint 25 then swept southerly roughly parallel to Highway 19 a klick west of the road. The fields were unplanted and most of the few hooches were abandoned. The RFs were split up among the platoons and Wells directed the platoons to separate areas to search, keeping everybody in sight. The RF officer was with First Platoon, but the RFs with the other platoons just joined in whatever the Cav troopers were doing.

At 1045 we turned southwest and started moving further away from the Highway. We stopped for lunch at 1115, about five klicks from Xom Bao Don. After thirty minutes for lunch, we were off in the same direction. By 1230 we had reached an intersection of cart trails that was about halfway between Highway 19 and Route 22. We checked the immediate area of the intersection and there was a huge explosion in one of the hooches being searched. Immediately after the explosion Wells called in a dust off for the two RFs who had been massively injured. The chopper came quickly, but one of them died before it arrived.

After the dust off, we turned back toward Highway 19. Our search patterns were about the same as for the morning, but the troops all moved a lot slower. We were back to the highway at 1500. We had unloaded the RFs at their compound by 1530 and the Troop was parked inside Hampton by 1630. Our evening briefing was that Division expected attacks on Tay Ninh City and the Cav was the fire brigade. Squadron had orders to put one Troop just south of the city tomorrow night and be ready to move the other two up to support. If an attack came, our initial job was to screen south of the city.

June 14

The platoons were out of Hampton by 0700 to clear the roads. First Platoon went north to the Little Rubber, Second to Checkpoint 18 and

16—CRIP

Third to Trang Bang. Wells reassembled the Troop halfway between Checkpoint 18 and Go Dau Ha. Six or seven kids from a cluster of huts on the north side of the road assembled to stare at us. We moved south off the road on line into an area with sparse vegetation and no rice dikes.

When we pulled off the road, we were roughly two klicks north of Hampton. It didn't seem that close because we couldn't see it. The tree line 200 meters north of Hampton masked it from sight. As soon as were a little away from the road, Wells sent the platoons on separate searches.

Today's rain was a short downpour just after we stopped for lunch. Most of the troops moved inside a track. One man in each cupola got drenched. The tracks were still wet when it was time to move, but the sun came back and dried them quickly. Nothing before lunch and nothing after. I guess we were ready to move to Tay Ninh all day if needed. We returned to Hampton. Wells held an evening briefing. Tomorrow we were going out with the Triple Deuce CRIP Platoon again, along with some RFs from the same Company we had with us on June 9.

June 15

Extra noise woke me before 0600. Many of the line track Track Commanders yelled to wake some of their crew and nobody made any effort to keep quiet any more. We normally got to bed early and, even with an hour on radio watch, a full night's sleep was pretty much done by 0600. I wasn't hungry for breakfast. I was rarely hungry anymore.

We were out on Route 1 headed south by 0750 and by 0815 were stopped at the road fork between Highway 19 and Provincial Road 6A at the north end of Trang Bang. The CRIP platoon was waiting for us there. They didn't come out of any fortification, they were just by the side of the road, about twenty of them. They were half U.S. infantry and half Vietnamese. A U.S. Second Lieutenant appeared to be in command. He and a U.S. Sergeant with a radio and two Vietnamese noncoms got on the Medic Track. The rest climbed on the nearby tracks.

We took the right fork up Road 6A to the RF fort about 200 meters on. We stopped for thirty RFs. The last two men down the path through the barbed wire were an RF Captain and his RTO. Wells said the Captain was the RF Company CO. Pete got down to greet him and escorted him and his RTO to the Medic Track. The RF Captain appeared to know the CRIP Platoon Leader. The rest of the RFs boarded the APCs behind the ones carrying the CRIPs.

As soon as we left the RF fort, we pulled off the road to the right continuing to the north paralleling the road for three klicks. We crossed to the west side of the road on line and stopped. Wells called our platoon leaders, the RF CO and the CRIP Platoon Leader over for a conference. They met standing next to Six Track on the CO's side. I didn't get down, but I moved over to the CO's seat to listen. From the discussion and pointing, we were going to sweep west. We were pointed at a hedgerow a klick west, about a klick south of fight on the 9th.

We moved out at 0900 and broke through the hedgerow ten minutes later. Scattered rifle fire came from the next hedgerow, about 200 meters to the west. The gooks usually started any fight a lot closer and with RPGs, but there was no question it was the enemy, and several of them were firing. Wells cleared fire and the Troop opened up with .50 calibers. The fire was steady and loud, but not a frenzy with flechette rounds.

Once the Troop started firing, I couldn't hear any more enemy firing. I radioed in that we were in contact, where we were and where I thought the enemy was. I didn't call a fire mission immediately because where I would normally have started was too close to Highway 19. We also didn't appear to need it. I yelled at Wells to be sure. "Boss, you want artillery?" "No, first fire team's almost here."

We had been moving very slowly forward for several minutes and were about 100 meters closer to the enemy than we had been at the first shots. There were two distinct explosions to the right mixed in with the machine gun fire. The First Platoon Sergeant's Sheridan had been hit. The rest of the line tracks stopped almost immediately. The volume of machine gun fire on the right increased and the First Platoon mortar track joined in, spraying fire to the north. By the time I saw two men dragging a third between them behind the hit Sheridan, the Medic Track had already taken off that way.

As soon as that had unfolded, a single explosion in front of us punctuated the steady roar of the machine gun fire. No one bailed out and I couldn't tell which track had been hit. Within a few seconds each of the remaining Sheridans fired two flechette rounds to our front. Then there were five or six smoke grenades marking our front and our firing stopped just seconds before a Cobra crossed our front firing rockets into the hedgerow in front of us. In the short gap between our cease fire and the rocket run, there was no sound of enemy firing. As soon as the first gunship cleared, another followed. There was a slightly longer interval before the first gunship returned for a second firing pass with the second close behind again.

While the rockets were going in, the Medic Track came back to near where we were with the two wounded from the Sheridan. By the fourth rocket pass, Doc popped smoke for a dust off landing behind us.

When the gunships began minigun runs, our tracks began backing

16—CRIP

up slowly with the CRIPs and RFs behind the tracks moving the same way at the same speed. The Sheridan that had been hit moved back with the rest of the Troop. Obviously someone was driving and there was a man behind the .50 caliber. We were almost back up against the hedgerow behind us when the gunships left. Pete spoke in the brief silence, "Here comes the napalm. They've been watching the choppers mark the target."

The first F100 came across on almost the same path the gunships had used, from right to left down the hedgerow. Two napalm canisters started tumbling down from the jets wings a long way before it was in front of us, but they were just about in front of us when they hit and the orange balls flashed out from the impact points. Several of our troops cheered the first run. The pair of jets took more time between their runs than the choppers had, but their eight tanks of napalm still went fairly fast.

The last napalm run was over about 0950. A few minutes later we started forward very slowly behind steady, moderate machine gun fire into the hedgerow across the field. After 100 meters of advance, there were two explosions and some incoming zings on the right flank. The volume of our fire on that end increased immediately. I saw a Sheridan back off line, pivot to the north, move to the end of the line and fire two flechette rounds into the open field to the right of our line. The RFs behind the tracks near the right flank started drifting toward the center. While this was going on I could hear fragments of Wells calling for a dust off. I saw no sign of any enemy in the stretch of field the Sheridan was firing into, but if there were any, they should have been trying to stay entirely inside any available hole.

Within five minutes the fire from our line had petered out to almost nothing. By the time the dust off landed behind Six Track to pick up three wounded, there was no fire going out or coming in. As the dust off was pulling away my FDC advised me that a company of the First of the Fifth Infantry was moving into position on the other side of Highway 19 and that I would not be allowed to call in any fire closer to them than 200 meters east of the road.

"Pete, Artillery says First of the Fifth is setting up on the other side of the road. You know where?" "That's what I hear, Foxy, but no specific location. A Delta Troop scout says they have spotted moving VC about a klick northwest. Gun team's about to go in." We couldn't see exactly where the fire was going, but the firing runs of two Cobra gunships were to our northwest.

For the next three hours little happened. Pete had radio traffic, but nothing important enough to tell me about. I heard nothing of note on the Artillery net. There were a lot more choppers in the air than usual, but mostly scouts. A couple of times we could see nearby firing runs by gunships. We had lunch. It was almost surreal to casually eat a can of pineapple sitting in the same place we recently were being shot at. Pete said First Platoon had pulled some bodies out of nearby holes, but we hadn't swept any of the areas the fire seemed to have come from.

C-rations had been passed out to the CRIPs and RFs. The CRIP Platoon Leader called his people to eat on the ground behind the line of vehicles. They sat in spaced groups of two and three facing to our rear. As they ate their lieutenant moved from group to group stopping to talk to each a bit as he ate something out of a can. Most of the RFs ate clustered right behind the vehicles at the south end of our line.

About 1315 Wells got busier on the radio. "Time for us to move, Foxy." The CRIPs walked in an evenly spaced line behind Six Track. The RFs stayed clustered in the lee of line vehicles. We moved forward at a slow walking speed. It took us about five minutes to get to within 100 meters of the tree line on the other side of the field. Enemy fire started again. It wasn't much fire. The enemy fire was distinguishable for only a few seconds but then disappeared into the noise of the Troop's .50 caliber machine gun fire and steady salvos of flechette rounds from the Sheridans.

When our firing began I had a clear field of fire between two widely spaced tracks to the hedgerow beyond. I fired several magazines into the hedgerow as fast as I could fire a magazine in three or four bursts and reload. At the end of my outburst, I noticed the CRIP Platoon Leader standing next to the right rear of Six Track with his RTO. The Lieutenant was firing also, single shots in groups of two—pop, pop, pause, pop, pop, pause. I wondered if he took it seriously with such half-ass shooting until I remembered he had to carry his ammunition. The 20mm ammo can in front of me held more loaded magazines than he could carry and we had twice as many rounds more in bandoliers inside the track. He must have thought that I was shooting like a fool.

After a few minutes our firing was slowing down a little when the Medic Track peeled off to the right and I noticed a small smoke column coming up from one of the Sheridans. I heard Pete calling in that the Sheridan had taken an RPG round and that one of the APCs at the other end of the line had been hit also. Our fire peaked again, then petered out again. There was no sound of any enemy fire. In the relative quiet, I heard Pete calling for the dust off again for four wounded, two urgent. By the time the dust off arrived, our line tracks were into the hedgerow without any more enemy fire. At 1430 Wells radioed in a total body count of 27 for the day. He also reported that the Troop was down to a third of our basic ammunition load.

As soon as Wells was through, there was scattered AK47 fire from the north. First Platoon's far right track in the hedgerow and mortar track in the open behind them opened up in response immediately, both with .50

calibers at maximum rate of fire. The line track was firing almost straight up the hedgerow, the mortar track sweeping the hedgerow near the top of the dirt between twenty and fifty meters north of the north end of our line. An M60 was firing from the line track and both crewmen on the mortar track were firing their M16s into the hedgerow. There wasn't much chance they had actually seen anything to shoot at, but the likely places were obvious and they sprayed them. While they fired, the First Platoon Sergeant's Sheridan, apparently now with a full crew, backed out of the hedgerow and pulled into the space between the end track and the mortar track. As soon as it stopped it fired its main gun, then again three more times, then silence. There was no sound of enemy fire. First Platoon began slowly checking the hedgerow to its north.

Within five minutes after the firing to the north stopped, a Delta Troop slick landed near Six Track and unloaded fifty boxes of .50 caliber ammunition. The ammunition was quickly distributed to the three platoons. It wasn't really a material resupply of ammunition, but it was a reassuring gesture.

Our dismounts, the RFs and the CRIPs continued searching the hedgerow positions, but found little more. At 1515 Wells reported to Squadron that First Platoon had two new enemy bodies to the north. The end of his transmission was punctuated with scattered AK rounds coming from somewhere in the brush behind us. Unless we had passed over people who had waited patiently for a very long time, gooks were moving in behind us. The three mortar tracks turned to face to the rear and fired into the distant brush. Doc fired the Medic Track's .50 caliber over its rear deck. Each platoon moved one APC to join the rear screen and the seven tracks kept up a steady .50 caliber fire back across the field. The CRIPs moved to join the rear line. The RFs moved to the front of the line tracks still facing the other way. Within five minutes the gunships started strafing and rocketing the hedgerow behind us while our firing was suspended. When the gunships left, the rear screen began firing again until the next fire team was on station and ready to begin.

By 1545 the gunships were done and Wells shut off our firing. Then we just sat while he talked on the radio. From what I heard, it sounded like discussion of where the enemy had gone. Just after 1600 the debate about where the enemy had gone was interrupted by a burst of AK47 full automatic fire, close in and directly to our front. Second Platoon responded with a burst of maximum fire and the RFs moved behind the line tracks again. Second Platoon's fire ended so quickly I assumed that they actually had a target and obliterated it. The fire was over before Wells radioed for an urgent dust off. Doc had run forward when the enemy fire started and was coming back supporting a kid with a field dressing on a neck wound.

The kid was walking, but poorly. Doc popped purple smoke and the dust off landed between the Medic Track and our rear screen.

We started forward again, moving up to where the line tracks thought the last burst of AK fire had come from. They found foxholes, but no sign of the last gunman. After twenty minutes of careful searching we loaded up and went a klick southwest to Highway 19 and turned left toward Trang Bang. At the intersection with 6A we dropped off the RFs and CRIPs. The RFs started up 6A to their fort without any apparent formation. The CRIPs disappeared between the houses next to the road. At Route 1 we turned right toward Hampton and headed home at the speed of the civilian traffic on the road. There was no hint that anyone in Trang Bang had paid any attention to the fight going on nearby for much of the day. We were inside Hampton at 1800.

After dinner, we had a briefing at the Cav headquarters. Colonel McGowan announced he was allocating 15 of our body count to the RFs, six to Bravo Troop and eight to air support. Wells spoke, "Sir, you know we don't care much about body counts, but the RFs didn't do anything." The Platoon Leaders nodded their heads.

"Pete, I'm sorry, this is a matter of policy. I know what you mean, the Division Commander knows, maybe even the USARV Commander, but we are going to assist the South Vietnamese forces gain confidence. This is part of it. Another part is that the RF CO is being written up for a Bronze Star."

"Shit!" I felt sorry for Colonel McGowan. He didn't have the same freedom to complain as a Lieutenant in for two years. Colonel McGowan never inflated our body counts. Our body counts were toe tagged, no estimates, no extrapolations. For a career officer, a policy of "helping to build ARVN confidence" had to be accepted. I also felt sorry for the RF Warrant Officer who was with us on June 9. He displayed personal bravery and leadership and got nothing. His worthless CO would get a medal.

June 16

There wasn't any wake up call. The mud on the ring road around Hampton was almost liquid. It was raining enough now that the ring never dried out and each passing track stirred it up.

We finally left Hampton at 1120 and were in the center of Trang Bang in less than twenty minutes. We turned north, then took the right fork to Road 6A. The RF fort looked empty again. Just past the fort, we pulled off to the left side of the road and continued in the same direction as the road.

At 1210 we stopped for the first time. We were six klicks from Trang

Bang just northwest of a cluster of huts on the map called Rung Cay. On the ground there weren't many hooches any more. The Troop spent the next two hours searching in the immediate vicinity of where we stopped. The platoons searched independently. Six Track and the Medic Track parked in the middle of the area. I read a paperback. We headed back the way we had come at 1430. Our total haul had been some books and a newspaper in a hole plus one 82mm mortar round.

When we reached east of yesterday's fight, we stopped and turned to face west on line. Then we started west toward the first tree line. I looked over at Wells. He didn't say anything, just gave me a tight little smile. I tensed as the line tracks approached the tree line. They all climbed the dirt mound at about the same time, broke the brush and bamboo on top, paused briefly at the top, pivoted down on the other side and drove on without incident. We who followed them approached and passed without concern after that.

In the field on the other side, we crossed the same ground we had covered the day before at a steady pace. I tensed again as we came up to the tree line on the west side of the field. The result was the same, the line tracks moved through without incident and the tension disappeared. On the other side there was fairly heavy scattered brush, but it just didn't seem as sinister as the places we had been shot at from the day before. We reached Highway 19 near Checkpoint R, turned south to Trang Bang and reached Hampton at 1645. We were greeted by a short rain.

We had an evening briefing at the Squadron Headquarters. Charlie Troop was laagering on the southern outskirts of Tay Ninh City and the Squadron was still standing by to respond to an assault on Tay Ninh. At the end of the briefing, Colonel McGowan handed over orders promoting Murray to First Lieutenant.

17

Defending Tay Ninh

June 17

Our serious work started when we got to the strip separating the Upper and Lower Boi Loi Woods. One of the tracks spotted a 55 gallon drum with a removable top. It was empty. When we reached the end of the southeast arm of the X cut in the Upper Boi Loi we turned toward the center of the X. About two klicks in, all the vehicles turned right on line and went into the brush on the side of the cut. It was the densest part of the Woods left. I could see the crews of nearby tracks almost all of the time, but usually couldn't see the body of any other track, or the ground next to me. A small rain cloud decided to improve our day by emptying on us as it passed.

At 1115 we stopped. Six Track was in a substantially cleared area big enough to hold four or five properly spaced tracks. About half the area was taken up by three meter deep craters B52 bombs left behind. Each crater was six meters in diameter and much closer together than those I'd seen before. Some touched and a few overlapped.

When we stopped, the line tracks in front of us had snaked through the bombed area and we were near its middle. As soon as we stopped, an ordnance sergeant who had been loaned to us came back for a 155mm dud near Six Track lying on the ground next to one of the craters. I watched with no particular interest as he walked up to it. That changed to amazed terror as he bent over, picked up the round, lifted it to his chest and threw it into the crater. The round went up a little as it moved away from him then turned down sharply into the hole. I couldn't see it land, but it didn't go off. It was the stupidest thing I'd ever seen. There was no way to know why a dud hadn't gone off or what it would take to set it off. A 155mm round detonating on the surface was supposed to kill half of everybody standing within fifty meters. I was ten meters away. If the round had gone off when he picked it up, it would have killed him a microsecond before me. If it had gone off hitting the bottom of the crater, I probably would have survived him. There wasn't any reason to do it. Before we left, he had to climb down and stand in the water and mud at the crater's bottom to rig a charge on the dud. It was blown behind us on a long fuse, just like it would have been if he hadn't moved it.

Our route through the Woods very slowly turned left. About 1230 we broke out of the brush into the northeast arm of the X cut and stopped for lunch. After lunch we headed toward the center of the X with First Platoon on the right edge of the cut, Second Platoon on the left edge and Third Platoon with Six Track and the Medic Track in the middle. When we reached the middle of the X, we turned back down the southeast arm in the same alignment. We reached the lower edge of the Upper Boi Loi without incident and turned westerly along the strip that separated the Upper and Lower Boi Loi Woods. Once we were into the open fields west of the Woods, it seemed a lot cooler.

We laagered near the east side of Highway 19, a klick south of the village. The cooks' truck towing a water trailer, a cargo carrier with fuel and two repaired APCs joined us at 1740. I told Wells about the ordnance sergeant throwing the dud. The sergeant left on the evening chopper.

After dinner, we got a coded message, "Several enemy PT76 light tanks sighted nearby in Cambodia. Review anti-tank procedures." The armor on a Russian PT76 was about the same as the Sheridan's. Its main gun was half the size of the Sheridan's, but it was a high velocity anti-tank gun. Pete instructed the Platoon Leaders to get a count of the shaped charge anti-tank rounds on each Sheridan, spread them out evenly and make sure that the loader on each crew knew where they were. He also told them to inventory their LAWs and make sure they were in the hands of someone who remembered how to fire one at a tank. His final instruction was to remind the Track Commanders to fire their .50 calibers at any enemy tanks. A .50 caliber round might penetrate PT76 armor and the noise of .50 caliber rounds hitting a vehicle should scare its crew. Fortunately, if there were enemy tanks nearby in Cambodia they didn't visit us.

June 18

We were up at 0545. After breakfast, Third Platoon cleared Highway 19 south into Trang Bang. The rest of us headed north. We dropped our trains at Checkpoint 18 cleared north to Xom Bao Don where we picked up a small party of RFs. We went back down Highway 19 to meet the Third Platoon a klick south of Checkpoint 12. Wells announced that we were sweeping on the west side of the highway this time. One of the APCs hit a mine as soon as we pulled off the road. When the smoke cleared, one of our troopers and an RF were wounded. Wells radioed for a dust off and an M88.

A few minutes later the dust off landed on a blocked a stretch of the road. The RF walked to the chopper, but our trooper was on a litter with an IV bottle mounted. When the dust off was away, we began our sweep, leaving the damaged APC and a guard APC to wait for the recovery vehicle.

We found nothing for the rest of the day. Just before lunch the repaired track and its guard rejoined us. Two short rains after lunch elicited general discussion about the rainy season. No one on Six Track had been through a rainy season before, but we all thought that really wet ground would restrict our movement to generally safe places. When we went back to the highway at 1415 the rain was so thoroughly ended that the roads were already dusty. We took the RFs to their compound then came back south and laagered near where we spent the night before.

June 19

Morning drill was road clearing and picking up RFs at Xom Bao Dom, just like yesterday except we went east of Ap Suoi Cao to sweep. But then we didn't sweep. Wells got a long string of radio traffic. In a break, Pete gave me a report. "Charlie Troop made contact south of Tan Ninh, just off Route 22. Three tracks on a resupply run were ambushed. One destroyed. That's under control, but they're reporting that the entire village along the side of the road is abandoned."

For a while we moved in fits and starts in the open space south of the Woods, but didn't search anything. We spent a lot of time stopped while Pete had unusual radio traffic and when we moved, we stayed in totally open space. At 1115 he said we were going to join Charlie. We dropped the RFs at their compound and reversed course back to Go Dau Ha then headed north on Route 22. We went faster than usual and crowded the civilian road traffic more than usual. I radioed in the checkpoints as we passed the Little Rubber, then the Big Rubber and on further north on Route 22 than ever before.

We stopped five klicks south of the southern edge of Tay Ninh City, at the intersection with Provincial Road 241 that went off to the northeast from Route 22. The village of Ap Nam Troung Hue began at the intersection and stretched for four klicks as a strip along the road. After Wells had a short discussion on his radio, we turned northeast onto Road 241. A klick in, we turned through a gap between two houses along the right side of the road, then left again, heading northeast parallel to the road about 200 meters away from the back edge of the village. The ground was open, no brush to speak of, but no sign of recent cultivation. Pete said the gap we went through was just short of where on Road 241 the Charlie Troop trains had been fired at.

Pete said that the RFs we were going to pick up were all Cao Dai. Cao Dai was a religion that had originated in South Vietnam fairly recently. They revered religious figures from many prior religions and historical figures from many countries. The Cao Dai main temple was in Tay Ninh City and they dominated the adjoining area. The Cao Dai were supposed to be dedicated anti-Communists.

As we kept moving away from Route 22, I heard the Charlie Troop FO reporting on the Artillery net that they were behind us. We reached the RF compound just beyond the end of the strip village a little south of the road about 1215. It was a dirt berm with firing bunkers built into the wall surrounded by barbed wire barriers and entanglements.

When the RFs came out to load up, I noticed that they were all fully equipped. They all had boots like ours, steel pots with cloth covers and all their fatigues matched. I didn't recognize their web gear, but they all wore the same gear. Seeing these RFs raised the question of why all the other RFs we saw looked so ragged. The RF Captain and his RTO got on Six Track. The Captain sat right behind Wells and his RTO next to him on the cargo hatch. There wasn't any interpreter and I don't think either of the RFs spoke English. It didn't seem to bother them; they certainly looked ready to go.

Before we started anywhere, Wells announced the Colonel McGowan was coming in and we were getting a recon flight over the village we had bypassed on the way in. Wells, Lieutenant Hughes, and Lieutenant Wright went up in the first LOH flight. As soon as the chopper was off, Colonel McGowan came over toward Six Track. The RF Captain got down and saluted, Colonel McGowan returned the salute and shook his hand. McGowan broke off to visit nearby troops and the RF Captain remounted.

A few minutes later the LOH was back and Colonel McGowan waved me and Lieutenant Murray toward the chopper. It was the first time I was the senior officer on a recon flight. I got in the right front seat and Murray got in back. I put on the flight helmet, looked over my shoulder to make sure that Lieutenant Murray was settled and gave the pilot a thumbs up.

Ap Nam Truong Hue was a narrow string of houses and hooches along both sides of the road. We were flying parallel to and a little north of the road at about 1000 feet. Matching the ground to the map was easy. The pilot's voice came over the intercom in my flight helmet, "Have you seen enough? There's a .51 caliber reported in the village." He didn't sound eager to linger over the village. "Yeah, let's go back." He pulled a sharp turn away from the village and we headed back to the Troop. We landed next to Six Track. Colonel McGowan boarded and left.

When we moved away from the RF compound at 1245 we went to the northwest, then formed up on line facing southwest straddling a trail that paralleled Road 241 about 600 meters north of the road. Pete said Charlie Troop was on line with us straddling Road 241 and would be sweeping through the village.

There was a noticeable gap between our left flank and Charlie Troop's right flank. We couldn't see all of Charlie Troop, but we could see enough of them to stay on line with them. They had harder ground to cover, maneuvering around houses, hooches and other obstacles. Pete said the RFs had suggested we sweep down the trail. We were moving through cultivated fields, probably destroying a good part of the crop. Several times Pete called a halt to avoid getting ahead of Charlie Troop weaving through the village to our left.

The first firing came when Charlie Troop had swept back to about a klick from where their trains had been fired at. It was a shock, but almost immediately it was clear no one was shooting at us, just at the part of Charlie Troop in the village. The line stopped, Charlie Troop opened up, we did not. After a few minutes of intense fire by Charlie Troop, we and they slowly backed away 200 meters.

Captain Thomas radioed in a fire mission targeted on the village ahead of where Charlie Troop had stopped. Air support was prompt, but almost leisurely in application. Two jets with napalm and bombs then two gunships with rockets then two more jets, then two more gunships. Captain Thomas' fire mission was fired whenever the airspace over the village was clear. When the last air support was done, about half an hour from start to finish, we moved forward again. Charlie Troop began firing when they approached their contact point. Their fire swelled, the line stopped then backed out. With only a short delay, the aerial assault began again.

After roughly the same air support and intermittent artillery fire, we moved forward again. In the process of moving up and back, Bravo Troop's line had moved left to close the gap between the two troops. This time we got just a little further on than where we stopped last time before the enemy started firing again. The left end of Bravo's line took scattered RPG and small arms fire from the village and returned fire. There was no significant further progress and after a few minutes we withdrew again.

The next air strikes were all napalm from two jets coming down over Road 241 from behind us dropping on or near the road just beyond where we had last stopped. Because light was fading, our line was marked for these strikes with three or four smoke grenades in front of each platoon.

After the jets finished their runs, two slicks dropped flame baths in front of Charlie Troop.

After the flame baths, we started forward again. Again, Charlie Troop started firing as they approached the last contact point. The left side of our line joined in shortly thereafter. The line stopped almost as soon as we joined the firing. I heard Wells radioing someone that we had stopped because the right flank of Charlie Troop had stopped and we were getting too far ahead of them.

It was almost dark. Six Track was near the corner of one of the scattered houses near the trail. It had a corrugated steel roof. Wells had an intense burst of radio traffic, then the track made a high speed turn to the left that almost slammed my helmet into the edge of the roof. My absorption with that near miss ended when I noticed we were driving at high speed down our line toward the sounds of heavy firing around Charlie Troop. Almost as soon as I refocused, we stopped, turned around and headed back. Pete had more radio traffic I couldn't hear, then he yelled at me, "Carlson's dead. Charlie's disorganized. We're going to sweep across their front."

As we moved, I could see Bravo's line pivoting to face the back side of the village just beyond where Charlie Troop's line had stopped. Moving across Charlie Troop's front while they were disorganized didn't seem too good an idea to me, but I wasn't asked. For a while all the fragments of Pete's radio traffic that I heard were about getting Charlie Troop not to shoot at us as we crossed their front.

As soon as we were on our new line, about 1830, the Troop opened up steady .50 caliber fire to our front, into the back of the village, and we started forward. Our fire hid the sound of any enemy fire. Our line tracks had almost reached the edge of the village in front of us when there was an explosion somewhere nearby and something was wrong with my neck. I don't remember being hit. I just lost track of what was going on around me for a while. The next thing I remember was sitting still while Charlie tied a field dressing to my neck. The pad was on the right side and he was knotting the two pairs of cloth straps on the left side. I had no sense of bleeding. There was no pain, other than being choked by the straps. "Charlie, that's too tight. It's not a tourniquet." Charlie retied both knots, a little looser. I noticed the RF RTO working on his Captain's broken arm.

There is a blank in my memory that begins just after being bandaged. I don't know why. No one ever said that I passed out; I just don't remember anything for a while. Wells told me later that Bravo crossed part of Charlie's front, getting almost to the road that ran down the middle of the village before we pulled back. He said the RFs were relentless in assaulting bunkers dug into strips of vegetation just inside the village. It was dark, but gooks were visible coming out of the bunkers to fight as the tracks got near. Pete said he shot a gook who came out of a bunker with his back to us on my side of the track, firing his .45 pistol just in front of me. I don't remember any of it.

What I remember next was the Troop stopped well north of the village, back in the field where we started. We were in an unusually tight formation, two columns of nose to tail, side by side tracks, headed north. In the dark I could see the two tracks in front of us and some people on them, but nothing beyond. When we began moving, Well's radio traffic was mostly about the benefits and risks of illumination. Apparently the risks prevailed because we continued on without. I didn't like moving in the dark and I didn't like being that bunched up, but we took no fire. We went on in the same direction for a while, then turned right and ended up pointed at a flare fired over the RF compound. When we arrived, the RF Captain and his RTO got off, the RFs went into the compound and a chopper landed to take off wounded.

As soon as the chopper took off, Wells said we were joining Charlie Troop for the night. When we started again, I had little idea what direction we were heading. It was past 2030 when we found a partial circle of tracks that was Charlie Troop.

I was standing next to Six Track when Colonel McGowan came over after we stopped. "Can you stay the night? Charlie Troop's FO was dusted off. We'll get you out in the morning." "I'm fine sir. But I don't know where we are." "Good man." He put his arm on my shoulder and started me toward the back of the track. "Let's go into the light and I'll show you where I think we are and where the RFs are."

About 2140 Colonel McGowan was called to the Six Track radio. He had already arranged a program of harassing helicopter and artillery fire into our contact area, but this was special. The choppers had located a Sheridan that Charlie Troop had reported missing. They had seen a light on the ground, hit it with a spotlight and confirmed that it was a Sheridan. The light the chopper first saw was coming from inside the vehicle through an open turret hatch. Now they were seeing that light flicker. The best explanation for the light flickering was someone moving in and out of the hatch. The pilots were asking special permission before firing at the Sheridan. Charlie Troop still had several men unaccounted for. Colonel McGowan hesitated, then said there was no sign of fighting and no chance that U.S. troops were holding out in the Sheridan. He released the gunships to fire using the Sheridan's light as their aiming point.

Because I was going in in the morning, I took all of the radio watch for the rest of the night. There wasn't much radio traffic on the Troop net,

17—Defending Tay Ninh

just the half hourly reports from the Platoon Leader's tracks. Several times during the night, I heard artillery hitting somewhere in the village.

June 20

When the sun came and the sleeping troopers started stirring, I started getting tired. We didn't move out until after 0800. As we pulled out, leaving Charlie Troop behind, Wells said that the RFs that had been with us the night before were already in the village and the enemy was gone. The RFs reported the missing Charlie Troop Sheridan was on the road in the middle of the village with its engine still running. The gooks had stripped both of its machine guns, but fortunately they didn't have anyone who could drive it. Our first job was to go collect it. There wasn't any obvious damage to the Sheridan when we arrived. Its engine was still running and one of our drivers confirmed that it could be driven out. There wasn't any blood around it.

Six Track stopped in the road in the center of the built up area of the village while the platoons poked through the area we hadn't been able to get through the night before. About 1000 Wells told me to get on the next chopper coming in and go back to Hampton. I checked with Captain Thomas on the Artillery net and he concurred. I changed into my rubber boots for the Hampton mud before the chopper came.

When I got to Hampton, I reported to a makeshift aid station. After months of VD and lower back pain, the Squadron Surgeon finally got to handle casualties. Dust offs usually went directly to the 12th Evacuation Hospital in Cu Chi, but our fight had produced enough lightly wounded that they were sent to him at Hampton. He took the field dressing off my neck and gently rubbed the side of my neck near the wound with his index finger. It didn't hurt, but I could feel something hard under his finger. "There's a small piece of shrapnel in the muscle. I don't want to cut it out now. It's still moving around a lot and I don't want to have to chase it. Let's let it build up calcium for ten days or so then cut it out. It shouldn't hurt, but if it does, let me know." As he talked, he cleaned my neck and put a band-aid over the wound. I was happy it wasn't serious, but felt a little silly that my wound could be covered with a band-aid.

After I got my band-aid, I went to the Squadron Headquarters. Most of the talk was about Colonel McGowan. He came back to Hampton as soon as it was confirmed the village was clear. He went directly to his tent and hadn't come out. Colonel McGowan had been Carlson's geography instructor at West Point.

There was a lot of talk about our fight. The main attack on Tay Ninh

City had been by parts of the 88th, 271st and 272nd NVA Regiments. I hadn't known yesterday that there were other attacks on Tay Ninh City. We had been fighting two VC main force battalions. By midday Bravo Troop had found 98 enemy bodies. The RFs said they'd found another 60 bodies near the fight area. Most of the enemy had fought in positions inside a rectangle of about 600 by 400 meters that was hit with air strikes, napalm, helicopter gunships and prolonged artillery fire before, during and after our attempts to overrun the position.

Charlie Troop had lost five killed, including Carlson. Bravo's only killed was a kid who quietly bled to death before anyone realized how serious his wound was. Both Troops had many wounded. When Gary was hit, his FO was seriously wounded and his Track Commander, Spec 4 Ogas, was blown off the track. The kid climbed back on and used the Squadron radio net to tell Colonel McGowan what had happened. One Platoon Leader was somewhere else, one was seriously wounded and the third, a new guy, had lost radio communications. Colonel McGowan told Ogas to run the Troop for a while. I'm sure McGowan helped, but the kid got most of Charlie Troop back in formation with hand signals and ran the Troop until it was out of the immediate mess. Ogas was promoted to Sergeant that night and was written up for a Distinguished Service Cross.

Bravo and Charlie arrived at Hampton about 1600.

June 21

We weren't going anywhere, so there wasn't any rush to get out of my cot. When it got noisy about 0630, I hugged the cot and snoozed. When I finally got up and finished my ablutions, the cooks still had some food out and I picked at half a breakfast. I had no idea which Vietnamese holiday it was that had suspended the war, but no one complained about a day inside Hampton. Probably the gook attack on Tay Ninh had been timed in hope that the truce would slow down counterattacks if they took the city. Colonel McGowan was back out and about, but he didn't spend any time visiting with the troops.

June 22

Stand to was at 0545. To leave I climbed up on Six Track, scraped the mud off my rubber boots, put on my field boots and stowed the rubber boots inside the track. Absent some crisis, I wouldn't dip my field boots in the Hampton mud anymore. We left at 0805 headed toward Checkpoint

18. As we went past the eastern edge of Go Dau Ha, a PF in a tiny outpost waved at us. The outpost had always been there, but it was the first time I paid any attention to it. There was a small circular wall of sandbags about shoulder high and no more that twenty feet in diameter. There were three strands of concertina barbed wire starting about ten feet outside the wall and a crooked path leading to an opening in the wall. A man sitting in a rickety wooden observation tower in the middle of the circle waved to us. The tower had a crude thatch roof and looked like it could only hold one man in a chair. He had a good view across the fields outside the village. Aside from his wave, what caught my attention was his rifle hanging on its sling from the roof frame. Even at the distance the shape was distinctive. It was an AK47. Recycling enemy weapons made sense, but still seemed odd.

We got to Checkpoint 18 at 0845, turned right on Highway 19 and pulled off the east side of the road just south of Ap Suoi Cao. Pete was on the radio off and on, but I couldn't hear anything of what he was receiving in his helmet earphones. His transmissions were short and usually no more that confirming that we were holding at the same location. Some of the troopers got down and stretched out on their backs on the ground next to their vehicle on the shady side. About 0945 the CO radioed for everybody to mount up and we headed east along the southern edge of the village's fields. Didn't see much of anything on the way except a couple of water buffalo being driven back toward the village by a kid.

We spent the day sweeping an area where we'd never found anything before. At 1445, we stopped, mounted everybody and went back to laager two hundred meters south of Ap Suoi Cao and the same distance east of Highway 19.

June 23

About 0730 we picked up some RFs in Trang Bang. The puddles in the road didn't change our road clearing speed. Forty RFs were waiting in the center of town, just north of Route 1. We were down to about twenty vehicles total, but we still took up a lot of road when we parked and waited for them to mount. The RF command group rode with the Second Platoon leader so we had no extras aboard Six Track. When they were all loaded, each of our vehicles reversed direction and we went back the way we had come. We passed Checkpoint Z north of Trang Bang at 0830.

On the other side of Checkpoint Z we pulled off the road to the east and formed on line pointing north. All the RFs and ten or fifteen of our troops dismounted and we began a slow sweep to the north, headed toward the south end of the Citadel. Most of the area was open, wet grasslands and there wasn't much to stop and check. We still stopped a lot to find nothing. Three hours later we had passed through the southern boundary of the Citadel and stopped for chow a hundred meters inside the Citadel.

The RFs ate their offered C-ration cans in small groups scattered behind the tracks. Most of our people ate on their track or right next to it. I ate a canned date roll and a can of fruit and drank a warm Coke. Then back to reading. At 1230 we were on our way again, moving southeast out of the Citadel and finding nothing. When that was done, we crossed two klicks of open space back to Highway 19 about where we had left the road in the morning.

After dropping the RFs, we came back north and laagered just east of Highway 19 a klick south of Ap Suoi Cao. Twenty minutes later our trains and two repaired APCs arrived to join us. A quarter hour of rain started when the trains arrived. For the troopers, the worst part was having it rain while they were digging in for the night.

June 24

Today we made up for the easy days before. Our trains departed and we headed toward the Lower Boi Loi Woods. We headed east south of the Woods for a while, then formed on line and headed northeast toward the center of the big end of the Woods. Lunch was just stopping where we were at 1200, surrounded by dense brush up against the vehicles. After lunch we swept south for about three hours to the southern edge of the Woods.

Once we were out of the Woods, we headed west. There was still a little brush where the Country Store had been, but we went through it at almost the same speed as the open space on either side. I was very careful to call in our location whenever we approached the Country Store. Past the western end of the Woods, we turned south into the Citadel to laager a little north of the Citadel's center. Within fifteen minutes of our arrival, three returning tracks and our trains came through the western edge of the Citadel to join us.

Colonel McGowan landed inside our laager just after our trains arrived and headed for Six Track. Pete had talked to him before he landed and then went off to do something without waiting. I had my defensive targets called in and was reading in my jeep seat. "Good evening sir." "Evening Watson. Chico, radio First Platoon to send Super Lou over."

McGowan made small talk with the crew for a few minutes until Lou ran over. McGowan walked out to meet him a little away from my side of the track. Lou stopped, straightened and saluted. Colonel McGowan returned the salute. When I saw the saluting, I stopped reading and paid attention.

"Lou, I hear you've asked for compassionate leave." "Yessir. My girlfriend was just pregnant when I left. I need leave to marry her. I want the baby to be born with my name."

"Son, some people worry it's too much to expect a man to come back to the field. If I let you go home will you come back and finish your tour?" There was no hesitation. "Yessir."

The Colonel was silent, then looked to the side and saw me watching. "Lieutenant Watson, what do you think?" "He's a fine troop sir."

McGowan looked back at Super Lou. "Yes he is. Specialist, I'm going to approve two weeks compassionate leave. Your orders will be ready when the Troop comes in on stand down tomorrow night. You will need to see the Red Cross office first thing the next morning to arrange stateside travel. You should be on an evening flight out of Tan Son Nhut." "Thank you sir." "Good luck, son. Your wife's getting a good man."

McGowan came into Six Track to use our radio to call his chopper back. He walked to one of the line vehicles, greeted the crew and got a smoke grenade. When the LOH appeared, he walked outside the circle and popped his own smoke. I was happy for Super Lou. He was a good troop. I was also happy to hear about stand down.

June 25

Out trains pulled out to the west about 0700 with a couple of tracks from Second Platoon as escorts to the road. The escorts were back by 0730 and the Troop moved to the north. As soon as we passed through the brush at the northern end of the Citadel, we stopped in the open space. Pete said our fuel truck had broken down at Checkpoint 18. We held there half an hour until it was confirmed that an M88 had arrived and our trains were going back to Hampton.

We headed east and were coming up on the western side of the Country Store at 0900. We kept moving east with only a few stops and by 1015 were another five klicks on, almost to Provincial Road 6A. We stopped in a very big circle and our dismounts searched the area we had circled and a little outside the circle. After less than half an hour, we mounted up and headed back about the way we had come. We were passing through the remnants of the Country Store at 1130, a little further north than on the way in. As soon as we were all on the other side, Wells noticed a rain cloud coming and stopped the Troop in a tight circle for lunch.

After lunch we headed southeast and passed through the Country

Store again, this time the furthest south of our three trips through. We searched some scattered brush east of the Country Store then turned around again and headed west. About 1320 our lead Sheridan arrived at Highway 19 and turned south as Pete got radio confirmation that the tail end of the convoy had cleared Trang Bang on Route 1. We reached the intersection with Route 1 in Trang Bang, and headed toward Cu Chi.

Almost as soon as we made the turn to Cu Chi base camp Wells called for cleared weapons and confirmation. Pete passed the message to Chico on the track intercom and Chico cleared our .50 caliber. Pete looked over at the rest of us as he pulled the clip from his pistol and pulled the action back to be sure no round was chambered. We all did the same to our M16s. All three platoons reported all weapons cleared within a minute after Six Track had done our clearing. Pete radioed for a double check and got the confirmations suspiciously fast.

The MP at the gate waved the column in with big circles of his right arm at 1505. Six Track parked next to the Troop Headquarters hooch less than ten minutes later. I went to the officers' hooch as soon as we pulled in to deposit my gear. Almost immediately there was a knock on the door. It was Super Lou. "I'm off to the Red Cross. Thank you for what you said." "It's true. Has the Army pressured you to get married?"

"Foxy, no sir. I want to." "Has she said yes?" "Yessir." "Congratulations."

Dinner was followed by a few beers at the Squadron Officers' Club. The air conditioner took the heat down a notch. I spent most of my time talking to Captain Dearborn, the Squadron S1. I asked him why the Squadron had so many West Point officers.

"It works like this, Foxy. Replacement Lieutenants and Captains are sent to Division without specific assignments. Whenever we have an open slot, or one opening up, I check on the incoming Armor officers. When there is a West Point Armor officer coming in, I go over to the replacement detachment to greet him. I tell him that the Division gets far more Armor officers than it has Armor jobs and that some Armor officers end up in Mech Infantry units or worse. I tell them that 2nd Battalion of the 34th Armor is usually guarding something in one or two tank outposts or parceled out to Infantry units one platoon at a time, which is definitely not proper work for an Armor officer. Then I tell them the Cav is the only unit in the Division where an Armor officer can be part of Armor being used the way it's supposed to be used. After all of that, I offer to ask for him by name if he will request the Cav. All of it is true, except the part about the Cav being used the way it's supposed to be, but that's close to true."

An unspoken message was clear and the process was efficiently self selecting. Anybody who heard Dearborn's pitch had a clue that asking for the Cav wasn't the path to a tranquil year. Not all accepted, but many did. When a unit and an officer asked for each other, why should Division personnel say no? The Cav officers weren't all West Pointers, but a lot more than a random share.

June 26

I got up with the Platoon Leaders. My early morning project was getting paid. I was due three months pay. Charlie borrowed a Cav jeep and drove me to the 1st of the 8th area. I took off my Cav brass as we pulled in, but didn't see anyone but the S1 in his office. I don't think he was the least bit embarrassed that he didn't come out to pay us. I got about $300 in bright new MPCs together with paperwork for the money that had been sent directly to my bank account. And I left.

We got back in time for the memorial service. Two empty pairs of boots this time. Instead of normal dinner, the Troop had an outdoor barbeque. The beer was paid for by some unit fund. The steaks and other food were from normal rations.

It was rumored that all of the Donut Dollies and nurses had been invited. Steaks were done and ready to eat before any women arrived. The cold beer was in tubs of ice, but nobody drank very fast. The food was better than usual and the mood was good, but the area wasn't really set up for a party. Most of the troops just sat on the ground in small groups near the charcoal grills. I visited a few of the groups I knew best before getting a meal. Wells and the Platoon Leaders also visited while waiting until all the troops had been served. We ate together on the ground near the center of the clusters.

I had finished eating and downing two beers when three Donut Dollies had arrived, two white, one Black. All three wore pale blue uniforms, like hospital volunteers wear, but with shorter skirts. They were experienced in dealing with lonely men in groups, organizing good, clean fun with only a subtle reminder of sex, but they still looked a little lost. Their arrival was noted by all fairly quickly but only ten or so of the troops got up to assist them in getting their meal. The others looked for a while and went back to talking with their friends.

The Donut Dollies ate, stayed a polite time moving from group to group chatting, then left. About that time I noticed some people getting carried into the showers, then one who looked like Lieutenant Murray, who had wandered away from our group. I decided it was time to go back to the officers' hooch. I worked on mounting maps on cardboard and covering them with salvaged clear plastic wrapping. Before I was done, I heard a mob headed toward the XO's room at the other end of the hooch. I put my work aside and left quietly through our front door while they were coming in the XO's door. I went to the Squadron Officers' Club. I really didn't want a beer, but thought I would be safe there.

I had just started sipping a beer when Nowak and Murray came in dripping wet. My two brother officers offered me a chance to chug my beer then picked me up and carried me outside to a waiting crowd of about twenty equally soaked troopers who assisted in carrying me to the shower hooch, anointing me with beer as we went. On arrival, I was deposited under a shower and drenched. The troops were acting like a bunch of college kids, which was about the right age for most of them.

June 27

No one spoke about the night before at breakfast, but there were a few sly smiles. There was an unusually early rain right after breakfast. After dinner all five of the Troop's officers and I shared three bottles of champagne at the Officers' Club to celebrate Wells' and Lieutenant Murray's recent promotions.

June 28

After breakfast I went to have the fragment in my neck checked. July 5 was picked as the date to cut it out. About 1600 I caught a ride to the Division Headquarters complex. I wanted to check in with Warrant Office Walker. I was directed to the 25th Military Intelligence Company and asked for Walker. He was in his office was next door. "Walker, Watson from the Three Quarter Cav. We put in a motion sensor south of the Boi Loi Woods."

"Good to see you, Lieutenant. Sit down."

"I'm curious about your toy. I've been very careful to radio in our position when we pass near. Has it worked out?" "Not sure. It's dead now. For a few nights we got some readings and fired at them, but it lasted less than ten days. Don't know if we hit it, Charlie found it or it just ran out early."

"Will you replace it?" "No plans to."

We talked more, then went to dinner at the Division officers' mess. During dinner, Walker talked about interrogating a Vietnamese woman. She was well documented as VC cadre. Like most Vietnamese women, she had long straight black hair.

"The Vietnamese really don't like being around us. Not so much disliking us as being uncomfortable with anything outside their own culture. So, we always use cultural isolation, question them with no other Vietnamese present, nothing Vietnamese in the room and more of us than needed in the room. Vietnamese women place great value on their hair. Government interrogators sometimes cut off a woman's hair to break her spirit. We don't. For this woman, we just clustered close to her and I touched her hair a couple of times. She sang. She answered every question and all of her answers that we could check were true."

We stayed for a movie shown in the mess hall. It was *The Night They Raided Minsky's*. The walk back to the Cav area was too long to be called fun, but I hadn't taken a walk in the relative coolness of the night for a long time.

18

Checking Out

June 29

We left Cu Chi at 0730. Less than an hour later we were picking up a large group of RFs at the north end of Trang Bang, about twenty per platoon. We went north on Highway 19 to Checkpoint B, pulled off the road just over the culvert and headed east on line. We swept slowly without dismounts through scattered brush then through the western hedgerow of the Citadel. Wells halted in the middle of the Citadel and called the platoon leaders to Six Track, together with the RF commander and his U.S. advisor. The plan was for separate platoon sweeps with their RF reinforcements. Six Track, the Medic Track and the First Platoon mortar track stayed in the middle of the open space and waited. The RF commander decided to go with one of the platoons.

Our day amounted to nothing. After I had radioed in our search areas, I was done for the day. The major excitement for our day was Pete repeating radio reports about Charlie Troop's recovery of a General's air conditioned house trailer that had some problem on the road to Tay Ninh City.

Pete and I moved inside Six Track with the rest of the crew for a rain front that passed at 1400. The rain was violent, but short. Pete called the Troop back together to return the RFs to Trang Bang about 1620. The return was done quickly and by 1720 we were pulling into a laager about 500 meters south of the western end of the Lower Boi Loi Woods. Our trains, plus a Radar Track, had met us when we returned from dropping off the RFs.

June 30

By 0700 we were ready to go, but stayed in our circle. Wells said Colonel McGowan was coming to give us a recon flight over the day's sweep of the Upper Boi Loi Woods. When Colonel McGowan's LOH landed on the south side of our laager Pete, Wright and Murray walked toward the chopper. Colonel McGowan headed toward Hughes and me. "Hughes, Watson, fine morning. Do you know where we're headed today?" "General direction, yes sir."

"Fine. They should be back in a few minutes. You load up as soon as they're back." "Yes sir." "Time to check in on some friends."

He headed toward the nearest track to talk to the crew. He was at the next track when the LOH came back from the north and landed about where it had taken off. Lieutenant Hughes took the front seat, I took the bench in back. As many times as I had done it, it was still surprising how much the land looked like the map. The pilot didn't fly over the Woods, but we were close enough to the edge that we could see almost all of it. As for recon, if an enemy soldier stood in an open spot and waved his arms I might have seen him.

Our trip was shorter than the first. We jumped off as soon as the LOH touched down and passed Colonel McGowan on his way to leave. As soon as I mounted Six Track, we started moving. We headed to the western edge of the Upper Boi Loi Woods a little north of the strip separating the two Woods. When we reached the strip, the Troop entered as a line facing roughly north and our left end just inside the western edge of the Woods. Once we started the sweep to the north, we were engulfed in the dense brush and the hot air that clung to it. Men jumped off individual tracks as there was something to look at, but we found nothing.

At 1200 we stopped for lunch near our April fight. After lunch we headed east toward the X cut. The drill remained the same, slow going through very heavy brush. We were a klick on from lunch at 1350 when the Third Platoon took several rounds of rifle fire. Two troopers were hit, one seriously.

There was no further incoming fire and the Troop never fired in response. I don't know how they got there so fast, but there were two gunships alternating firing runs to our right front almost as soon as the rifle fire started. "Foxy, flame baths next."

While five flame baths were dropped, someone found a clearing large enough to dust off our two wounded. When the last flame bath was dropped, we moved forward slowly into the area we thought the shots had come from. The area had been strafed and bombarded, but I saw no signs of the aerial attacks at all. We left the way we had come, passing under a heavy rain front. At 1630 we were out of the Woods and less than half an hour later laagering behind Ap Suoi Cao.

July 1

We moved south past the Lower Boi Loi Woods to the southern edge of the open space south of the Woods. Wells picked a relatively dry patch in the open for Six Track and the Medic Track and dispatched the platoons on separate searches.

At 1100 Second Platoon reported that one of its APCs, 22, was stuck in a mud puddle. We could see it from Six Track. At first it was funny watching it strain to get out and just spinning its tracks. Spewing mud behind both tracks trying to go forward and them giving up and spewing mud off the front of both tracks trying to go backward. Finally 22 stopped struggling and two other Second Platoon APCs lined up in front of it. They were cross cabled together, then the backs of the two were connected to 22 by two cables connected end to end. While the cables were being connected, Wells moved us to join Second Platoon and called First and Third to join us.

When the cables were all rigged, the lead APC took the slack out of the crossed cables and both tow vehicles moved forward slowly pulling 22 out of the pool. As soon as all three tracks were well clear of the mud they stopped and disconnected. Wells said 22's transmission was blown. As he spoke, an APC towing 22 started back toward Ap Suoi Cao. Pete radioed the platoons we'd be staying put long enough for lunch.

After lunch, we moved north to the southwest arm of the X cut and up toward the center. At the unoccupied hard site we reformed on line headed south into the point of the uncut quadrant of Woods between the southwest and southeast arms of the X.

Over four hours and many cigarettes later we broke out into the strip between the Upper and Lower Boi Loi Woods. In a few minutes we were moving to laager behind Ap Suoi Cao. As we were pulling up, I could see two APCs parked in the open. The white triangles on the upper rear corner of the side of the vehicle that marked them as ours were visible from a considerable distance. "What are our tracks doing there?" "They couldn't tow out. We've got an M88 coming out tonight. Two Two's going back to Cu Chi in the morning for a new transmission." An M88 came to join us with cooks and a repaired track.

July 2

My morning activities took a little extra effort to avoid the really wet spots. We were moving toward Checkpoint 18 by 0730. The M88 towing 22 moved as if there wasn't anything was attached. When we reached the edge of the village south of the Checkpoint 18, Second Platoon stopped on the east side of the road and the rest of the Troop headed north up Highway 19. Apparently we were clearing the road to Xom Bao Don because the seven klicks to the RF compound took almost half an hour. Our pickup was thirty RFs.

We rejoined Second Platoon and by 1000 we were searching scattered brush on the southern edge of the open area below the Woods by platoons. The platoons with RFs got the bigger clumps and the few hooches in the area.

After lunch we headed east into the brushy area along the western side of Provincial Road 6A, near where Lieutenant Nelson had been killed in March. The drill was searching by platoon again. At 1330 one of the RFs found a booby trap the hard way and Wells radioed for a priority dust off. That was as far east as we went. When the chopper left, we turned west. Wells dispatched platoons a little to the left or right of our center line to check one thing or another. I could make no sense out of what he chose to check and didn't. Our path took us through the southern end of the Country Store and 1500 meters further west by 1540. Another thirty minutes beyond that and we were approaching the Ap Suoi Cao fields.

That was the end of our searching for the day. Wells made sure that all the RFs were on First and Third Platoon tracks, then sent them on to take the RFs back. Six Track and the Medic Track stayed with Second Platoon to begin a laager two hundred meters from where we had spent last night. First and Third Platoons joined the laager with our trains at 1720.

At our evening briefing Pete passed on a warning from Division that a B52 strike was planned next morning in the Upper Boi Loi Woods, four klicks north and a klick east of our laager. We didn't worry about their accuracy, but it wasn't too pleasant to know that somebody thought there were enough gooks in the Woods to justify a B52 strike that close.

July 3

Getting up was the same as usual, but once we were packed at 0830 we formed on line in the open pointed a little east of north and waited. As soon as we broke our circle, our trains and one track in need of repairs headed toward the highway. Pete showed me on the map where the bombs were going in. It was near the area of the Upper Boi Loi that we had swept on the first.

At 0845 Pete said, "It's about time now." Two minutes later it came. The first impact was visual. A column of dirty grey smoke and dust jumped straight up out of the Woods, then swept from left to right like a curtain drawn sideways. It ended with a dull grey rectangle drawn in the sky resting on the Woods at its bottom. When the curtain was fully drawn, the rumble in the ground and the sound of the explosions reached us together. Feeling the ground shake below us was more of a shock than how loud the explosions four klicks away were. Immediately the grey rectangle began to lose its sharp outline, changed into a dirty, low cloud and then disappeared. It came and went too fast to be confident of estimating anything, but I think the smoke and dust had risen 300 meters into the air and swept across an 800 meter front.

The entire Troop sat silent for at least a minute after the noise was over. When the spell broke, we headed north. Four klicks north we came to the Highway 26 trace a klick west of the edge of the Upper Boi Loi Woods. We stopped short of the road for a while. Pete was on the radio a lot and we were obviously being held in place for something. Several LOHs took turns crisscrossing the Woods two to three klicks east of us.

By 1000 whatever we had been waiting for was over. We turned toward the Woods on the south side of the road. At the edge of the Woods we formed on line. Again there was a delay for something. At 1020 we started east again. Because the road went off to the southeast, that meant that we slowly crossed the road as we angled across it. We moved very slowly in the brush at the edge of the Woods and stopped from time to time without apparent reason. The LOHs still buzzed back and forth well in front of us. In half an hour we did less than 400 meters and then stopped. "They've spotted gooks on the move in front of us. We're holding here for the fireworks."

One of the LOHs had a minigun mounted and it began a firing run a klick in front of us as Pete spoke. It was followed shortly by two Cobra gunships for a conventional series of rockets and minigun runs. We sat quietly and watched. We hadn't even been sniped at and the firing runs were much farther away from us than usual. Just before the gunships pulled out I heard Captain Thomas calling in a fire mission on the Artillery net. His first rounds landed a klick east of us. He got four volleys of "battery two" spread out a klick in front of us before he was shut down for the next batch of choppers. That installment was four Hueys dropping flame baths beginning about 1110. They were followed by two F100s making two napalm passes each. We could see the planes and the top of the napalm fire balls, but we were too far away to feel the heat. The planes cleared about 1125 and Captain Thomas called for another twelve rounds in the same area. Three times after that he waited about five minutes, moved the rounds a little and repeated the battery two. He called end of mission after the last twelve, about 1145. Almost immediately two LOHs appeared to flit over the target area.

By then, most of the troopers I could see were eating as they watched

18—Checking Out

the show. I heard Pete radio the Platoon Leaders to get anybody who hadn't eaten yet fed quickly. Our call came at 1220 and we started east at a steady slow pace. The scout choppers moved much further east as soon as we started moving.

At 1230 Pete reported on the latest development, "Colonel McGowan just cleared an airstrike on some gooks they caught swimming in a bomb crater." They had been spotted about six klicks east of us, near the northern edge of the Lower Boi Loi Woods. Apparently our fireworks display was far enough away they saw no reason to skip their bath. Nobody will ever know if they got away, but their bath was supplemented with white phosphorus rockets followed by five hundred pound bombs.

We didn't stop for the airstrike in the distance. About 700 meters further in we came on the edge of the B52 bomb impact area at 1300. The craters didn't have any water at the bottom and still had rough edges. The big craters weren't continuous, or even regularly spaced, but they were close enough together that it was hard to imagine that anyone had been in the impact area and lived. After searching for half an hour, we found one RPG round and some clothes with fresh blood stains, but no bodies. Moving and searching continued at a snail's pace. The craters were not dense enough to stop us, but each was too big to cross. Another hour brought us 600 meters further in and to the eastern edge of the impact area. We headed back though the impact area again for another hour that found nothing.

When we quit the search, we moved north to the southwest arm of the X cut and turned toward the center of the cut. At the center we turned left and went up the northwest arm to Highway 19 northeast of Xom Bao Don. From there we were inside Hampton by 1800. Track 22 was waiting for us with a new drive train. A Cav pay call was set up with dinner. I told Charlie to go in for pay tomorrow. The dinner line was closed early by a half hour downpour. Hampton had no drainage. Most of the water collected in the perimeter road and reliquified the mud pudding.

July 4

We left Hampton at 0815 to sweep and outpost Route 22 to Checkpoint 22. As the convoy passed our outposts on its way to Tay Ninh, Wells ordered early chow. After eating, the Troop assembled on the east side of Highway 22 at the middle of the Little Rubber.

We started on line northeast up the spaces between the neat rows of trees. With frequent stops we reached the end of the trees about three klicks from the road at 1250. We pivoted to the right and headed back to the road. There was steady rain all the way back. My rain jacket fit over my flak jacket and kept my torso dry, except for the sweat it trapped. My steel pot was waterproof. My pants and boots got soaked. I was using a cardboard mounted map covered with salvaged clear plastic sheeting that stayed reasonably dry. Most of the troopers put on ponchos, the rest just ignored the rain. The rain stopped when we got back to the road at 1445. We were settled inside Hampton by 1520. Charlie was waiting when we arrived. I told Lewis he went in tomorrow.

Darkness fell and the day's business ended without any notice of Independence Day.

July 5

The Troop headed for Ap Suoi Cao at 0730. We spent the day moving slowly through the heavy green embrace of the Lower Boi Loi Woods. We exited the Woods about 1445 and were back in Hampton at 1545. Lewis was waiting. When we parked, I got a message from Squadron to be at the Hampton helicopter pad at 1615 to take the evening hash and trash chopper back to Cu Chi for my neck to be examined.

The Squadron clinic building was just across the paved road from the Delta Troop pad. The Squadron Surgeon was there with one medic when I arrived. "Watson, just in time. We were about to shut down for the day. Sit here."

I sat on the edge of his examining table. He rubbed the side of my neck where the fragment was, stopped then did it again. "I was wrong. It's not moving much and it's a lot deeper than I thought. It may move later, but unless it gives you some problem, I don't want to cut that deep to get it out. If it hurts, we'll dig it out." I said, "Thanks for that happy thought."

July 6

The chopper left the Delta Troop pad at 1000. Bravo in the Citadel was the first stop. The big open space north of Trang Bang was easy to identify. When I got off, there was only Six Track, the Medic Track and a mortar track in the middle of the Citadel. Six Track's rear ramp was down so I bent down to walk in then climbed up to my jeep seat.

Wells didn't speak until I climbed up; "Well, are you all fixed?" "No. He changed his mind. He's going to leave it in." "Third Platoon's in the brush at the north end. Second Platoon's working the tree line on the west. Third Platoon's in the brush at the south end. We're just sitting here until they find something interesting."

18—Checking Out

Pete went back to his radio and I reached for mine. Charlie should have called in our location, but I wanted to make sure by doing it again. Then we sat. I read and smoked. At 1115 Pete called a chow break. The platoons went back to work at noon.

At 1320 I heard rifle fire to the south. Pete got radio traffic immediately. Second Platoon had almost reached the southern end of the tree line when their dismounts spotted three gooks in a hole and fired. There was no return fire. One was killed and the other two captured. They had no weapons, but wore pieces of uniform and carried enemy identification cards. Pete was satisfied that it was under control and left it to the platoon leader to load the two prisoners on a chopper without our help. After the prisoners were gone the platoons went back to searching without further excitement.

About 1530 Wells moved Six Track four hundred meters south and called the platoons to laager around us. Our trains, with an escort of two returning tracks, arrived through the west side tree line about 1610 and the line track crews started stretching their concertina.

July 7

Our departure was delayed waiting for a POW guide. One of the prisoners taken the day before had agreed to show us a cache near where he had been captured. About 0830 Second Platoon left with the trains to escort them through the western tree line to Highway 19. As Second Platoon left, I got a radio message that all the Cav FO teams had been transferred to a new artillery battalion. Call-signs and everything else remained the same, just as part of a different unit. The message came from the FDC call sign. I had no idea who it actually was on the other end.

Second Platoon was back in thirty minutes, just as a slick was landing with the POW, a military intelligence type and an interpreter. Wells met with them to get the location of the cache. They looked at the maps and I saw the POW pointing south toward where he had been captured. The POW and his minders rode on the Medic Track. We headed in the direction the POW had pointed and on through the western tree line and stopped fifty meters on. The POW and his minders got down with a First Platoon escort and started looking for the cache. When the POW said he had found it, the hole they dug out was empty. It looked like the cache, if there had ever been one, had been emptied the night before. Pete advised Squadron and the POW and his handlers were picked up by 1030. We continued a search to the south until 1130 and broke for chow in a fair sized clearing.

Chico was on radio watch, "Foxy, there's a chopper inbound with visitors for you." When the chopper radioed in again, I popped smoke behind Six Track. A LOH landed, two officers got out of the back and it took off again. As they walked toward me, I identified a Lieutenant Colonel and a Major, both Field Artillery. I saluted the Colonel, "Welcome to Bravo Troop, sir."

He returned the salute, as did the Major. "Lieutenant Watson, welcome to Third of the Thirteenth. We wanted to meet all of our new teams at the Cav." That was my new unit, 3rd Battalion of the 13th Artillery, and the Colonel was its CO. He introduced himself and the Major, the battalion's S3. The battalion had taken over responsibility for artillery support for the Cav and Captain Thomas and all the current FO teams had been transferred with the change. The Battery at Hampton was part of my new battalion, but that had never mattered in calling for fire. Wherever we were, if I called for fire, it came from the closest available battery.

"I checked your file Watson. You've done a great job. How long have you been out?" "Since January, sir."

"I thought so. I'm surprised you've been out that long. As soon as we have a replacement, we'll be bringing you in." They talked to me a little more, then spoke briefly to Charlie and Lewis. While they were finishing up, they had Chico call their chopper back. I opened a can of mixed fruit as soon as they were gone.

After lunch, it was more of the same. We found nothing. We broke off the searching at 1540 and moved west to Highway 19. We went north four klicks and set up our laager on the east side of the highway. Our trains arrived almost immediately. I only asked for two defensive targets, east and south. A klick north was in the village and a klick west was an area of scattered occupied hooches.

At evening briefing Pete shared the latest directive from Division. "The Cav is to be prepared to engage enemy forces in the vicinity of Tay Ninh City on thirty minutes notice. We will be committed in the city if that is where the enemy is. Intelligence is that the gooks will launch a five day attack trying to get enough of Tay Ninh to set up a capital. Division has instructed us to get the enemy, wherever he is, before he has a chance to dig in. These orders supersede our earlier instructions to avoid fighting in the city. Any questions?"

"What if it rains?" "You'll get wet. Go tell your lads the good news."

July 8

Puddles on the ground showed that I had slept through a heavy rain during the night. First Platoon and our trains left at 0700 to open Highway

19 north to Checkpoint 25. Second Platoon followed to do the same into Trang Bang. Third Platoon stayed with us. When First Platoon had cleared to Checkpoint 18, our trains stayed to wait for someone else to clear the road to Go Dau Ha.

Both road platoons were back by 0920 and we headed out on our day's work. It wasn't all that much. Our searches found nothing and were finished at 1500. We headed back the way we had come. We laagered 200 meters south of the night before.

July 9

Stand to was 0540. Puddles from the morning's rain spotted the entire laager. The Platoon Leaders were called to Six Track just before 0730. Colonel McGowan asked for smoke inside the laager and landed twenty meters from Six Track. As soon as Colonel McGowan got off the LOH, the pilot pulled out to loiter overhead until called back.

Colonel McGowan held a 1 to 100,000 map up against the side of Six Track and pointed as he spoke, "If we get called to Tay Ninh, Bravo's most likely route will be to Xom Bao Dom then up Highway 26 all the way to the east side of Tay Ninh. Exactly when you get off Highway 26 will depend on the situation. You were as far as the Cau Khoi Rubber last March. Right?" "Yes sir."

"Good then you know most of the way. Do you all have the 1 to 25,000 that covers the city?" "Yes sir." "If we are called to fight in Tay Ninh, you are authorized to fire into any building that appears to have enemy soldiers in it, other than the main Cao Dai Temple. No firing into the Cao Dai Temple without specific permission from Squadron. Foxy, I don't know what the Artillery rules are. Any questions?"

"When is this supposed to start?" "We really don't know. It could be as early as today. Pete, call the chopper back. Have him take you and two platoon leaders up the route to the east side of Tay Ninh and come back. I'll take Foxy and a platoon leader when you get back."

Wells, Wright and Murray were gone almost half an hour. While we waited Colonel McGowan visited tracks with Hughes. Chico monitored the Squadron radio net. When the pilot asked for smoke to land, Chico tossed one from the CO's seat. Colonel McGowan and Hughes headed over as soon as they saw the smoke. By the time the chopper landed, both were at Six Track.

Colonel McGowan got in front and Hughes and I got in back. I'm not sure why we took the trip. Highway 26 was a straight line from Xom Bao Don to a point east of Tay Ninh. It was reassuring to see that the ground looked like the map, but I didn't learn anything. When we arrived over the outskirts of Tay Ninh the pilot turned and we headed down the straight line that we had come up. When we got back the Troop had moved to south of the Ap Suoi Cao fields. We landed to the side of Six Track. Hughes and I jumped as soon as the chopper touched and it left immediately. I had a short walk to Six Track and climbed up. Pete waited until Hughes got to his track and started again.

We turned north toward the gap between the Upper Boi Loi and Lower Boi Loi. It was about 1000 when we headed east into the gap. The ground was completely saturated and the going was slow. The lead Sheridan didn't do too badly, but the APCs behind it were often temporarily stuck and any stuck vehicle stopped the whole column. After a while Pete radioed something about "essentially impassable" and we turned north on line and moved into the Upper Boi Loi Woods. It took us an hour and a half to get to the southeast arm of the X cut. We stopped for lunch in the cut.

We started again at 1240 to the center of the X then down the southwest arm. We weren't stopping on purpose anywhere, but the wet deadfall jumble slowed us considerably. We were out of the Upper Boi Loi Woods at 1430. We continued south past the Ap Suoi Cao fields then turned toward Highway 19. On our way out I saw the usual contingent of three or four kids and a couple of water buffalo staring at us from the southern edge of the fields. At 1610 we laagered 400 meters south of last night.

July 10

Our day was a repeat of July 8. From our laager we swept the road between Checkpoint 25 and Trang Bang, then went in past the Ap Suoi Cao fields. At the end of the fields, we turned southeast and started searching our way toward Provincial Road 6A.

At some point, Wells must have decided that a particular clump of brush seemed unusually threatening. Without any warning, a Sheridan fired its main gun into the brush. I snapped to look toward the sound of the explosion, but relaxed quickly when I recognized the smoke near the barrel and the rocking of the vehicle as signs that it had fired, not been hit. The next thing I saw was Doc sky walking. He looked like a cartoon character standing still in midair before gravity finally kicks in. In response to the explosion, he had immediately stepped off the top of the Medic Track, running to the sound of the guns. When I saw him, he had his portable kit in one hand and a look on his face that showed he had just realized his leap was for nothing. He landed hard then climbed back on.

That firing without warning was the only notable event of the day. Our route out was about the same as our route in. We got to our laager, almost on top of our July 8 laager, at 1550.

July 11

I was up about 0600. When Chico and Lewis had the tarp down, I showered standing in the relatively dry area that had been under cover during the night's rain.

Second Platoon went north to Checkpoint 25 and Third south to Trang Bang. A few minutes after they left, Colonel McGowan radioed in to offer Pete a chance to overfly our route for the day. Pete quickly showed Hughes and me a rough path through the Upper Boi Loi Woods on his map. We got on the LOH as soon as it landed. We were over a thousand feet high when we crossed the edge of the Woods. We came in over the southwest corner of the Upper Boi Loi, passed over the center of the X cut, and flew back to Bravo. We saw nothing other than features we knew already with the random pox of bomb and shell craters.

We were back on the ground with First Platoon by 0820. We had seen our trains pulling up to Checkpoint 18 before we landed. Third Platoon rejoined us at 0830 and Second Platoon ten minutes later. We headed straight for the southwest corner of the Upper Boi Loi then formed on line and swept into the Woods at 0945. We spent the entire morning moving to the northeast, making very slow progress. The saturated ground compounded the problems of keeping formation. In the two and a half hours until we stopped for chow at 1215, we managed little more than a klick.

We were off again at 1300 and managed two klicks in the same direction in two hours. However, the reward at the end of the two hours was breaking into the southeast arm of the X cut. A Third Platoon Sheridan threw a track on its first turn in the cut. It took an hour to get the track remounted. First and Second Platoons searched the edge of the cut in the immediate vicinity while we waited. As soon as the Sheridan was put back together, we moved to the center of the X cut then down the southwest arm to the edge of the Woods. From the edge of the Woods it was our normal route around the Ap Suoi Cao fields and on toward Highway 19. We didn't go all the way to the road, turning south to laager 400 meters east of the night before.

July 12

Road clearing was the same as yesterday. When it was done the Troop assembled on Highway 19, then swept east into the Citadel. When we were through the Citadel's western tree line, Second Platoon headed south while the rest of the column continued east across the open area. Pete said Second Platoon would be checking the area just south of the southern end of the Citadel.

When we crossed the Citadel and passed through the tree line on its east side, Third Platoon turned to the southeast and we went on with them. First Platoon continued on to the east, but almost immediately stopped to check a brush cluster. Third Platoon continued on for a klick toward Provincial Road 6A before stopping for its first detailed search of an abandoned hooch.

The rest of the day the platoons searched separately. Six Track and the Medic Track stayed with Third Platoon. Most of the day passed with nothing of note. At 1430 Pete called for First Platoon to join us. A few minutes later came an embarrassed report that one of First Platoon's APCs was stuck in a flooded rice paddy. Pete changed his plans and we went with Third Platoon to them. From half way there we could see an APC almost alone in the middle of a small pond. There were scattered puddles throughout the area, but the water around the stuck APC was the largest pool in sight. It looked suspiciously like someone had decided to run through the water for the fun of it.

When we arrived to watch from near the edge of the water, another First Platoon track had backed part way into the water in front of the stuck track and two troopers from the stuck track were wading in the water to connect them with two cables connected end to end. A third track was backing up to be cross cabled to the middle track.

When all the connections were in place, all three tracks tried to move forward. The two tow tracks had little tread slippage, but were clearly straining. The stuck track's treads spun free and threw up small plumes of water in the rear. I heard Wells radio that the stuck track should disconnect power and just idle. The stuck track was still just barely pulled forward by its tow team. After the stuck APC had moved a few feet, Pete radioed for it to try gentle power and it moved forward steadily out of the water.

When the cables were all recovered and stowed, we headed across the driest land available to the southwest toward Second Platoon. When we arrived south of the Citadel, they were waiting in a column pointed in the same direction and fell in at the end of our column. Fifteen hundred meters further on we reached Route 19 and turned left toward Trang Bang. Next was a right turn on Route 1. Bravo was settled inside Hampton by 1600.

July 13

We left Hampton at 0730. First Platoon went out first to clear the road to Checkpoint 18, then went south to Checkpoint 12. Six Track went with Second and Third Platoons to clear Route 1 into Trang Bang and pick up forty-five RFs at the intersection with Highway 19. As soon as they were settled in, we started north on Highway 19 at road clearing speed.

First Platoon was waiting at Checkpoint 12. We stopped and Wells arranged for some of the RFs to move over to First Platoon APCs. As soon as that was done, we moved east off the road on line. Just off the road, Pete called a halt to put down the RFs and our dismounts and we headed east at a slow walking speed with stops to check anything of interest. There wasn't much to check, but we checked it all and found nothing. At the western tree line of the Citadel we found bits and pieces of gook debris in some foxholes of indeterminate age. We continued into the Citadel and stopped for lunch at 1130. Some of the RFs had packed cold cooked rice, but most of them happily ate C-rations.

We were back in business at 1230. We moved through the brush at the south end of the Citadel and Pete cut the platoons loose to search the area immediately south. As we had done in that area several times before, Six Track and the Medic Track spent the afternoon parked in the middle of the area. We could see all three platoons most of the time moving in and out of the brush and homesteads around the perimeter of the open space.

The day's rain was a quarter hour beginning at 1315. Less than half the RFs carried any rain gear. Most of the ones who did had something like a U.S. poncho, but smaller. It looked like it was made from green plastic sheeting. A couple wore makeshift ponchos cut from clear plastic sheeting. When the rain stopped, they rolled their ponchos back up and tied them back on their belts. By 1430 Third Platoon was at the southern end of the search area about two klicks north of the northern edge of Trang Bang. Pete called the other platoons to move to Third Platoon and we joined them. The Troop then moved to Highway 19 and took the RFs back to where we had picked them up.

Up Route 1 to Hampton through light civilian traffic went quickly. Super Lou checked in at Six Track as soon as we stopped. He flashed a wedding ring and a smile. Wells sent him back to First Platoon, "I think your slot in the Mortar Track is still open."

July 14

Road work began at 0740. Troop assembly was two klicks south of Checkpoint 22, at the turnoff we had taken to get to the fight on February

2. We spent the morning sweeping the area south of the eastern end of the Little Rubber. Heavy rain slowed us down for twenty minutes in the morning. When we broke for lunch we were a klick north of our fight on February 2. After lunch it was a little more of the same then north into the Rubber itself and a slow drive down the rows between the rubber trees back to the road. We were back at Hampton at 1500.

At evening briefing Lieutenant Wright reported that some of his vehicles were so undermanned that their crews weren't getting enough sleep because of night watches. I volunteered for the first watch in the cupola of one of his APCs. Watch began shortly after dusk. When I started, I could see better in the half light than through the starlight scope. Even when it was full dark, I couldn't use the starlight scope all the time. It did increase the light, but the result was a harsh green and white picture. If you looked at anything for very long through the scope, it was almost hypnotic. I wish I'd known what a man moving in the distance looked like in the scope before I started looking for one. I did two hours of half hourly radio reports to the Platoon Leader's track, then woke the Track Commander and went to bed back at Six Track.

July 15

The Troop left Hampton at 0720 to Checkpoint 18 and then over the well beaten ground south of Ap Suoi Cao. At the end of the village fields we turned north. Wells said nothing, but I knew where we were headed. We were moving slower than usual because the wet ground made a considerable difference. The tracks slipped frequently and had to pick their path far more carefully. While we were still in the open area east of the village fields, I got a radio message from my Battalion S1. My replacement was arriving tonight. I was to show him what he had to do for three days and leave the evening of the 18th. When I passed this on to Pete, he gave me a big smile.

When we got to the edge of the Upper Boi Loi, we formed on line and went into the brush 500 meters south of the opening made by the southwest arm of the X cut. We moved northeast, paralleling the cut. Despite my good news, being in the Woods was as unpleasant as usual as the tracks slipped and zigzagged through the wet green junk. Every bomb crater we came near was about half full of water and the shell craters were almost entirely full.

At 1100 we reached the edge of the southeast arm. We turned to sweep southeast parallel to that arm with the left flank vehicle of our line at the edge of the cut. The line of vehicles was about a hundred and fifty meters wide, so our right flank was well into the uncut Woods. We covered the two klicks to the gap between the Upper and Lower Boi Loi Woods in just a little over an hour and stopped for lunch. Word of my replacement had spread. Everyone who came over to Six Track had some passing comment about the general worthlessness of people who got transferred to cushy jobs.

When the lunch break was over, Wells had each platoon send a foot patrol into the scattered brush directly to our south. The low land next to the stream was fully saturated with water and would not have been suitable for the tracks. They didn't go much beyond visual contact with the vehicles and didn't find anything. When they came back, we loaded up and started up the middle of the cut toward the center of the X. Third Platoon was bringing up the rear and one of its Sheridans threw a track. It took two vehicles to help the Sheridan drive back over its track after it had been disconnected and stretched out. After that it was track jacks to reconnect the two ends of the track.

Other than my news and the broken tread, it was just another day in the Woods. We went to the center of the X, turned left and went down the southwest arm to the edge. From there we went to laager two klicks east of Ap Suoi Cao at 1540. Our trains arrived twenty minutes later.

When the evening hash and trash chopper called for smoke, I went out to meet it. A First Lieutenant got off and introduced himself, Ed Wahnee. He knew who I was. I had no idea if there was a formal drill, but some things were obvious. The first introduction was to Wells, then Charlie and Lewis. Next was Chico and Baker. Then a walk to meet each Platoon Leader before dinner. After dinner we went over radio call signs and I showed him where my signal order was. He actually had been briefed at Battalion on radio procedures before he was sent out. He had the 1:25,000 map that included where we were. I showed him where the rest of my maps were and explained my drill of parking Six Track pointed north with four standard defensive targets.

An extra cot showed up from somewhere and we crammed it under the tarp. I had radio watch from 2300 to midnight and Wahnee stood it with me. There wasn't anything doing on the radio and so we just talked, mostly about him. He was a Comanche whose family lived near Ft. Sill.

July 16

When we got up I went through my morning ablutions. Wahnee watched the activity around us without saying much. Nobody was nasty to him, but there was no rush to meet the new FO. As soon as I was dressed,

I explained about the laundry procedures and dropped off what would be my last bundle through the Cav's laundry as we walked over for breakfast. I didn't know if I outranked Wahnee, but I assumed it was my show to run. I told him I'd do the work today and he'd watch. Tomorrow morning it would be his and I'd watch.

We left the laager at 0740. It was as ugly a day as we had done in a long time. Four klicks north and a little east took us to the end of the southwest arm of the X cut. We started up the cut to the northeast, passed the center of the X and kept going to the far end of the northeast arm, a few hundred meters from the Saigon River. We got there just before 0900 and headed on line south into the Woods. Three hours later we broke through the edge of the southeast arm of the X cut, about a klick from where it ended at the southern edge of the Upper Boi Loi Woods. Throughout the morning, I pointed out landmarks and reference points. Each time I radioed in our position, I first told him where I thought we were and why. He followed on his map and said little.

We took our lunch stop in the middle of the cut and started moving again at 1240. This time we went southwest on line straight into the dense brush on the other side of the cut. Morning and afternoon we had found nothing. We broke out of the Woods at 1620. Once we were in the open, we took a normal route to the north end of the Citadel and laagered 500 meters in.

I reminded Wahnee about Six Track parking pointed north and went through the four defensive targets. The south target was in the middle of open space and easily visible, so I called in a fire mission to fire it in, one gun in adjustment. The first round landed due south, made me look good and I ended the mission.

July 17

Wake up was at 0550. Normal move time came and went without explanation. There wasn't much traffic on Pete's radios. Finally I asked what we were waiting for and he just said that we had been told to stand fast. I noticed that the cooks were still with us, there hadn't been any morning chopper to take them out. Wahnee was in the FO seat and monitored the Artillery net. For another two hours I just hung around Six Track, smoked and waited.

At 1000 a chopper arrived to pick up the cooks and Wells called the Troop to mount up. I sat next to Wahnee. We moved two klicks south down the center of the Citadel then turned left through the east tree line. Wahnee radioed in when we started moving, when we turned and when

18—Checking Out

we broke the tree line, about what I would have done. Five hundred meters east of the tree line, Pete halted to call the Platoon Leaders to Six Track. Our job for the day was searching an area about four klicks long and a klick wide stretched out along the near side of Provincial Road 6A. Pete assigned a third of the area to each platoon.

When the platoons took off on their own, Six Track and the Medic Track followed Third Platoon in the center. I reminded Wahnee about reporting independent movement by separate elements and he radioed it in. After that there wasn't much for us to do. I felt strange with somebody else sitting in my seat.

At 1415 Wells got a radio report that all of First Platoon was stuck. It must have taken quite a while and a lot of effort before Lieutenant Hughes was forced to admit that. Pete ordered Second and Third Platoons to move to where First was stuck. We stopped a fair distance from them. Today, First Platoon had two Sheridans, the Platoon Leader's track, a mortar track and three other APCs. They were in three clusters, in three adjacent rice paddies. Each rice paddy was covered with standing water. Two pairs of tracks were cabled together and apparently one of each pair had got stuck trying to tow the other. Most of the troops were standing on top of a vehicle when we arrived, all with wet pants legs.

I never heard Wells criticize Hughes on the radio, but he didn't rush to relieve his embarrassment. There was no dry land close enough to the stuck vehicles to just drive up and tow them out. Third Platoon cabled three APCs together directly on the line of travel of one of the stuck vehicles. The APC closest to the stuck vehicles was pointed toward it and the other two were pointed in the opposite direction. When all three were lined up and connected, they drove in close enough to connect cables to the stuck vehicle. There was a little slippage when they started pulling out, but the stuck vehicle was towed to firmer ground.

Wells didn't use Second Platoon for extractions. He just kept them on solid ground away from the mess. If we needed someone who could move, it would be them.

The First Platoon vehicles came out one at a time and each was a slow task. By 1630 we had recovered five of First Platoon's vehicles. Still stuck were the platoon leader's APC and a Sheridan. Both were well stuck, apparently in the deepest water. Before tackling them, Wells sent Second Platoon to secure our laager site next to Highway 19 a klick south of Ap Suoi Cao. He gave Wahnee the coordinates and Wahnee relayed the information to the Artillery.

Recovering the last two vehicles took almost an hour. I suspect that leaving the Platoon Leader's track to last was a deliberate lesson, but Pete never said a word about it. All of First Platoon was mobile at 1730 and we all left on the same route Second Platoon had taken. When we arrived at the laager, Second Platoon occupied roughly the eastern third of a circle about the right size. Our trains had arrived and the cooks were already setting up for supper, a little closer to Second Platoon than the center of the circle. As soon as Six Track was parked pointed north in the center, Wahnee plotted four targets. I told him there was no point in asking for the north one in the village and he radioed in the other three.

After the laager set up, Pete called the Platoon Leaders. He said we were unlikely to be called upon to work in areas of significant standing water, but that if we were, it was the responsibility of each platoon leader to make sure that no more than one or two vehicles were committed until it was confirmed that the water could be crossed. After a short pause he went on to announce that our preliminary orders for tomorrow were to sweep between Highway 19 and the western tree line of the Citadel.

July 18

At 0715 First Platoon went north to Checkpoint 25. The rest of the Troop went to Trang Bang. Wahnee had radioed in First Platoon's route and reported the checkpoints on our route as we passed them. When we reached Checkpoint 07, we turned and went back to join First Platoon north of Checkpoint 12. Wells called the Platoon Leaders over and split up the area between the highway and the western tree line of the Citadel. First Platoon got the north, Second the center and Third the south. Six Track and the Medic Track stayed with Second Platoon. There weren't any hooches in the area, it was all checking clumps of brush. All morning long we found nothing significant. After a brief mid-morning rain squall, the sun quickly dried us as dry as a sweating man can be.

At 1100 Pete called the platoons back together to go into the Citadel. Once in, Wells sent the platoons to search separate nearby sections of the tree line. Six Track and the Medic Track parked well into the clear area. About 1230 the platoons were called into the open for lunch. I ate a can of fruit and read the new issue of *Stars and Stripes*. About 1330 Pete sent the platoons back to separate tree line searches. Wahnee paid attention to what the platoons were doing, Pete worked his radios, the crew napped and I read.

I had just started on the crossword puzzle in the *Stars and Stripes* when Pete called the platoons in and the laager formed around us. Pete answered a radio call and spoke to me, "Hash and trash arrives in about ten minutes. Better get packed, Foxy, it's your ride."

I didn't carry much and it was all packed in one duffel bag. I was

18—Checking Out

wearing my helmet and flak jacket. I put the duffel bag and my rifle on the ground next to the track and went to say goodbye. Chico, Charlie, Lewis and Baker were putting up the tarp and the cots. I shook hands with each and exchanged wishes for good luck. Wahnee was in the FO seat calling in his night defensive targets. I reached up to shake his hand. Pete was inside the track talking to the chopper on the Squadron net. He switched nets and told a platoon leader to pop smoke. I picked up the *Stars and Stripes* inside the track.

Pete extended his hand, "Good luck, Foxy." I shook his hand, "Good luck, sir, take care of the boys."

The chopper was just over the western tree line and headed toward the smoke. I walked between two line tracks and the troops who saw me gave a little wave and smiled. Lots of people knew I was leaving, but carrying my duffel bag made it clear to all. I smiled and nodded in return. I got to the Huey just as it was through unloading. No one else was getting on. I got on the back bench facing forward and the pilot took off as soon as I sat down. I started back to work on the crossword puzzle. I paid no attention to where we were going until the chopper started swerving sharply from side to side and I looked up to see why.

We were over the southern edge of the Ap Suoi Cao fields, headed toward the village. Out the chopper's door I could see we were very low and had just flown over two kids on a wide dirt path. Three running water buffalo were almost directly under us, headed toward the village. The pilot was trying to herd the water buffalo with his chopper. I went back to the crossword puzzle.

Glossary

105—105mm howitzer. A U.S. artillery piece that fires a projectile 105 millimeters, about four inches, in diameter.

155—155mm howitzer. A U.S. artillery piece that fires a projectile 155 millimeters, about six inches, in diameter.

3/4 Cavalry—3rd Squadron, 4th Cavalry. Bravo Troop was part of the 3/4 Cavalry.

Aerorifles—The Infantry platoon in Delta Troop.

AIT—Advanced Individual Training. The next stage of training for an enlisted man after basic training. Training for a specific branch, such as infantry, artillery or armor.

AK or AK47—Ubiquitous Russian/Chicom assault rifle. Full or semi-automatic with a thirty round banana shaped magazine. Primary weapon of the NVA and VC.

APC or Armored Personnel Carrier—Any armored vehicle designed primarily to carry troops into combat. In Bravo Troop an M113.

ARVN—Army of the Republic of Vietnam. Used to identify any South Vietnamese army personnel, unit or equipment. Spoken as "Arvin."

Bunker—Any of a broad range of fortifications and protective structures, from a simple hole in the ground with some overhead cover to elaborate multi-room constructions above or below ground.

C4—Army plastic explosive.

Cav—Contraction of Cavalry.

Chicom—Contraction of Chinese Communist. Usually used to identify something of Chinese Communist design or manufacture, such as a "Chicom grenade."

Chinook—A CH-47 helicopter. Bigger than a Huey. Twin main rotors and interior space for twenty or thirty troops.

Chopper—Any helicopter.

CO—Commanding Officer.

Glossary

Cobra—An AH-1 Attack Helicopter. Designed solely as a gunship.

Concertina—A slinky like roll of barbed wire about three feet in diameter that can be compressed into a donut or stretched to form a barrier.

CS—A form of tear gas.

Delta Troop—The 3/4 Cavalry's Air Cavalry Troop, made up of helicopters and the Aerorifles.

Dust off—Evacuating wounded or removing dead by helicopter. Also the helicopter used for the evacuation.

FDC—Fire Direction Center. The part of an Artillery unit that receives fire requests, decides whether to fire and forwards firing data and commands to the guns.

Fire Support Base—A semi-permanent U.S. fortification containing all or part of an artillery battery.

FO—Forward observer. The person, usually a Field Artillery Lieutenant, who requests and adjusts artillery fire.

FSB—Fire Support Base.

Gook—Any enemy soldier.

Gunship—A helicopter equipped and used to provide fire support.

Hooch—Vietnamese hut-like home or small, semi-permanent U.S. Army building.

Huey—A UH-1 Utility Helicopter. The standard U.S. Army helicopter in Vietnam. Used as a transport, ambulance or gunship.

IO—Information Officer. An Army press agent.

Klick—Slang for kilometer. One thousand meters, about six-tenths of a mile.

Laager—An all-around defensive formation of an armored unit. The word was adopted into English during the North African Campaign of World War II from the Afrikaans word for a defensive circle of wagons. As a verb, to form or set up a laager.

LAW—Light Anti-tank Weapon. A light anti-tank rocket packed in and fired from a single shot, expendable launcher.

Liaison Officer—A Field Artillery officer, usually a Captain, who acts as artillery advisor and forward observer for a battalion or squadron commander.

LOH—OH-6A Light Observation Helicopter. Spoken as "Loach."

LP—Listening Post. An outpost, usually at night, in front of a defensive position to warn of an enemy approach. Usually intended to withdraw without fighting. For Bravo Troop two or three men about fifty meters outside the concertina.

LRP—Long Range Patrol unit or member of the unit. Spoken as "Lurp."

M16—The standard U.S. rifle in Vietnam by 1969: 5.56mm, full or semiautomatic with a 20 round magazine.

Glossary

M60—The standard U.S. machine gun in Vietnam. Fed with an ammunition belt of 7.62mm cartridges linked together with disposable metal clips.

M79—40mm grenade launcher. Looks like a single shot, break-open shotgun with a short, fat barrel.

M88—A tank recovery vehicle used by 3/4 Cavalry Squadron.

M113—The standard U.S. armored personnel carrier in Vietnam.

NCO or Noncom—Non-commissioned officer. Sergeants, Corporals and Specialists.

NVA—North Vietnamese Army or one of their soldiers.

PF—Popular Forces or one of their soldiers. Lightly armed South Vietnamese local militia.

PFC—Private First Class. Usual rank for any short service enlisted soldier who has finished initial training and hasn't messed up.

PRC 25 or Prick 25—A man pack radio. The FO's radio on Six Track.

RF—Regional Forces or one of their soldiers. South Vietnamese local forces. A step up from the PFs in armament, unit size and training.

RPG—Rocket propelled grenade. A Russian designed, light, shoulder fired, shaped charge, anti-tank weapon. The VC and NVA still had some RPG2s, but mostly they had the newer and more powerful RPG7s. Though designed as anti-tank weapons they were routinely used against a wide variety of targets including personnel.

RTO—Radio Telephone Operator. A man carrying or responsible for a radio.

S1—Army staff for personnel or the officer in charge of the personnel staff for a unit.

S2—Army staff for intelligence or the officer in charge of the intelligence staff for a unit.

S3—Army staff for operations or the officer in charge of the operations staff for a unit.

Seabees—U.S. Navy Construction Battalions and their members.

Sheridan—M551 Armored Reconnaissance / Armored Assault Vehicle. Technically not a tank, but it looked like one.

Six Track—The Troop Commanding Officer's APC in a Cavalry Troop.

SKS—Russian/Chicom semi-automatic rifle comparable to a U.S. M-1 rifle.

Slick—Another name for a Huey.

SPEC4—Specialist 4th Class. One rank above PFC, the same pay grade as a Corporal, but with some "specialized" training or responsibility.

Track—Any tracked vehicle, usually an APC.

Track Commander—Man in charge of a track. Usually communicates with his Platoon Leader by radio.

VC—Viet Cong.

Viet Cong—Vietnamese Communists. Name usually used for the armed forces of the National Liberation Front. In 1969 Viet Cong units were often partially composed of NA troops.

XO—Executive Officer. Second in command.

The Author's Service Record

The author, William Watson, volunteered for Army ROTC on enrollment in college in September 1961. He was commissioned a Second Lieutenant in the Artillery upon graduation in May 1965, with a delay in call to active duty to attend law school. While in law school Watson was enrolled in the individual reserve and promoted to First Lieutenant in the Field Artillery.

Watson was called to active duty on August 6, 1968, with an initial assignment to Field Artillery Officers Basic course at Ft. Sill, Oklahoma. Following that, he completed Jump School at Ft. Benning, Georgia.

Watson's next assignment was to USARV, arriving in Vietnam on January 11, 1969. On arrival he was assigned to 25th Infantry Division. From there he was assigned to 1st Battalion, 8th Artillery, and sent to Bravo Troop, 3rd Squadron, 4th Cavalry as forward observer. He joined Bravo Troop on January 22.

On July 7, 1969, Artillery support for 3/4 Cav was reorganized and Watson was transferred to 3rd Battalion, 13th Artillery, while remaining Bravo Troop's forward observer.

On July 18, Watson was recalled from Bravo Troop and assigned to a firing battery as Executive Officer. After brief service as Executive Officer, he was assigned to 18th Military History Detachment, part of 25th Inf staff, to assist its commanding officer.

On August 6, 1969, Watson was promoted to Captain. Shortly thereafter, he was made commanding officer of 18th Military History Detachment.

Watson left Vietnam in early January 1970, assigned to the Field Artillery School at Ft. Sill as an instructor. At Ft. Sill he taught courses in the International Laws of Land Warfare and in Riot Control. He was also responsible for initial development of a course presenting the history of African American soldiers in the U.S. Army.

Watson was relieved from active duty on August 5, 1970.

For his service with Bravo Troop, Watson was awarded five Bronze Stars for valor, a Bronze Star for achievement and a Purple Heart. After leaving Bravo Troop he was awarded a Bronze Star for achievement and a Bronze Star for service.

Index

1st Battalion, 5th Infantry 123, 221
1st Battalion, 8th Artillery 11, 239
1st Infantry Division 182
2nd Battalion, 22nd Infantry 66
2nd Battalion, 27th Infantry 87
2nd Battalion, 34th Armor 238
3rd Battalion, 13th Artillery 11, 250
3rd Squadron, 4th Cavalry (3/4 Cav) 22–23
4th Battalion, 9th Infantry 35
7th Battalion, 11th Artillery 11
10th NVA Regiment 110
11th Armored Cavalry Regiment (11th Cav) 142–144
12th Evacuation Hospital 233
25th Aviation Battalion 200
25th Infantry Division 9
25th Military Intelligence Company 202–203, 240
25th Replacement Detachment 9
60th Land Clearing Company 203
88th NVA Regiment 97, 107, 234
90th Replacement Battalion 6
155mm dud 226–227
271st NVA Regiment 234
272nd NVA Regiment 234
287th Replacement Company 6

Aerorifles 35
Alpha Troop 108–110, 44, 53, 55, 57, 74, 121, 123, 174, 204
Ap Bien Hoa 2, 34, 45, 72
Ap Nam Truong Hue 229
ARVN first lieutenant 184–189, 193
ARVN Marines 54, 57–58
at my command 52

B52 172, 226, 245, 247
Baby Dumpling 212–215
Bear 27–30, 41–43, 51, 56–57, 69, 79–80, 111
Bien Hoa airport 5
Big Rubber 27
body count (bodies) 39, 92, 97, 133, 141, 191, 213–214, 222–224, 234

Cambodian Border 21, 30, 32, 35, 39, 43, 62, 87
Cao Dai 229, 251, 353
Cau Khoi Rubber 123, 126
Cav brass (crossed sabers) 24, 114, 154
Charlie Troop 54–55, 57, 73, 83–84, 92, 94, 96, 102, 105–106, 121, 137, 139, 145, 171, 174, 209, 214, 225, 228–234
chieu hoi 88
Citadel 134
claymore mine 18–19
click-click 143, 157, 176–177
Colt Commando 30, 40, 172
command detonated mine 164
concertina 36, 48
convoy 60, 86, 123
Country Store 72–73, 140–141, 282
CRIP 66–67, 219–224
Cu Chi 19, 22–24, 88–90, 111, 115, 154, 159, 199, 201, 213, 238, 242

Dau Tieng 142
Delta Troop 208
division information officer (IO) 173, 175
Doc 173, 193, 198, 212–213, 215, 223–224, 252
Donut Dollies 239
Duster 123, 125–126

enemy forces 12
enemy mines 13–14

F100 94, 174–175, 193, 221
Fire Support Base Hampton: location 30–31; mud 210
Fire Support Base Wood 115
flame bath 162
flechette round 40, 81, 91, 100–101, 110, 134
Fontana 23–26, 28–29, 32, 34–35, 44, 48, 53, 56

grenades 16–17

helicopter mine 161
Hobo Woods 157–160
Hoi Chan 29, 188–193

269

Index

ice 54, 186, 194
IV needle 193-194

Killer Junior 37, 40, 47, 49

laundry service 43
Little Rubber 43
LOH 157-160
Long Binh 2, 6-9
LRP 76, 79, 137-140, 144, 146, 210

M16 19-20
M88 74
maps 28, 141-142
McGowan, LTC Robert: body count 224; burning hooches 195-196; dustoff 207-208; long trench 100-101
Michelin Rubber Plantation 141-143
military civilians 154
MPC (military payment certificates) 7-8, 48, 239

niner 41

Pall Malls 63-64
Patrol Base Diamond 72, 86, 88
Princeton coeds 169
PSP 37
PT76 227

radar track 41-42, 51-53, 59
radio procedures 32

Rome Plow 198, 203-204
RPG screen 36

S1, 1st Battalion, 8th Artillery 22, 68, 239
S1, 3rd Squadron, 4th Cavalry 238-239
say again 91
Second Wolfhounds 86
Secretary of State 173
Senator 136, 201-202
Sheridan: arrival 61-62; blown up 73-74; demonstration 77-78; main gun 81; night light 87
signal operating instructions 26, 103, 180
Soul Track 217-218
splash 131-132, 183
Squadron Duty Officer's Log 1
Starlight Scope 256
sucking chest wound 14-16
sundries pack 63-64
Super Lou 139, 236-238, 255

Tay Ninh City 218, 225, 228, 233, 250-251
television news interview 147, 199
Thumb 182
track jack 160-161, 257

Vulcan 183-185

wait 41
war correspondents 173-175
West Point 101, 177, 233, 238-239